AF251919

OF DREAMS AND ASTRONAUTS

John P. Schreitmueller

VANTAGE PRESS
New York / Los Angeles / Chicago

To Kristen and Lauren

FIRST EDITION

Published by Vantage Press, Inc.
516 West 34th Street, New York, New York 10001

Manufactured in the United States of America
ISBN: 0-533-08340-0

The future doesn't belong to the fainthearted. It belongs to the brave. Nothing ends here. Our hopes and our journeys continue.

—Ronald Reagan
January 28, 1986

Contents

Preface

As I neared completion of *Of Dreams and Astronauts*, business took me home to Connecticut. Conveniently, I stayed with my parents. I slept in my old room. It was autumn, the trees were in glorious color, and the air carried the scent of thousands of leaves.

I visited my old high school. I hadn't been inside the building since 1971. As I walked through the hallways, I was engulfed in a wave of memories. Had it been so long?

The peace signs were gone. "Stop The War Now" graffiti no longer adorned locker doors. And, strangely, the halls were less crowded—evidence of the Baby Boomers' departure.

Still, as I walked past my old locker and home room, memories of the space program and the Vietnam era were vivid. Wasn't that coverage of *Apollo 10* I heard on a television in one of the biology rooms? And wasn't that the sound of the Doors coming from somewhere down the hall?

Recognizing me after sixteen years, several teachers paused to talk. I prepared to explain why I was in the hall between classes without a lavatory pass. When I realized no explanation was necessary, I realized, too, that we were all older.

Ackowledgments

Of Dreams and Astronauts is a story about growing up with the space program. Part of the book consists of personal memories, another part is narrative in nature, and yet another part consists of basic history of an era.

A lot of people helped to make this book possible. Three veterans of the NASA astronaut corps helped by taking the time to talk with me. They are former astronaut and current U.S. senator from Ohio John H. Glenn, Jr., who signed my copy of *The Right Stuff* when he stopped in Atlanta one rainy afternoon in 1984, Eugene A. Cernan, whom I met at the Beech Aircraft Corporation's plant in Wichita, Kansas, in 1981, and John Young and his lovely wife, Susy, who so patiently answered our questions at our AWA (Aviation/Space Writers Association) dinner one evening in 1986.

In compiling data on the music of the sixties and seventies, Debbie Nugent of Informart/Dallas, Frank Holler and Gary James of WDRC Radio/Hartford were invaluable. Steve Nesbitt and Mike Gentry of NASA (Johnson Space Center) were most kind in providing assistance.

Fellow AWA members Robert Parke and Norman "Pete" Bulban provided support and constructive criticism. I also must thank Jack and Judy Westerman, Linda Bowman, Jim Van Gilder, and Jay Miller for their welcomed assistance.

Lora McGrath, Janie Burke, Phyllis and Bill Salmon, Jim Telinda, Cathy and David Holmes, Richard Mott, Jim

Rapp, Joy Tyson, Joy Anderson, Doug Grove and Annie Reid were constant sources of ideas and inspiration.

And I owe special thanks to my family. My brother Bob was an outstanding consultant, always ready to assist. My parents lent their total cooperation, including taking my frequent frantic telephone calls from Texas late at night. And most of all, I thank my daughters, Kristen and Lauren, and my wife, Cathy, for their unwavering patience and support. They know what it is like to have a man in the house who dreams about astronauts, and they survived to tell about it.

Introduction

All of this happened in my lifetime.

This is not a scholarly research volume, although you will find the descriptions of events quite accurate. This is a story, and it was written to capture and to provoke feelings.

An entire generation of Americans grew up with the space program. I was fortunate to be among them. There are lots of books about the history of manned spaceflight, but few of them offer perspective from those mere spectators whose lives were deeply touched by our efforts in space.

My childhood dreams—and the dreams of millions— were captured by the lure of spaceflight. The dreams remain. They are special.

Growing up with the space program was a unique experience. This book is a description of that experience. I tried my best to recapture how it felt to watch those magnificent rockets, many of them bearing fragile human lives, thunder into the heavens.

To appreciate the story, one must "taste" the flavor of the times that surrounded each mission into space. This was accomplished via a sampling of the music, television, movies, and events that influenced my perceptions of the era, represented chronologically. The result, a snapshot of one American's life prior to the demise of *Challenger*, may be both humorous and sobering; the "golden era" of our manned space program took place during very turbulent times. Describing them accurately demanded discussion of the best and the worst of an era scarred by assassinations, social upheaval, and war.

Nevertheless, even during a tragic period in our nation's history, the space program was a vast source of pride. Since the loss of *Challenger,* a vacuum has existed in place of that pride. And Americans who were born after *Apollo 11* landed on the moon may never realize the intensity of that accomplishment or the positive ramifications of a bold manned space endeavor. An understanding of our achievements in space is important to the future of our nation. Clearly, it is time to share the story.

We are between chapters in the history of our manned space program. The destruction of *Challenger* placed us there. As our manned space program struggles to regain direction, we can put this interim to good use if we plan aggressively and wisely, as we did when we first set sail for the moon. The decisions we make or fail to make today will determine how we will use space—or how we might be forced to misuse it—in the future.

In 1961, when Yuri Gagarin and Alan Shepard were the first to taste the thrill of spaceflight, I thought the achievement of leaving our planet for the "new ocean," as President Kennedy called it, was one of the boldest, most honorable adventures the human race could embark upon. I still believe it is.

See what you think. I hope I have captured a fragment of history to which many of you can relate.

The men and women who got us into space were dreamers. Their dreams materialized into feats of such importance that they are still difficult to comprehend. Robert Kennedy once said, "Some men see things as they are and say 'Why?' I dream things that never were and say, 'Why not?' " If this writing in any way causes you to look up at the stars and say, "Why not?", my goal has been achieved.

Of Dreams and Astronauts

No Downlink

The design flew successfully in twenty-four missions. There were problems with the craft, but none of them severe enough to cause grave concern; at least none of the problems known by the public or by the flight crews themselves indicated catastrophic potential.

On Saturday, the mission was postponed for twenty-four hours because the weather forecast called for too many clouds in the launch area. Even the next day, January 26, 1986 (which happened to be my thirty-third birthday), was, meteorologically, unfavorable for the launch. The vast fire machine remained silent for another night.

Monday was cloudy, too, but the experts predicted some clearing later in the morning. The countdown continued and the sky did eventually clear. Unfortunately, by the time an overtorqued screw on the crew access hatch was replaced, the period of clear skies was replaced by more clouds. So the launch was scrubbed until Tuesday, the twenty-eighth.

There was anxiety in this for the crew, the NASA personnel responsible for the flight, and, certainly, many who still found the launch of a manned flight into space thrilling. But this was not 1962, and it was not the flight of John Glenn. So frustration caused by launch delays for NASA Space Transportation System (more commonly known as the space shuttle) Mission Number 51-L were more personal in nature; these were setbacks that influenced the crew, its families and friends, but not the national mood.

It had only been ten days since the last flight, Mission 61-C, had landed after a week in orbit. According to NASA, the Space Transportation System had achieved "operational" readiness and manned flight in and out of space was becoming a very common occurrence. Even to a space enthusiast, a couple of days one way or the other regarding the flight of Mission 51-L were hardly worth concern.

Tuesday morning was clear and cold in Plano, Texas, where I lived with my wife and two daughters. It took about thirty minutes to commute from Plano to my office, and as I crept through the maddening traffic between Plano and Richardson that morning, I listened to my favorite news station on the car radio. There was discussion about interest rates, pessimism over the price of oil, and the sagging Texas economy. Well, it certainly wasn't 1962. Welcome to the eighties.

When news of Mission 51-L's imminent departure finally received some attention, I turned up the volume so I would not miss the scheduled launch time, which was expected to be around 11:30 A.M., EST. That's 10:30 A.M. in Dallas; I would have to catch rerun footage of the launch on the evening news. No big deal. . . .

It was cold in Florida, too. In fact, at the Kennedy Space Center launch site, the entire area had been bathed in freezing temperatures. Scientists call it a cold-soak. On the Pad 39B launch complex, where mighty *Saturn V* rockets once departed for another world, the space transport launch vehicle, tethered to the orbiter (the flying component of the system, the orbiter carries the crew and is approximately the size of a DC-9 commercial jet airliner) for Mission 51-L, sat in the chilled air, its load of 528,000 gallons of supercold liquid hydrogen and liquid oxygen hissing.

The unusually low temperatures and a frozen water pipe on the pad caused icing around the vehicle. Icing is bad news in the space flight business. Ice can cause a "no-go" condition, scrubbing a launch until better conditions prevail. So NASA sent a special ice inspection team to the pad area ninety minutes prior to the scheduled launch time, just to make sure the ice would cause no damage to the highly sensitive thermal tiles on *Challenger*, the orbiter that was about to fly on its tenth mission.

When the ice team measured the temperatures on the lower portions of the vehicle's massive solid rocket boosters (SRBs), they found curious readings. The right booster only indicated a surface temperature of -7 to -9 degrees F., while the left SRB indicated about 25 degrees F., a more normal temperature for the weather conditions that existed at the time. In engineering letters and memos dating back to the initial design of the SRBs, personnel indicated concern over the effects of cold temperatures on the seals that held the SRB casing sections together. Some thought extremely cold temperatures, below 40 degrees F., might cause the seals to "erode" or fail. But this concern never reached NASA top management. And the flight crew of *Challenger* was not aware of it either. Perhaps unaware of the implications, the ice inspection team did not report the low temperature they found on the right SRB to flight management in charge of the launch.

Seal erosion was no new topic to those who dealt with the SRBs. During the spring of 1985, it had become clearly evident that the dual-seal system incorporated in the SRB casings could lead to disaster.

The concept is simple. The pressure and temperature inside a running SRB are high. The SRB itself is constructed of several casings that come together at common joints. It is difficult to seal those joints, because the superhot gases, under great pressure, naturally tend to vent through the joints. Gases escaping through the joints in flight could easily cause a catastrophic explosion.

To solve the problem, an initial and secondary seal system was designed into each joint, which was also insulated with putty. Because the SRBs tend to flex while in use, it is critical that the seals "seat" themselves immediately upon ignition, with the putty forming an additional layer of insulation against the possibility of hot gases venting from any joint.

The problem was, the system didn't work. The primary seals showed signs of erosion as early as the second mission, STS-2, in November 1981. Since then, five other missions had yielded unmistakable evidence of seal erosion.

Documentation dating back to 1982 discussed leakage of the primary seals. The topic caused enough concern to get it on the SRB Critical Items List in February 1983. A critical item, in aerospace jargon, is an item or system that, having failed, could result in loss of life.

In each case of seal erosion up until 1985, the primary seal was able to contain the "blowby" of hot gases. The secondary seals were not used. But on January 24, 1985, as *Discovery* carried its crew of five (including Ellison Onizuka, who would later be scheduled aboard *Challenger* for Mission 51-L) toward orbit, two joint seals had failed. One failure was great enough to cause soot behind the primary seal and to also cause heat damage on the secondary seal. Given more exposure to the extreme heat, the secondary seal was subject to failure and Mission 51-C could have been lost with all aboard. Mission 51-C was launched following colder temperatures than those experienced prior to any earlier mission. The cold temperature made seating of the joints more difficult.

On April 29, 1985, during the launch of Mission 51-B,

another primary seal failure of significant magnitude occurred, causing the secondary seal to act as the last defense against a massive explosion and loss of the vehicle and crew. The secondary seal received considerable erosion damage. That made two close calls.

In July 1985, a NASA SRB engineer brought the matter to the attention of the NASA associate administrator for spaceflight, Jesse W. Moore. The engineer, Irving Davids, told Moore that, given primary seal failure following fatigue of an SRB joint to seat properly after ignition, the secondary seals could not be expected to prevent hot gases from escaping through the failed joint and disaster would follow.

NASA tried to determine whether the problem at hand posed immediate danger. There were a lot of missions to fly. NASA was trying desperately to convince a skeptical administration of the shuttle's effectiveness, and the launch schedule was brutal.

When managers from Morton Thiokol, the manufacturer of the SRBs, briefed NASA on the joint problem on August 19, 1985, they admitted considerable improvements were necessary immediately, but that it was still safe to fly missions before the improvements could be implemented.

The crew had entered *Challenger* several times during the last few days, ready to be vaulted into space, only to climb out again when the mission was delayed. But they all wore smiles on the morning of the twenty-eighth; delay was part of the business, and it was always important to maintain a positive attitude. Spaceflight may have seemed a common occurrence, yet this team of seven represented a very privileged few. Millions had dreamed of the experience for which these seven had trained.

To Christa C. McAuliffe, thirty-eight, being a member of the flight crew for Mission 51-L was an honor and the thrill of a lifetime dedicated to her family and to education. For McAuliffe was not an astronaut/pilot, a mission specialist, or a payload specialist, the three categories of flight personnel who normally flew the space shuttle. She was an ordinary secondary education teacher—if one could call such a remarkable woman ordinary.

McAuliffe entered the NASA Teacher-In-Space program, which was created to afford the adventure of spaceflight to highly qualified members of the education community who were not employed by NASA and who were not pilots by profession. McAuliffe was the first teacher selected—from eleven thousand applicants—to fly on an actual mission. With her would ride the hopes and dreams of countless Americans: her students, those who hoped to earn seats on future missions, those who saw McAuliffe as a peer, and many, many more who simply wished her well on an incredible accomplishment. The reality of spaceflight was nearing the grasp of the "average" American, NASA told us.

For Francis R. (Dick) Scobee, this mission was a reunion with the airless void above the earth's atmosphere. Scobee had flown as the pilot of *Challenger* before, during Mission 41-C in April 1984.

Scobee, like so many of his predecessors and peers, loved to fly. He originally entered the Air Force as an enlisted man, working on piston aircraft engines. It didn't take long before Scobee opted for an officer's commission and flight training, which he completed in 1966. After a combat tour in Vietnam, Scobee returned to flight school, this time the vaunted Aerospace Research Pilot School at Edwards Air Force Base in California. He qualified in more than forty different types of aircraft.

Scobee's responsibilities for Mission 51-L were immense; he would command it.

The pilot for the mission—and Scobee's assistant—was Navy Commander Michael J. Smith, forty. Smith had a flying record most can only envy.

As pilot of an A-6 Intruder over Vietnam, Smith won the Navy Distinguished Flying Cross, three Air Medals, thirteen Strike Flight Air Medals, the Navy Commendation Medal with combat "V," the Navy Unit Citation, and the Vietnamese Cross of Gallantry with Silver Star. One could say Smith was quite a pilot, a "hot stick" by an aviator's standards. He was also smart as hell, having earned a B.S. in naval science at the U.S. Naval Academy at Annapolis and an M.S. in aeronautical engineering from the U.S. Naval Postgraduate School, not one of the easier grad schools one may select.

Smarts was a common quality among this crew. Also flying a second mission into space aboard Mission 51-L was Dr. Judith A. Resnik, thirty-six. Resnik had flown aboard one of *Challenger*'s sister orbiters, *Discovery*, in August 1984 as a mission specialist during Mission 41-D. Call it piggy, call it anything you want, but I remember watching television coverage from that mission and I remember seeing Judy Resnik's beautiful long hair floating, weightless, in the *Discovery*'s cockpit as she expertly handled a massive solar array panel and thinking how pretty she was. I admired her tremendously.

Resnik was one of those types who just didn't know the meaning of the word *quit*. She had earned a B.S. in electrical engineering from Carnegie-Mellon University. Then she had earned a Ph.D in electrical engineering from the University of Maryland. Then she served as a biomedical engineer in the laboratory of neurophysiology at the National Institute of Health in Bethesda, Maryland.

And then she became a NASA astronaut at the ripe old age of twenty-nine.

When Mission 41-B flew in February 1984, mission specialist Dr. Ronald E. McNair became the first to deploy the Canadian-built robotic arm, assisting his fellow crew members during EVA (Extra Vehicular Activity or "space-walking") operations in *Challenger*'s cargo bay. So this was a reunion for McNair, not only a reunion with spaceflight but a reunion with *Challenger*, having logged 191 hours aboard her during Mission 41-B.

McNair was another shining example of the kind of smarts NASA assembled to fly these STS missions. He had earned a B.S. from North Carolina A&T State University and a Ph.D. from the Massachusetts Institute of Technology, both in physics.

At Hughes Research Laboratories, McNair built upon his experience at MIT developing laser equipment by contributing to research in laser technology for satellite communications. And in 1978, at age twenty-seven, Ron McNair was selected by NASA as a mission specialist astronaut.

On January 24, 1985, the first dedicated Defense Department mission was launched aboard *Discovery*. Among the crew members for Mission 51-C was Air Force Lieutenant Colonel Ellison S. Onizuka, thirty-eight.

Onizuka, like Scobee and Smith, had the kind of flight record that caused other aviators to seethe with envy. As an aerospace flight test engineer, Onizuka had participated in flight test programs for nine different high-performance jet aircraft. He had logged over seventeen hundred hours in the air. To boot, Onizuka came to NASA sporting both B.S. and M.S. degrees in aerospace engineering from the University of Colorado. He was selected as an astronaut by NASA in 1978.

Astronauts chosen from various segments of industry typically fly as payload specialists. For Mission 51-L Gregory Jarvis of Hughes Aircraft Company was chosen as payload specialist.

Jarvis, like all of his fellow crew members, was eminently qualified for the job. He had earned a B.S. degree in electrical engineering from the State University of New York. Then he had earned an M.S. in electrical engineering from Northeastern University. As Mission 51-L prepared for its voyage, Jarvis completed studies for yet another M.S. degree, from West Coast University in Los Angeles in management science.

Gregory Jarvis had become a satellite expert, working in electrical systems design at Raytheon and then at Hughes. In 1983, two satellites he helped to create were placed into orbit. Jarvis, forty-one, was selected by NASA as a payload specialist in 1984.

In STS operation through mission 51-L, the actual boarding of an orbiter prior to a mission was different from the days of Mercury, Gemini, and Apollo. There typically was no traditional "launch day breakfast," which used to consist of steak and eggs (too much cholesterol perhaps). There was no lengthy "suiting-up" procedure, with technicians applying body sensors and assisting the crew into bulky pressure suits. The once-familiar portable air-conditioning units (now in use again because crews are using pressure suits for launch and re-entry) held by the veterans of Mercury, Gemini and Apollo as they walked from the transfer van to the gantry were gone. And the process of getting inside the orbiter remains radically different from squeezing into an Apollo command module, a Gemini spacecraft, or, most certainly, a tiny Mercury spacecraft.

An STS crew typically woke up about five hours prior to launch time. They have kept a sleeping schedule designed to accommodate their particular mission. Exposure to outsiders is held to a minimum to prevent possible infection and sickness during the flight. Through mission 51-L, the crew donned fire-resistant flight suits very similar to those used by military aviators and flight personnel. Even the boots worn by pre–Mission 26 STS crews were like those worn by military flyers. The sole giveaway that the crew was about to do something a bit beyond a typical military mission was the helmet worn by each crew member once aboard the orbiter. The helmet was designed to protect upon impact, protect against noise, and provide emergency oxygen via "air packs," located behind each crew seat, in the unlikely event of fire while on the ground. The apparel worn by the crew during launch and throughout the mission (except, of course, during EVA) was not designed to protect them against decompression in space or at extreme altitude within the atmosphere.

Within reason, crew members can have whatever they wish for breakfast; the drama that surrounded the pre-launch activities of earlier space pioneers is gone. Launch-morning breakfast is more like those shared by airline crews about to depart on a scheduled flight, professional but not profound.

At the time, no portable air conditioners were required, because the crew was in a "shirtsleeve" environment. Indeed, on the morning of January 28, 1986, as the crew of Mission 51-L departed for the pad, one was more concerned with staying warm than with cooling equipment.

Climbing aboard the orbiter is accomplished by walking across an access ramp at orbiter level in the support structure, at Level 195, to be exact. The crew, commander first, climbs aboard via the round crew access hatch. Since the orbiter is poised nose-up, one must lie on his or her back once inside the orbiter, like in Mercury, Gemini, or Apollo craft. But the resemblance ends there. While the orbiter is not spacious, it is a vast improvement over the cramped cockpits of its predecessors. The commander and pilot occupy positions the size of a Boeing 747 flight deck. Behind them, two additional crew members, typically mission specialists/engineers, occupy their seats. Below the flight crew, in the middeck section, are additional seats for mission and payload specialists. The middeck section houses much of the living space for the crew in flight and it is quite comfortable compared to the inside of Mercury, Gemini, or Apollo craft.

For Mission 51-L Scobee would occupy the left front seat. Smith would sit to Scobee's right. Behind Scobee and Smith, Resnik and Onizuka would occupy the specialist/engineer flight crew seats. And in the mid-deck section, McNair, Jarvis, and McAuliffe would occupy crew seats located there. The arrangement was close but relatively comfortable; the orbiter is designed to fly easily with seven aboard.

As in the case of all manned space missions, the preparations for Mission 51-L had been taking place, in a sense, for years. NASA took well-deserved pride in the painstaking planning that surrounded a flight, and it was this planning that earned the United States its enviable safety record: fifty-five manned missions into space over a period of twenty-five years without a single flight fatality. (The deaths of three Apollo astronauts in 1967 occurred during a routine test on the pad.) In January 1986, the public had no reason to believe any phase of preflight planning had been compromised.

The coordination necessary for a successful STS mission is awesome. There are foreign alternate landing sites to be considered. There is a tracking network of immense proportions to be at the ready. The computer, telemetry, and related ground equipment are so complex they have created a separate industry of their own. And all this in addition to the launch vehicle itself, clearly the most sophisticated machine man has ever launched into space.

In the case of Mission 51-L, the preparation ritual was followed to the same standards as in every STS flight. The postponement of the mission on several occasions clearly indicated NASA's reluctance to launch under anything less than what they thought were optimum conditions. Yet there were concerns—like those indicated by engineers about the SRB seals—that publicly were left unsaid.

Spaceflight is an extremely risky business. John H. Glenn, Jr., the first American to orbit the earth and now a U.S. senator from Ohio, has often spoken of discussions he had with his fellow Mercury astronauts speculating on how many of them might survive the Mercury program. Although we have come a long way since those daring Mercury missions, launching frail human beings strapped to equipment capable of millions upon millions of pounds of raw thrust remains a very potentially dangerous endeavor.

But men and women accept risks to better themselves. Walking down the street can be dangerous. Riding in a car is even riskier. And flying on a commercial airliner certainly has inherent risks, but most of us accept these and additional risks as part of our daily rituals, because facts and experiece have proven these methods of transportation to be safe and dependable. Considering all the people who walk down streets, ride in cars, and fly in airplanes, few of them are injured or die as a result.

The story is similar for NASA flight crews. During

Mercury, Gemini, and Apollo, everything possible was done to eliminate human error and we launched one mission after another, confident of a successful flight and the safe return of the crew. We took that standard for granted as we entered the shuttle age.

The problem with outstanding safety records is the development of trends. With the completion of every successful flight, a tendency may develop to relax just a few of the requirements for the next flight, et cetera. This process of deterioriation was increasing as the STS program went "operational" in 1984. In fact, the trend had developed even before the first STS mission was launched in 1981.

The Space Transportation System was born of different stuff than were Mercury, Gemini, or Apollo. For the first time in NASA's history of manned spaceflight, there was more attention to the dollar than there was to the ultimate safety of the flight crew. And this priority was established in 1972 when the Nixon administration announced the shuttle program in terms of "reducing" the cost of access to space.

While reducing the cost of access to space is a credible goal, making it the top priority can be lethal to those who must fly the equipment involved. In the case of the Space Transportation System, the reversal of priorities from safety to dollars went against the strict foundations of excellence set by the brillant teams who made the successes of Mercury, Gemini, and Apollo possible.

Aside from the SRB joint problem, which is a classic example of shoddy handling of a safety-related problem with the shuttle, other examples of how safety standards were relaxed are plentiful when one compares the shuttle program with its predecessors. Before the drastic budget cuts of the seventies, NASA would never have even considered launching humans aboard a booster system that was not "man-rated" by a series of stringent unmanned flight tests. The Redstone, Atlas, *Titan II*, *Saturn 1-B*, and *Saturn V* all flew repeatedly before NASA astronauts found themselves strapped atop them. The Soviets beat us into space in 1961 because NASA, at the urging of Wernher von Braun, insisted upon additional tests before placing Alan Shepard in his *Freedom 7* spacecraft for our first, timid suborbital attempt. Shepard could have flown as early as January 31, when Ham, the chimp, became the first living creature to ride a Mercury spacecraft into space. Instead, Shepard did not fly until May 5, nearly a month after Yuri Gagarin's fantastic flight. But the threat of humiliation by the Soviets was not enough to cause NASA to take chances with a Mercury pilot . . . and that is to NASA's great credit; they did it right. When Shepard flew, there were no skeletons hidden in some engineer's closet concerning the Mercury/Redstone system. Everyone had done everything humanly possible to ensure Shepard's safety. If catastrophe had struck on May 5, 1961, it would have come as a surprise to those who had prepared so well for the flight.

The very design of the shuttle is an utter compromise. The craft was originally to have both air-breathing (jet) and internally oxydized (rocket) engines, allowing the craft to accelerate above the atmosphere and also allowing it to maneuver once it reentered the atmosphere. The inclusion of air-breathing jet engines of one type or another would have given the shuttle "go-around" capability, meaning the craft could attempt a landing at one site, abort the approach, and repeat it again in search of more favorable conditions . . . or seek an entirely new landing site, like a commercial jetliner. Instead, to save money, the STS was designed with only pure rocket engines and no propulsion system—aside from the kinetic energy derived from trading vast altitude for range—to power the huge vehicle within the atmosphere. In short, if for some reason a returning STS crew found themselves faced with a rejected approach situation, the results could easily be fatal for the crew and the $1.5 billion orbiter would be destroyed. For once inside the atmosphere, the shuttle is a big glider and nothing more. One chance is all the crew gets.

In Mercury, Gemini, and Apollo, considerable effort was made to provide a reliable escape system for the crews. Mercury and Apollo both had a separate escape rocket system, capable of pulling the entire spacecraft away from an exploding booster within a split second's notice from internal sensors that were designed and tested to work right the first time. In Gemini, which used a less complex booster, the crew was provided with fighter jet-style ejection seats that would get the pilots away from a massive failure in a most expedient manner. Fortunately, none of those escape systems was ever used in a manned mission. The closest a NASA crew came to ejecting was in the case of *Gemini 6* in December 1965, when its *Titan II* booster ignited and shut down on the pad . . . and astronauts Wally Schirra and Tom Stafford decided—correctly—that they were not in immediate danger. They flew another day.

When Mission 51-L flew, the STS did not have an escape system for the crew. There are elaborate plans for returning the craft for a landing near the launch site, but the maneuvers required for such an abort (it is called a RTLS, for Return to Launch Site) are extremely difficult. Furthermore, a RTLS abort is not possible unless the craft has reached sufficient altitude from which it can glide safely, and the rate at which the shuttle trades altitude for distance is more similar to a road grader than a layman's concept of a "glider."

And there are other compromises. On mission 51-L, the braking system was utterly susceptible to overheating when it was needed most, to slow the massive craft down following landing. At places like Edwards Air Force Base, where there are tens of thousands of feet of straight, dry runway available, the overheat problem was of concern, but not potentially fatal. In the case of the Kennedy Space Center in Florida, where far less footage is available for landing, badly overheated brakes on a returning orbiter could have serious consequences.

For years, engineers worried about the heat-absorbing tiles that are, literally, glued to the orbiter. The tiles protect the vehicle from thermal destruction during the reentry phase of each mission. As we saw from the very first mission, STS-1, in April 1981, the tiles can and do fall off in flight. Tile loss caused no problems on STS-1, not that many of them fell off. But what would happen if too many tiles fell off? As a pilot, I cannot believe the shuttle flies with doubts about the tiles.

Most salient is the compromise we made in our lifting capacity when we literally abandoned our world-class *Saturn V* for the shuttle, which cannot loft nearly as great a payload as *Saturn V* and, furthermore, can only place the orbiter into low earth orbit. We put all our eggs into one confused basket when the Nixon administration choked NASA down to the compromise we now call the Space Transportation System.

Gone is the terrific expendable launch capability we once had in the form of a ready supply of Atlas, Titan, *Saturn 1-B*, and *Saturn V* boosters. And we have no well-defined plan for space exploration in the future. The Soviets may have taken second place to our magnificent Apollo program. But since Apollo ended, the Soviets have demonstrated a well-planned, organized program for access to earth orbit and beyond. They use space like their lives may someday depend upon it. We seem to have failed to recognize the inevitable.

And yet, on January 28, 1986, Scobee, Smith, Resnik, Onizuka, McNair, Jarvis, and McAuliffe boarded *Challenger* once again, prepared to demonstrate America's manned space capability. They were proud, and rightfully so, to be there.

After McAuliffe was secure in her seat in the middeck area, it was obvious to the crew that *Challenger* was "alive," with hundreds of thousands of gallons of supercold fuels that would slam them up through the atmosphere and into orbit within a brief eight minutes and fifty seconds. Indeed, *Challenger* actually moved with the groaning and screaming of the external tank.

Around 10:47 A.M. the crew helped align the IMU (Inertial Measurement Unit), which allows the spacecraft to determine its true position relative to the solar system. And at 11:08, the personnel who assisted the flight crew during boarding moved away from the "white room" at Level 195 to a safe area about three miles away, to observe the lift-off.

At about 11:18 A.M., the ice inspection team made another external check of the launch vehicle. No icing problems were found. The crew was already in position in the orbiter, assisting with entry of final mission data, which typically is linked at this time, twenty minutes before liftoff. Then there was a planned ten-minute hold, affording the launch crew time for final weather determinations and systems clearances.

Kennedy Space Center personnel fielded a phone call from a Rockwell International engineer in California at about this time. Rockwell International is the primary builder of the orbiter. And the engineer was calling out of concern for launching in such cold temperatures. The closed-circuit television picture of the launch proceedings the engineer was watching worried him. He expressed his concerns about launching with ice visibly in the area of the orbiter. He thought it might be dangerous.

There was still time. The launch could have easily been delayed—or postponed altogether—from the vantage point of the planned hold in the countdown. But the launch director elected to continue. He did this, probably, because he had no reason not to continue. Based upon what he knew—or did not know—at that point in the launch process, there was little reason to delay the launch.

The day before, January 27 (the nineteenth anniversary of the *Apollo 1* fire), there was extensive discussion between NASA management at the Kennedy Space Center, the Marshall Space Center in Huntsville, Alabama, and representatives of Morton Thiokol in Utah, where the SRBs are manufactured.

Clearly, Thiokol engineering managers within the SRB project struggled to convince NASA not to launch Mission 51-L the next day. They were not comfortable with the unusually low temperatures and the possible effects of the cold on the SRB joints. Thiokol pressed for a delay until at least the following day, when warmer temperatures were forecast, or longer.

NASA protested, indicating that valuable launch schedule time would be lost by delaying Mission 51-L until warmer temperatures prevailed. One gets the impression, upon researching the vast amount of materials published in the aftermath of the Mission 51-L launch, that NASA management expected Morton Thiokol to prove to them why they recommended a delay.

At this point of frustration, Thiokol top management stepped in and pressured their own engineers, who had argued against a decision to proceed with the launch, to make a "management" decision instead of an "engineering" decision. In other words, top management wanted the engineers to play ball! There was a launch at stake, and they had to demonstrate their confidence in their product.

The engineers were overruled. Thiokol's manager in charge of the shuttle project issued a statement to NASA recommending launch as scheduled. Thiokol had no conclusive evidence, he reasoned, related to blow-by of hot gases through the primary "O" ring seals on the SRBs. According to the postflight documentation, the Thiokol decision then appeared unanimous; no one at NASA who was involved with the Thiokol-NASA teleconferences that took place on the twenty-seventh believes they were aware of the opposition to launching within the Thiokol organization.

But the final decision to launch was still NASA's. (Had he been properly informed of the gravity of the SRB situation, the final decision should really have been Scobee's, and, in speculation, he surely would have rejected the launch.) Some Thiokol engineers still requested delay, based upon poor weather conditions in the SRB recovery area in the Atlantic, where thirty-foot seas were reported and the wind was gusting at seventy knots. That request was also rejected.

At the time of Mission 51-L's launch, NASA management operated on a series of levels. Each level had decision authority for certain activities associated with the launch of an STS mission. The requests for delay because of weather at least reached NASA Level 2 management. But all the concern over the SRBs never got above NASA Level 3, where officials at the Marshall Space Center felt the booster decision belonged. The NASA Space Transportation System director, at NASA Level 1, indicated he heard nothing of the NASA-Thiokol discussions prior to the actual launch.

At T-minus nine minutes, the countdown for Mission 51-L resumed and all appeared normal. The walkway leading from the white room to the orbiter swung away, and the massive vehicle stood alone. The spectators in the Kennedy Space Center bleachers, several miles from Pad 39, were shivering in the cold. McAuliffe's parents were there. Her husband was there. They wore badges with her picture and "STS 51-L" emblazoned on them. They were there to celebrate.

Aboard *Challenger*, Smith prepared to start the orbiter's auxiliary power units, which enable the craft's hydraulic pumps. This was accomplished at approximately 11:33 A.M., at T-minus five minutes. Scobee and Smith then put the orbiter's main engines through a series of preplanned maneuvers, to ensure the massive nozzles gimbaled properly. In flight, the nozzles moved constantly, helping to balance the huge vehicle as it climbed.

Challenger was now operating on its own internal power. The huge loads of liquid oxygen and hydrogen in the external tank began to pressurize, in preparation for ignition of the orbiter's main engines. The crew closed the visors of their helmets. They were ready.

At T-minus ninety seconds and counting, the mission was pronounced "ready to go" by the NASA public affairs commentator at the cape. Aboard the spacecraft, the crew on the flight deck level carried on a light but professional conversation. As the sixty-second mark went by, Scobee spoke over the crew intercom, "One minute downstairs," to Jarvis, McNair, and McAuliffe, seated in the middeck section. At about the same time, *Challenger*'s on-board computers accepted management of the launch from the Launch Control computers inside Kennedy Space Center. And at T-minus eight seconds, the water tower near the Pad 39B complex let loose thousands of gallons of water into the base of the pad, to dampen the sound shock waves of the launch; the noise alone could damage the orbiter as it climbed away from the pad.

When the T-minus three second mark was reached, *Challenger*'s main engines came to life, building in power to their full 1.12 million pounds of thrust. *Challenger* lurched toward the external tank some two feet as the main engines ignited—a normal reaction—and then the nose settled back to a vertical posture. At that point, at about T-minus two seconds, igniters in the noses of the two SRBs shot flames through the solid fuel inside the boosters, igniting the aluminum inside and causing the material to burn uncontrollably, which is how solid-fueled rockets are supposed to work.

In a split second, the SRBs were blasting their combined strength of 5.2 million pounds of thrust out of their exhaust nozzles. The exhaust from the SRBs was as white as raw sunlight; the exhaust from the liquid-fueled orbiter main engines was a pale blue. And as the SRBs ignited, NASA cameras caught first a rush of white steam—which was ice evaporating from where it had formed inside the right SRB aft joint—and then a cough of ugly black smoke as it exited from the failing joint. The smoke was caused by sealing material that was burning. But no one noticed.

It was 11:38 A.M. *Challenger* cleared the tower of Pad 39B, and control of Mission 51-L changed from the Kennedy Space Center at the cape to the Johnson Space Center in Houston, Texas. Steve Nesbitt, the NASA public affairs narrator in Houston, took over routine announcements about the flight's progress.

The sound of *Challenger*'s departure was awesome, reminiscent of the Apollo days when the shock waves from a *Saturn V* launch sent tremors through the ground for miles and the air crackled with the raw energy unleashed by the massive F-1 engines. While the *Saturn V* packed a 7.5 million-pound thrust, the shuttle is no shrinking violet, with 6.3 million pounds of combined main engine and solid booster thrust. And, in the case of the shuttle, the launch event is much faster. Saturn/Apollo craft rose slowly, almost imperceptively at first. But a departing shuttle is something else. The vehicle rips away from the pad at a startling rate.

Within seconds, *Challenger* was far above the pad, arcing out over the Atlantic Ocean and rolling into its climb attitude, with the orbiter riding below the external tank, so that the crew of Mission 51-L was riding inverted as they accelerated. "Go, you mother!" shouted Smith as they climbed.

NASA cameras saw the last traces of black smoke from the failed joint as *Challenger* completed its roll maneuver, at about twelve seconds into the flight. As a result of *Challenger*'s keen acceleration, the crew experienced about three "G's," meaning the sudden acceleration produced a competition of sorts with normal gravity to produce three times its normal force. And it was bumpy. Smith commented to Scobee, Resnik, and Onizuka, "Looks like we got a lotta wind here today."

Soon, at about thirty-five seconds into the flight, Scobee monitored a throttle manuever with the orbiter's main engines, reducing their thrust to about 65 percent of full power. This was done to prevent *Challenger* from passing through the zone of maximum dynamic pressure (it is called Max Q by the flight crews) too quickly. If the vehicle continued at maximum thrust, the atmosphere, which was still relatively thick at *Challenger*'s altitude, could not clear the leading edges of the accelerating vehicle fast enough and damage—or possible disintegration—could result.

Steve Nesbitt continued to keep the public audience informed. He spoke of three good APUs (Auxiliary Power Units) and a speed of some 2,257 feet per second. At forty seconds elapsed, *Challenger* reacted to a wind shear condition aloft, according to telemetry data. "There's Mach one," Smith added. *Challenger* was supersonic.

At 58.3 seconds into the mission, NASA long-range cameras again saw black smoke coming from the aft joint area on the right solid booster. At 58.7 seconds, the cameras caught a plume of roaring flame emerge from the side of the right booster.

"Feel that mother go!" Smith called from his pilot's seat as *Challenger* bored up through the atmosphere at 60.2 seconds into the flight to orbit. Simultaneously, telemetry noted a drop in chamber pressure for the right solid booster, the first indication that gases were escaping through a leak somewhere in the booster. Also, around this time, additional data indicated *Challenger* was reacting to high winds aloft, because the craft's elevons were commanded to move and the engines were gimbaling at significant rates. The vehicle's pitch angle changed as it fought with the wind.

About four seconds later, the NASA cameras confirmed additional fire spots were visible on the right solid booster. The leak was getting larger. Pressure within the external tank began to change, indicating a possible leak in the tank.

When the sixty-four second mark was reached, the flight controller at Houston gave Scobee a "go at throttle-up," which meant the zone of maximum pressure was essentially behind the flight (it occurred at fifty-nine seconds) and that *Challenger*'s main engines were properly throttled up to full power again. Actually, the engines were producing 104 percent of their rated thrust in the cold, high-altitude air.

Scobee confirmed the throttle-up sequence at seventy seconds after lift-off. "Roger, go at throttle-up," was the simple reply; the crew was not yet aware of their predicament. *Challenger* was approaching an altitude of forty-eight thousand feet and was travelling at Mach 2, twice the speed of sound.

"Uh-oh." The comment came from Smith about .3 seconds after Scobee rogered for the throttle-up sequence. It was the last comment recorded on the crew intercom communications loop before all voice data was lost from the ascending vehicle.

Challenger was breaking up as a result of a massive explosion that began about 72.1 seconds after lift-off. The failed joint on the aft section of the right booster was venting exhaust gases at a volume so great that one of the lower struts that held the booster to the external tank failed, causing the nose of the malfunctioning booster to pivot toward the external tank. This movement was confirmed from data taken from the booster's rate gyro, and it occurred at about 72.2 seconds into the flight.

Shortly thereafter, the base of the failing booster swung back toward the orbiter, probably breaking off *Challenger*'s right wing and burning the side of the orbiter with hot exhaust gas. At the 72.6 second mark, the entire vehicle began yawing to the left with considerable momentum, in reaction to the swaying of the failed booster's misdirected thrust.

Two-tenths of a second later, indications were recorded of lowered inlet pressures in the main engines. That meant the external tank had ruptured somewhere or that the thick liquid oxygen line, which ran down the side of the external tank, had been damaged and was leaking.

At seventy-three seconds, the right booster was running a full twenty-four psi (pounds per square inch) lower in pressure than the left booster, which continued to function normally. The failed booster rotated into the top of the external tank, penetrating the tank and allowing a huge volume of either oxygen or hydrogen gas to escape. Cameras also recorded gases escaping near the bottom of the external tank, which indicates a possible puncture in the lower portion of the tank, too.

As the craft passed the 73.2 second mark, there was a large explosion near the top of the external tank, caused when the liquid oxygen and liquid hydrogen propellants mixed rapidly where the right booster inflicted massive damage to the external tank's forward end. Data from *Challenger*'s main engines indicated propellant fluctuations of huge proportions.

Seventy-three and one-half seconds after lift-off, the number one main engine shut down. At 73.6 seconds after lift-off, transmission of all data from the vehicle ceased. Shortly afterward, the entire vehicle was totally destroyed. And about thirty-five seconds later, range safety officers destroyed the boosters as they flew, uncontrolled, away from the inferno aloft that was *Challenger*.

On the ground, the pathetic explosion looked like a giant fireworks display. To any experienced observer it was obvious that something was terribly wrong. It wasn't the "staging" fireball so common during the Saturn days. It was sudden and final.

Yet inside the orbiter's crew compartment it is highly probable that Scobee, Smith, Resnik, Onizuka, Jarvis, McNair, and McAuliffe survived the actual vehicle breakup. NASA cameras recorded the crew compartment's departure from the vehicle, and the compartment, which can retain full pressurization, appeared intact.

Carried by the momentum of the vehicle's velocity of Mach 2, the crew compartment, free of the exploding launch vehicle, coasted up from about forty-eight thousand feet, the altitude at which the final explosion took place, to an altitude of about sixty-five thousand feet. It then arced over and fell toward the ocean.

The crew compartment survived in the air for two minutes and forty-five seconds before it hit the sea at a velocity of 207 mph. It was impact with the water—and not the explosion itself—that caused massive damage to the crew compartment.

Each crew member aboard *Challenger* was provided with a PEAP (Personal Egress Air Pack), designed to assist in ground evacuation in case of fire. Recovered items from the crew compartment indicate that at least three of four air packs from the flight deck level, where Scobee, Smith, Resnik, and Onizuka were seated, had been pressed into service after the explosion. Someone, probably Judy Resnik, had leaned forward and activated Mike Smith's air pack, which, as another unbelievable quirk of *Challenger*'s design, could not be reached by the commander or pilot. Those seated behind the commander and pilot could activate their own air packs because the controls for the system were located on the sides of those seats and not directly behind the seats, as in the cases of the commander or pilot.

If the crew compartment lost pressure as a result of the explosion, it is likely that some or all of the crew lost consciousness during the ascent beyond forty-eight thousand feet. Remember, the crew was not wearing pressure suits and the air pack systems did not operate on the pressure-demand principle that would enable that system to sustain the crew at such extreme altitude. But it is very likely, according to NASA's postflight data, that the crew compartment was not subjected to G-loads during the explosion and subsequent breakup that would have damaged the crew compartment badly enough to cause it to lose pressure. And the fact that at least three air packs, which were recovered, indicated their supplies had been considerably depleted demonstrates there were crew members alive—and probably conscious—as the compartment fell toward the sea. They knew what was happening, and they tried to take action.

Had the orbiter crew compartment been equipped with a parachute system similar to those that eased Mercury, Gemini, and Apollo to the surface with such success, it is entirely possible some or all of the crew of Mission 51-L would have survived.

Back at the Kennedy Space Center VIP observation area, where McAuliffe's family watched *Challenger*'s ascent, people at first just stared at each other. Indeed, McAuliffe's parents kept watching the fireball, expecting something normal to happen, when, unknown to them, at the split second the vehicle exploded the awful had already taken place.

And on television, the agony was prolonged. Steve Nesbitt, the NASA narrator, continued supplying normal ascent data even as the explosion covered the screens of televisions across the nation. Then he stopped for about forty seconds.

After what seemed a brief eternity, Nesbitt continued to do his job the way he was trained to do it: professionally. I will never forget his words. "Flight controllers are looking very carefully at the situation," he said, then, "Obviously a major malfunction." And finally, he added, "We have no downlink." In spaceflight jargon, to have no downlink is to have lost all contact with the spacecraft. Such was the case with *Challenger*.

The *Challenger* tragedy caused the entire U.S. manned space program to cease. In fact, following the disaster of January 28, 1986, the U.S. struggled to get even unmanned payloads into orbit, with two major failures occurring later in the year. Meanwhile, the Soviet Union launched mission after mission, proof of their evolutionary system of exploration and proof of the Soviet commitment to manned space exploration for the benefit of their people.

It is clear during this period as NASA continues to recover from the worst disaster in the history of spaceflight that the directions of our once-proud space program are off-course.

As astronaut Sally Ride recommended in 1987, we desperately need a concise program for the future of Americans in space. Should we just build a space station, using shuttle technology, and observe the earth from orbit? Should we return to the moon, where proud Apollo astronauts once walked, and build a permanently manned lunar base there? Or should we set our sights on the planets, probably beginning with Mars, since it is most like our own and the easiest to reach?

The answer is—or should be—"yes" to all of those questions. Certainly there are financial and technological restraints that will prevent all of those noble adventures from happening simultaneously. But we must start on them immediately, for reasons of world peace, national purpose, and the survival of mankind, who will one day turn to the stars for their solutions just as surely as the mariners of the fifteenth century turned to the west for theirs.

We have at our fingertips the potential for man's* greatest accomplishment: the exploration of the planets for the benefit of his knowledge and for the benefit of those who follow.

---

*(I use *man* and *his* to avoid wordiness; after men first flew in space, women went on to demonstrate their keen abilities in space. Future ventures into space must include women on equal terms with their male counterparts, for we would be foolish indeed to ignore the talents of current and future female astronauts. At the time of *Challenger*'s destruction, our program included many females. Two of them gave their lives aboard the *Challenger*.)

My oldest daughter frequently asks, "What was it like when John Glenn went up?"

My reply is, typically, "Well, what do you mean, what was it like? Do you mean, was it exciting?"

And she answers, "Yeah, Daddy, that's what I mean. Was it exciting to watch them make those first flights? How *did* it feel to watch them make those first flights? And how did you feel when they really landed on the moon? And what happened before *Challenger* blew up? Did others blow up? Tell me about it, Daddy. . . ."

What happened before the *Challenger*? What was it like to watch the space program as it developed . . . and fell apart? Those are interesting questions, questions that must be explained carefully if we are to preserve and put into perspective such an important part of our nation's recent history.

Challenger's loss marked the end of a period that began a long time ago. It all started when I was a little boy. It grew as I grew, right into that stage we call adulthood, whatever that is. I would like to tell you about it.

To the Heavens

I'm not a doctor or a child psychologist, so I don't know how early in life a person has memory of things. While I am sure I have memory of events before Easter of 1956, they are pretty vague. But I remember that Easter. I remember the big airplane.

That's right! For Easter of 1956 my grandparents gave me a beautiful model of a DC-7C airliner (one of the last giant piston-powered aircraft made obsolete in the late fifties by the Boeing 707). The model was huge, especially in the eyes of a three-year-old. It had running red and green lights and was painted in United Air Lines markings. The battery-powered propellers on the four engines whirled, and the landing gear extended and retracted. I loved that model airplane. Hell, I loved all airplanes.

Memories of those early years include trips with my father from our home in Connecticut to Newark and Idlewild (it's now John F. Kennedy International) Airports to watch planes taking off and landing. We always had a great time at the airport together. I usually got a new model airplane to help get me through those difficult periods between visits to the airport.

I could identify most of the commercial aircraft then in service with the major airlines. I could tell the difference between a DC-6 and the larger DC-7. I knew the difference between a standard Constellation and the advanced "Super G" model of that spectacular aircraft. And I often surprised the other folks on the observation deck with comments on new aircraft, like the exciting turbo-prop Viscount, whose peculiar shriek distinguished it from the conventional piston airplanes.

I must place at least part of the blame for my addiction to aviation on my parents, who supported "the sickness" right from the start. And I have loved aviation ever since.

My parents often reminded me that I was a very lucky boy, and they were right. We had a nice place to live, a new television, and a decent car. One only had to look at nearby New York City to see how poorly some people lived . . . and a few trips through the rougher sections of the Big Apple left me thoroughly convinced of my good fortune.

My folks often planned weekend trips to introduce me to various places of educational significance. I remember how impressed I was by the cadets at West Point and the scholarly students at Yale University. Because of my parents' extensive coaching, I knew a lot for a little kid. I could usually be found with the adults at family gatherings discussing phenomena such as the abominable snowman or President Eisenhower's health problems and the chances of Vice President Nixon becoming president should something happen to Ike. But my favorite topics remained airplanes and rockets.

Rockets were big news around 1957. The United States planned to put a satellite into orbit around the earth as part of the IGY (International Geophysical Year), a program in which participating nations would demonstrate technological expertise in the earth's upper atmosphere. IGY was my first exposure to space and our nation's desire to learn about it. My friends and I spent hours donning our imaginary space suits and piloting make-believe spacecraft to unknown worlds.

There was also excited talk about jet aircraft capable

of tremendous height and speed. Television reporters spoke of fantastic aircraft like the B-52 bomber, the Bell X-2, and the even more fantastic X-15 project. It seemed like there was a speed or altitude record being broken almost every week.

A barrage of science-fiction movies hit the screens. My favorite was *The Thing from Another World*. My interests were a happy conglomerate of airplanes, rockets, and spacemen.

On October 4, 1957, my father came home from work with exciting news. Some people called the Russians had launched a huge rocket and on top of that rocket was a satellite, which went into orbit around the earth. It was called *Sputnik*. Our scientists could hear *Sputnik* each time it flew over the United States, because it made a beeping sound. That was incredible news! But I was crushed to think the United States hadn't been first. I felt ashamed, and I was sure President Eisenhower was ashamed, too.

The television was full of *Sputnik* talk. One scientist after another spoke in grave tones about the consequences of Soviet technology in space. Pictures and articles filled the newspapers. The United States had to catch up—and I knew we would, because we were "the best."

Shortly after *Sputnik* went into orbit, the Russians placed yet another satellite, *Sputnik II*, into space. *Sputnik II* was so large, the Soviets put a dog named Laika inside it. *What a lucky dog*, I thought, until it was clear there were no provisions for Laika to return safely to earth. I wondered how long it would be before a man (or even a woman) would fly in space. I was certain the U.S. was doing something about it, and I listened and watched for the first sign of our participation.

Shortly after Laika's mission, the U.S. did do something. We tried to launch our first satellite, *Vanguard*, which blew up on the pad before the television cameras on December 6, 1957. The December 1957 *Vanguard* firing was only intended to be a test of the Vanguard system. A final version of *Vanguard* was scheduled to achieve orbit in March 1958. But in the commotion created by *Sputnik*, the press was hungry for a story and the test in December was treated like the real thing.

Our "second attempt," on January 31, 1958, was a success. The *Explorer I* satellite made it into orbit atop a Juno rocket designed by the famous German scientist Dr. Wernher von Braun. It made me very proud to be of German descent! That made up for all the teasing I got in school about my long German name.

There was such emphasis on men going into space around 1958 that there was even a television series called, you guessed it, "Men into Space." Watching "Men into Space" was a solemn responsibility if one was to have any credibility on the playground. I can't remember the leading actor's real name, but in the series he was Colonel McCauley, an Air Force officer. Each week Colonel McCauley and his men faced peril in space, and each week they lived to tell about it. I had a Colonel McCauley space helmet, complete with visor and microphones. I dutifully wore it for all missions flown in my big wooden toy box, which was large enough for one to climb into and close the sliding door—just like the real thing.

Another television show that was very popular because of the nation's newfound passion for great height and great speed was "Steve Canyon." "Steve Canyon" was about jet pilots, so watching it was also a solemn responsibility. And, of course, I had a Steve Canyon fighter pilot's helmet, complete with visor, oxygen mask, and microphone. For these jet missions within the atmosphere my toy box was instantly converted into an F-100 Super Sabre fighter jet.

I logged considerable hours flying that crate.

That summer, we went to Florida for vacation, in our new 1958 Chevrolet, replete with chrome. I remember talking about airplanes, space, and Elvis Presley on the long drive. Spaceflight was on my mind for the entire two weeks.

There was a lot of talk about space in Washington that summer, too. In fact, the topic was getting so much visibility that an entire civilian-run agency was created at President Eisenhower's request to address our efforts in space. The National Aeronautics and Space Administration (NASA), as the new agency was called, was charged with setting up a program to launch an American into space and return him safely.´

The formation of NASA, with its hopes to put Americans into space, was perhaps the most exciting single event of my childhood. I talked about NASA at show-and-tell at school. And soon replicas of the Jupiter and Atlas missiles joined the rows of model aircraft in my room.

The remainder of 1958 was spent visiting airports, building more models, and learning everything possible about NASA's projects. One of the hottest playground topics was, who would get to fly in space? Our astronauts, as the American space pilots were called, were to be selected from a group of military test pilots, and features in newspapers and on television describing the grueling selection process made the tension mount.

Finally, on April 9, 1959, NASA held a press conference in Washington and announced the names of seven military test pilots who had been selected to fly as astronauts in Project Mercury, the American manned space program. Their names? That's easy. I memorized them within an hour or two. They were: John H. Glenn, Jr., of the Marine Corps, Alan B. Shepard, Jr., of the Navy, Walter M. Schirra,

Jr., of the Navy, L. Gordon Cooper of the Air Force, M. Scott Carpenter of the Navy, Donald K. Slayton of the Air Force, and Virgil I. Grissom of the Air Force. My admiration of them was—and remains—immense.

Suddenly the stores were flooded with all kinds of "How and Why" books about Project Mercury and the astronauts . . . and I think my parents bought me every single one. I lapped the stuff up like ice cream. One of my favorites included special color stamps in the back. When you finished reading a chapter, you could go to the back of the book, find the color picture that matched what you had just read about, and place the stamp in the appropriate box at the end of the chapter. I got every picture right on the first try, which meant I should have been selected by NASA, too. They just didn't know there was some great young talent they'd overlooked.

1959. There I was, I thought, just a little kid, growing up in this great country with all that great stuff like the space program happening. More than anything else, I wanted to learn to fly and get picked to fly in space. My parents encouraged such idealistic dreams.

I got a lot of new airplane and rocket models in 1959. I also got my brother, Bob, who was born on July 25. I remember when my mother left for the hospital to go have him. That was back when big brothers and sisters were not allowed in the hospital. I think hospital personnel were afraid we would do something hideous if they actually let us know what was going on in there. Anyway, Bob was born and all I got to do was stand on the lawn in front of the damn hospital and wave to my mother! I never got any closer through the whole thing! Until the day I saw my mother again, I wasn't sure whether or not those hospital lunatics were going to keep her there forever.

While my mother was in the hospital, my father built me a model of a Piper Tri-Pacer airplane. That was special! I dreamed about flying a plane like the Tri-Pacer. I knew I could do it. It helped pass the time until that exciting day when we could bring my mother and Bob home. It was very hot outside, but I clearly remember my mother had Bob all covered up with blankets . . . and the blankets were over what appeared to be a tiny astronaut's pressure suit designed for babies. (It was actually a "sleeper" gown, but it looked a lot like a pressure suit to me.) Little Bob was sweating profusely, and I wondered if he'd make it home alive, despite all the protective clothing my mother had so wisely provided. After all, even though it was July, we could have had snow. Bob was a cute baby, but he fell far short of my expectations. I was essentially prepared to have this new partner with whom I could share my most sacred astronaut dreams. As it turned out, Bob didn't give a flip about Project Mercury or anything else, for that matter, aside from drinking his bottle, screaming, soiling his shorts, and sleeping. And I soon found out it would be years, literally, before I could effectively prepare young Robert for the conquest of space.

A combined total of five space shots were attempted by the U.S. and by the Soviet Union during 1959. We put two monkeys into orbit atop a Jupiter rocket in May. (They made the cover of *Life* Magazine.) Both nations were able to escape earth's gravitational pull in other attempts. Our *Pioneer 4* flew past the moon and continued into deep space. The Soviets missed the moon with *Luna 1*, but actually impacted the moon with *Luna 2* and took pictures of the far side of the moon with their *Luna 3*. The race was intensifying.

The following year, 1960, was a key year for the nation and for the space program. For starts, it was a presidential election year. While I vaguely recall people discussing the election in 1956, memory of the event is hazy. In the case of the 1960 election, however, my memory is very clear. President Eisenhower, having served two terms, was about to retire. A lot of people believed Richard Nixon, who had served as Ike's vice president for both terms, would easily win both the Republican nomination and the November presidential election. But there were quite a few strong Democratic contenders that year also. Among the Democrats was the junior senator from Massachusetts, John F. Kennedy.

After 1960, presidential politics was almost as interesting as the space program. I attribute the added interest to two things. First, the 1960 election was heavily covered by television. That type of exposure conveyed the magic of politics more easily than the print media, especially for a child who spent plenty of time in front of the television set. Second, Kennedy turned out to be quite special.

Reflecting upon 1960, it was a year of expanding horizons. My concept of who the Russians were had increased considerably since I first learned of *Sputnik* in 1957. The Soviet leader, a gent by the name of Nikita Khrushchev, was interesting but scary. During the spring of 1960, the Soviets shot down one of our magnificent U-2 high-altitude reconaissance aircraft. They held the pilot, an Air Force officer named Francis Powers, prisoner in Moscow. At first, our newspapers and the news on the television told us the U-2 had only been on a weather observation mission. But later we learned the U-2 had been on a "spy" mission over the Soviet Union.

I was intrigued with the U-2 incident because it involved high-altitude flight in an advanced superjet as well a global politics. Even NASA got involved in the attempt to explain away the spy mission.

Old Khrushchev had a ball with the U-2 incident. He used it to show what a sordid bunch we in the U.S. really were. The whole affair caused a field day for Soviet propaganda. In hindsight, I can hardly blame the Soviets for cashing in on a juicy opportunity. But it made us look really stupid at a time when we were feeling somewhat behind the eightball already. It finally took a major speech by President Eisenhower, who had authorized the U-2 flight and others like it, to put the issue to rest. And since this was 1960 and not the post-Watergate era and Eisenhower was a respectable guy, he was able to simply tell the truth and move on to other things. But we still looked dumb.

There was more from Khrushchev that year. He made some interesting appearances and provoked a lot of controversy. One of his most memorable performances took place when he removed one of his shoes and banged it on the conference table at an important meeting. On another occasion, Khrushchev held a little globe in his hand and, referring to the capitalist bloc, proclaimed, "We will bury you." That frightened a lot of people.

Because we had big bombs, big missiles, and guys like Khrushchev around, we had air raid drills at school. Fallout shelters were advertised on television. Dinner conversation in our new house (we moved to the town of Cheshire, Connecticut, in 1960) often centered on what we would do if the Russians started a nuclear war. And by 1960 I had the good, basic understanding of nuclear war required of every good little boy and girl in the 1960s.

Khrushchev even mattered out on the playground, where we created entire musical arrangements about him. A Walt Disney movie song, "Whistle While You Work," became

Whistle while you work,
Khrushchev is a jerk . . .

But despite the songs and our dislike of his shoe banging, Khrushchev scored a big hit in space in 1960 when his nation orbited a pair of dogs, named Strelka and Belka, in August. Even better, the dogs were returned from orbit aboard their *Sputnik V* spacecraft. There had been talk of a Mercury launch in 1960, and the flight of *Sputnik V* made a lot of people nervous.

Aside from the elections and Khrushchev, 1960 was also special because I became more interested in music that year. Despite the fact that he was severely deaf by the time I was born, my father is an outstanding pianist. We had a beautiful baby grand piano, and I often listened in amazement to his playing. He played almost anything, from his favorite Dave Brubeck jazz to Beethoven. I began to appreciate his music and the happiness it brought him.

My parents purchased a new "hi-fi" set that year. The sound it reproduced was incredible compared to that of conventional record players of the late fifties and early sixties. So there was music almost constantly in my house. If my father wasn't home playing his piano, my mother (who has a beautiful voice) would be singing along with her favorite Broadway musicals. I heard so much of *South Pacific* and *The Music Man* that I could recite the lines. I don't know how Bob, who was still pretty tiny, slept through all that noise.

I developed more of a personal interest in "popular" music, which really meant "rock and roll." Most of the popular music to which I listened prior to 1960 was recorded by Elvis Presley, although I distinctly remember "At the Hop" by Danny and the Juniors. In 1960, Elvis released what I've always thought was his best song—"Now or Never." All the girls I knew loved it, and I thought it sounded pretty neat, too.

This music, from my father's piano to the twanging of Elvis's guitar, was the early sound of the space program.

Autumn 1960. The presidential election was the hottest topic. For the first time in history, presidential candidates debated on television. I remember watching them.

As predicted, Nixon had won the Republican nomination. Kennedy was the Democratic nominee, and he was running much stronger against Nixon than my parents thought he would. My folks were great Eisenhower fans and, because Nixon was associated with Eisenhower as vice president, favored Nixon. But their criticisms of Kennedy faded somewhat by the time those first, historic "broadcast debates" took place.

Aside from the Eisenhower/Nixon popularity, the toughest obstacle Jack Kennedy faced in the 1960 election was his Catholicism, which was better known as "the religious issue." Kennedy handled the issue well, making those who questioned his ability to be both President and Catholic appear narrow-minded and naive.

After the debate, it didn't matter as much whether Kennedy was a Catholic or not; he just seemed to be the better candidate. His control under pressure during the debate was magnificent. Kennedy made the power of image a presidential prerequisite. His appearance was impeccable. In November, Jack Kennedy won the election, by a narrow margin. He was forty-three years old. And despite their earlier feelings about him, my parents went on to like Kennedy immensely.

The year 1960 ended with anticipation of a new administration and with no American in space. But we were on the threshold of, as Kennedy called it, the New Frontier. And everyone waited for something special to happen.

Mercury: Camelot's Magic Carpet

Connecticut usually gets lots of snow during the winter. That was especially true in the winter of 1960–61, when the drifts were so high I had to dig a tunnel from the front door all the way out to the street just so I could get on the school bus. My father took pictures of me on top of those snowdrifts with my friends that winter. When I look at these pictures now, I still can't believe how much snow was on the ground.

It is very beautiful in Connecticut after a snowstorm. There is a silence that is hard to describe, broken only by the creaking noises made by tree branches as they groan, bending under the weight of the snow. In 1961, our street was rather isolated, so the silence, especially in the early morning hours, was profound.

There was a little stream where I used to wait for the school bus, which was usually frozen over all winter. You could hear the cold water, fresh off the big hill in front of our house, rushing beneath the ice.

Since we were almost surrounded by forest, winter often brought wildlife down from the hill in search of food. For instance, one morning as I waited for the school bus, I heard a cracking noise coming from the direction of the stream. Wheeling around, I found myself face to face with a large deer. It regarded me momentarily with deep, lovely eyes and then continued to drink through the crack it had made in the ice. On another morning, a family of wild pheasants paraded proudly in front of me en route to the stream, barely acknowledging my presence. Memories of

1961 begin with special scenes like these—winter daydreams of beautiful New England.

There was a lot of snow south of New England that winter, too. In fact, on January 20, 1961, as Washington, D.C., recovered from a spectacular snowstorm, John F. Kennedy delivered his inaugural address in front of the Capitol. Deep piles of snow were everywhere and the sun was so glary that the poet Robert Frost, who took part in the inauguration ceremonies, had to quote verse from memory because he couldn't read his notes.

Even us school kids found Kennedy's speech stirring, and our teachers repeated the "ask not what your country can do for you; ask what you can do for your country" portion often. We were entering the Kennedy era. It was a very special time in our nation's history.

The story about growing up with the space program cannot be complete without President Kennedy, because in many ways he *was* the space program. What was so special about him? Millions of words have been written attempting to answer that question. Surely his cruel death turned him into a legend. William Manchester describes that aspect of the Kennedy mystique well in his excellent book *One Brief Shining Moment*. But in 1961, without any knowledge of his fate, we still thought President Kennedy was indeed a special kind of leader.

Young people found it easier to relate to Kennedy than Eisenhower. Eisenhower's image, especially to those of my generation, was more like that of a kindly grandfather. Kennedy, on the other hand, was like our own fathers. He was about the same age. He was a World War II veteran. And he had small children of his own. It was amazing to think that this young man was president of the United States.

Kennedy's brand of humor was refreshing. In fact,

his Washington press conferences were often so tastefully witty they were referred to as "the best matinees in town." He was a handsome man, and he dressed with natty, understated class. He wore his hair in a youthful style that was widely imitated. And he had an intelligent knockout of a wife who was the most elegant First Lady our nation would see for a long time. Just take a look at a picture of Jack and Jackie Kennedy together during their White House years. You'll see what I mean.

John F. Kennedy was a pragmatist. He had the ability to put himself in an adversary's shoes, look back at himself, and laugh. He was highly literate. And although he suffered terribly from back problems, he had the aura of an athelete about him, which went on to inspire a rather flabby nation.

Kennedy innovated new ideas like the Peace Corps and the President's Council on Physical Fitness. He appealed to the youth of this nation like no president ever has—to excel, to grow, and to dream. For that we took him as one of our own. We admired him and loved him.

With me, President Kennedy attained astronaut status without being an astronaut.

Speaking of astronauts, the new president had different views on our space program than did his predecessor, President Eisenhower. Ike was kind of lukewarm on the whole idea of sending men into space. Ike felt machines could do the job as well—if not better—than humans. So he agreed to a manned space program reluctantly, after considerable pressure from people like (then) senate majority leader Lyndon Johnson, who saw the Soviet successes as an outrage.

President Kennedy made the space program a top priority. His admiration for the seven Mercury astronauts became well known. He insisted upon precise communications with NASA managers. To eliminate the "clouding" of any space-related issues, he made it possible for the administrator of NASA to communicate directly with the White House without going through a lot of bureaucratic red tape. And while he urged the program forward he never encouraged sacrificing quality for speed.

When President Kennedy took office in January 1961, our efforts to get a manned Mercury mission off the pad were suffering. One technical setback followed another. There were problems with the Mercury/Redstone combination, which would loft the first suborbital missions. And the Mercury/Atlas combination faced even greater problems in its task of boosting an American astronaut into orbit and returning him safely. Even Kennedy's science adviser was questioning Mercury's success.

But eleven days after Kennedy's innauguration, a Redstone rocket with a Mercury spacecraft on top lobbed a monkey named Ham on a successful suborbital ride into space, similar to the first missions planned for the astronauts. President Kennedy was keenly interested.

In 1960, Kennedy ran on a premise to "get the country moving again." As part of that promise, he was determined to stimulate our schools of higher learning and our bastions of technology. NASA was a key to his goals. Kennedy had shown the voters he was the best candidate by using the technology of television to his advantage. Now, as president, he planned to show the world who really had the edge in space by using the technology available at NASA to the nation's advantage. Kennedy's plans went far beyond Project Mercury. Meanwhile, we waited for our first astronaut to thunder skyward.

To set the stage for the first Mercury flights, some Cold War history is necessary. Global tension was high.

During Kennedy's presidency, the threat of thermonuclear war was was more intense than at any time in history. Ads for fallout shelters greeted us constantly on television. The reality of it was awesome. There was even a model fallout shelter on display right in the middle of our town, with a sign that read:

A FAMILY OF 6 WILL SURVIVE HERE.

Anxiety was intense. It seemed only President Kennedy stood between us and Khrushchev's ICBMs (Intercontinental Ballistic Missiles, capable of lofting nuclear warheads at any city in the United States).

The shaky peace we perceived was strained even more when, in April, Kennedy suffered the biggest disappointment of his tenure as president. The culprit was a poorly planned invasion of Cuba by a band of Cuban nationalists. Originally planned during Eisenhower's administration, the so-called Bay of Pigs operation was encouraged by the Joint Chiefs of Staff and was backed by the CIA. Kennedy reluctantly gave his approval for the operation, basing his decision on the military's predictions of victory.

The operation was anything but victorious, and, even worse, it smacked of improper U.S. involvement. Kennedy and the nation were bitterly embarrassed. In a statement to the nation the new president took total blame for the operation, even though in reality the operation was not entirely Kennedy's fault. Amazingly, Kennedy's prestige, which was considerable during his first ninety days in office, surged. The president's forthright acceptance of responsibility played well with the American public. But the consequences of the Bay of Pigs ordeal internationally were potentially threatening. More than anything, we needed a "win."

Around the same time as the Bay of Pigs debacle, NASA announced that three of our seven astronauts were candidates for the first historic flight. The three were John Glenn, Alan Shepard, and Virgil "Gus" Grissom. NASA's announcement further intensified the anticipation. At Darcey Elementary School, we were confident the first man into space would be an American astronaut.

The Bay of Pigs incident was bad enough for American prestige, but what happened next was devastating. I remember my father came home from work on Wednesday, April 12, 1961, with big news. The Soviet Union had scored again by launching one of their cosmonauts (as they called their astronauts) not only into space but clear into orbit! A Soviet Air Force major by the name of Yuri Gagarin had flown a complete orbit of the earth in his *Vostok I* spacecraft.

I was happy for Gagarin because his accomplishment was truly admirable. And the fact that a man had actually flown in space was thoroughly exciting. But what about our Mercury astronauts?

The national mood was crushed. Kennedy called hasty meetings. Everyone was worried. NASA was clearly under pressure to make something happen. Days, then weeks, passed.

Freedom 7

On Friday, May 5, NASA prepared to launch Alan B. Shepard, Jr., into space on a ballistic flight atop a Redstone rocket. The "How and Why" books about Project Mercury prepared me well. I knew the difference between the Redstone flights, which were essentially cannonball lobs into and out of space, and the big missions, which were orbital flights launched via the mightly Atlas.

I was really lucky that day because I didn't have to go to school. My parents asked for me to be excused from class so I could go to New Jersey to visit my grandfather. That meant I could listen to the entire flight on the car radio without interruption.

It was a beautiful warm spring day. We stopped at a nearby American Oil (today it's Amoco) station in our 1960 Ford Fairlane 500 for gas before departing on the two-hour drive. You didn't have to pump your own gas back in 1961. A cheery gas station attendant *in a clean uniform* ran out to fill your tank. And while he filled your tank, he checked your oil, cleaned the windshield, and checked the air in your tires. And then he *thanked* you and asked you to come by again! And the whole thing cost maybe five dollars. Try to find that kind of service today . . . or that kind of price. Somehow the customer has lost.

A radio was blasting away in the gas station garage; the mechanics were listening to the lengthy preflight coverage. A guy pulled up in an outstanding brand-new '61 Impala convertible. He had the preflight on his radio, too. Everywhere people were watching or listening to NASA's first crack at flying in space.

The Mercury suborbital flights were not lengthy missions. Because the seventy-eight thousand pounds of thrust generated by the Redstone were insufficient to place a Mercury spacecraft into orbit, the result of a Mercury/Redstone launch was an elegant ballistic arc of about three hundred miles down the Atlantic Missile Range. An apogee—or peak altitude—or about 110 miles was achieved, and then the spacecraft descended back into the atmosphere for a splashdown target near Abaco Island in the Bahamas. Total flight time: about fifteen minutes.

But before Shepard lifted off, he spent hours inside his tiny spacecraft, *Freedom 7* (each manned Mercury mission was named by its pilot and ended in 7, representing the seven Mercury astronauts), as he waited through lengthy "holds" in the countdown for one reason or another. It seemed Shepard would never get to fly; the whole damn thing was just too complicated, and the Soviets had obviously mastered the technique of launching machines and men into space much better than our team.

That wasn't true. My books told me how utterly careful NASA was, and I was reassured, knowing near-perfect conditions would be met before NASA said, "Go."

A little after 9:30 A.M. (EDST), the Redstone ignited and Alan Shepard successfully flew *Freedom 7* to a well-placed splashdown. America had her first astronaut, and America was in love with Alan Shepard, the other astronauts, Project Mercury, and NASA.

It is difficult to describe the utter joy we felt that day. There was feeling of pride that enveloped everyone. On television there were special programs about Project Mercury. Shortly after Shepard's flight, a special show about the astronauts followed "My Three Sons," which we always watched on Thursday nights. My mother got so choked up with pride, she cried. God, it was great.

President Kennedy cashed in on the flight of *Freedom 7* by presenting Shepard with the Distinguished Service Award medal in a ceremony at the White House. There were pictures of the fanfare in all the magazines, and it was on the news on television. Shepard even got a big parade. Kennedy's prestige increased.

Then Kennedy made his move. On May 25, he asked Congress for funds to land Americans on the moon! His words were widely publicized, and they were typically eloquent and highly inspirational. The president declared, "Now is the time to take longer strides . . . time for a great American enterprise . . . time for this nation to take a clearly leading role in space achievement, which in many ways may hold the key to our future on earth.

"I belive this nation should commit itself to achieving the goal, before this decade is out, of landing a man on the moon and returning him safely to earth. No single space project in this period will be more impressive to mankind, or more important for the long-range exploration of space, and none will be so difficult or expensive to accomplish."

The national mood was ripe. As we prepared for the second manned Mercury mission, plans for our effort to land Americans on the moon before 1970 began in earnest. The lunar landing project was named Apollo.

Liberty Bell 7

The summer of 1961 was the first "space summer." Specifically, it was the first summer vacation dominated by manned missions in space. Among other things, I would spend the next twenty-six summers in some stage of anticipation of another flight in space.

I told you how beautiful it was in Connecticut during the winter. It's that way during the rest of the year, too. Summertime is the high season in New England. In 1961, I was having a great time playing outside with my friends or watching fallout shelter ads on television. President Kennedy went on TV and talked about some war in a country called Laos. I really didn't care.

There were more special shows about space. And on July 21 another Redstone rocket roared upward, carrying astronaut Virgil I. "Gus" Grissom into space aboard his Mercury spacecraft, *Liberty Bell 7*. Since we were all home on summer vacation, I watched coverage of the flight on television with my mother and Bob. Bob was basically unimpressed.

It was a great flight, just like Shepard's, until the splashdown. Grissom's Mercury spacecraft was equipped with several modifications that were not aboard Shepard's *Freedom 7*. One of the mods was a hatch designed to open easier at the end of the mission because it had an explosive-bolt system. Instead of leaving the spacecraft through its tiny neck or waiting until the recovery crew unlatched an array of bolts, Grissom only had to "blow" the hatch when a recovery helicopter snagged the top of the spacecraft and lifted it enough so water couldn't enter the interior. But somehow Grissom's hatch blew off prematurely. Sea water poured in over the open sill, and *Liberty Bell 7*, complete with a painted crack for realism, sank in deep water off the Bahamas.

Gus Grissom nearly drowned as Marine helicopters struggled to pull his sinking spacecraft out of the water. The Marines were still using piston-powered helicopters in 1961, and there just wasn't enough lift available to do the job. It was reported that one of the helicopters almost had an engine failure trying to rescue the water-laden *Liberty Bell 7*.

Despite the sinking, NASA said the mission was a success. And if NASA said it was a success, that was good enough for everyone. We had our second man back, a little waterlogged but safe from a ride into space. And I thought no less of Gus Grissom. He was a good man.

Our celebration only lasted about two weeks, however, before the Soviets did it again—in grand style. On August 6, the news on television described the launch of cosmonaut Gherman Titov atop another giant booster, in the mission of *Vostok 2*. Titov wasn't kidding around either. He flew seventeen orbits of the earth, which meant he was in space for about twenty-five full hours. That was 24.5 hours longer than Shepard's and Grissom's combined total time. I couldn't help but admire the Soviet accomplishment, even if we were supposed to hate them for it.

After Titov flew, with our efforts to orbit a man stalled by complications, we did the next best thing: we listened to Chubby Checker's "Let's Do the Twist."

There was a crisis in Berlin, Germany, when the Soviets actually built a wall to keep people from getting out to the "free" side of West Berlin. The pictures on TV were ugly, showing thousands of people staring at the wall, obviously wondering if anyone would risk their lives trying to escape. President Kennedy made a speech on TV about Berlin, and everyone wondered what the Russians would try next.

Before I knew it, winter arrived. Titov's flight convinced NASA to cancel any remaining suborbital flights and to go for the big one . . . the first orbital mission. Astronaut John Glenn was selected to be the first to ride the Atlas, and he was expected to fly before the end of the year. It didn't happen. Weather and other technical malfunctions prevented our chances of going into orbit until February 1962. But when the opportunity finally did present itself, it was spectacular.

Friendship 7

Waiting for John Glenn's flight was agonizing because of all the delays. Between December and February, Glenn suited up several times, climbed into the spacecraft, and sat for hours, only to suffer the disappointment of a "scrubbed" mission. But Glenn was a test pilot, well versed in technical delays. He accepted them as part of the business.

The American public had to learn to accept the delays, too, and it was difficult. NASA never wavered. They insisted on optimum conditions before they tried to boost John Glenn into orbit. NASA performed like true professionals. Safety was not up for a vote. It could not be compromised.

Glenn was quite a celebrity even before the mission. He was the only Marine in the Original Seven. He had a solid reputation as an outstanding test pilot, and he held a transcontinental speed record, set in a Marine Corps supersonic fighter. He even appeared as a special guest on television game shows. Somehow he seemed like the astronaut's astronaut. *Life* magazine showed many photographs of Glenn training diligently for his orbital mission. As clear evidence of my esteem for Glenn, my list of heroes in early 1962 consisted of my father, President Kennedy, Alan Shepard, Gus Grissom, and John Glenn.

The year 1962 began with a new car. My father arrived home one evening in a brand-new 1962 Ford Galaxy. This was a company car. And it was a real beauty, with a sparkling white exterior and a luxurious cardinal red interior, loaded with options. That new car epitomized the way we felt in 1962. We knew we produced the best of everything in the world: cars, watches, televisions, you name it. In 1962, American-made was a status symbol. If you couldn't afford a Ford or a GM car, your old man wasn't cutting the mustard. Mine was, and I thought he was as super as John Glenn for doing it.

There were other mores. In the White House, President Kennedy was setting a standard of class that had every American household talking. We saw articles about the gala dinners the president and Mrs. Kennedy hosted. The food they served was prepared by a celebrated French chef. The menus were printed in French. Artists like Pablo Casals played at the White House. So did modern jazz ensembles, ballet troups, and noted actors and actresses. As far as the sixties went, it was the age of class, gang, and we all knew it. Many compared the Kennedy era to a popular Broadway show of the time titled *Camelot*. How proud we were!

Tuesday, February 20, 1962, was clear and icy cold in Connecticut. A snowstorm had just left over three feet of snow on the ground, and the pleasant result was a snow day: school was canceled. What perfect timing! For NASA was ready to launch John Glenn into orbit. This mission was a television spectacular. The brief duration of Shepard's and Grissom's flights precluded extended in-flight coverage by the major networks. But Glenn was supposed to fly three full orbits, a mission that would take hours instead of a mere fifteen minutes.

In position before our TV at 7:00 A.M., I was thrilled to hear Col. John "Shorty" Powers, the "Voice of Mercury Control," as the countdown for *Friendship 7* progressed. Even though I watched the coverage in black and white (color TV was still an expensive luxury; few programs were available in color, and when they were, the people looked green or yellow), each live close-up of the magnificent booster, poised for flight aside its huge gantry, was outstanding. Glenn's Atlas was nearly a living thing as clouds of vapor poured from its sides, indicating that the super-cold liquid oxygen, which was used as an oxidizer for the hydrazine fuel, was aboard.

At 9:47 A.M., the countdown reached the long-awaited point of "ignition." It was immediately apparent that this launch was very different from the relatively "clean" ignition we saw with the Redstone. The Atlas belched torrents of flame. Vast clouds of steam abruptly surrounded the Pad 14 Complex as thousands of gallons of water cascaded into specially designed trenches to prevent damage to the pad by the brimstonelike power of the Atlas's 360,000 pounds of brute thrust. The viselike hold-down clamps fell away, and *Friendship 7* rose gallantly into the sky. Minutes later, with only a squiggled contrail remaining to mark his ascent, John Glenn was successfully in orbit around the earth.

As in the flights of *Freedom 7* and *Liberty Bell 7*, we couldn't see what the astronaut was actually doing while in flight; there were no television cameras aboard the tiny Mercury spacecraft. Our impressions of "real-time" events were derived strictly from voice communication with the astronaut (and those tranmissions were mighty sketchy), descriptions made by the TV commentator (gents who we would know later as anchors), and animation.

Glenn was having a great time. He carried out several medical experiments, and he squelched fears he would encounter the same disorientation problems Titov complained about during his flight in *Vostok 2*. Since the space program had begun, many had expressed grave doubts man could exist in a weightless state. Glenn was proving them wrong.

After a while, problems cropped up in the spacecraft's automatic control system. Glenn took over manual control and found he had no difficulty keeping *Friendship 7* properly aligned. The Mercury astronauts had fought desperately to have control of their craft. Prior to Shepard's flight, critics claimed the Mercury astronauts were merely passengers along for a ride in a totally automated system. For the astronauts, all of them proven test pilots, such an arrangement would have meant acute embarrassment. But the "passenger" scenario was not the case. The Mercury astronauts did pilot their vehicles during critical phases of flight, and Glenn's mission was a good example.

Then the serious story broke. Via telemetry, Mercury Control began receiving indications that the little landing bag on *Friendship 7* had deployed in orbit. This smacked of peril. The landing bag was supposed to act as a landing cushion, deploying just prior to splashdown. Since the landing bag was essentially a skirt attached to the blunt, ablative heat shield, a deployed landing bag in flight meant Glenn's sole protection against the deadly heat of reentry—the heat shield itself—was no longer in place against the spacecraft. A loose heat shield in orbit would mean a dead astronaut after reentry.

The drama on the ground was intense. The situation was so scary that Mercury Control only hinted at the problem to Glenn himself, who later in the flight finally deduced from the strange inquiries from the ground concerning the landing bag position light that something was very wrong.

On the Mercury spacecraft, a set of straps helped hold the small retro rocket pack in place against the exterior of the heat shield. Normally (or "nominally" in NASA-ese), the straps were jettisoned along with the spent retropack following retro-fire, leaving a "clean" heat shield surface. But, given the telemetry data, it was decided to leave the retropack and straps in place after retro-fire, so the straps might help hold the potentially deployed landing bag and loose heat shield in place.

After retro-fire, we all tensed up. On TV, we could see flight controllers at NASA praying. No one was really sure whether John Glenn would fry upon reentry or not. He didn't. The heat shield worked. *Friendship 7* returned safely from space, and John Glenn was the new hero.

Glenn was such a hero that he got a gigantic ticker-tape parade in New York. He addressed a joint session of Congress. And he got a visit from President Kennedy, who flew to Cape Canaveral to meet him when he arrived back in Florida from the spacecraft recovery area.

With the success of Glenn's flight, it was difficult to concentrate on anything else. I built models of all scales and sizes of the Mercury spacecraft. I taped pictures of each astronaut on my bedroom door. I answered questions by saying "roger," instead of "yes."

And even those who were less fanatical about space-flight couldn't ignore the exciting, positive impact the space program had upon the entire nation. We were still behind the Soviets in space spectaculars, but our plans were vast and we had President Kennedy at the helm. Few doubted our eventual success.

It was a strange interlude: our Cold War worries were many, but I remember most of 1962 as a very happy time. Shelly Fabares sang "Johnny Angel" on "The Donna Reed Show." (She played the teenage daughter, and I was in love with her.) Wally Cleaver dated Mary Ellen Rogers on "Leave It to Beaver." "The Beverly Hillbillies" went on the air every Wednesday night and left millions of households in stitches. And my father's hard work was paying off; our standard of living seemed to improve almost every month. We had nice clothes and two TVs. We went out to dinner regularly, and there were numerous "mini vacations" to great places like Boston; Newport, Rhode Island; and Mystic, Connecticut.

At school, I was elected president of my class. I was called upon frequently to talk about the space program, and I enjoyed that immensely. My baseball game improved. I learned how to run faster than any of the other guys. I even got notes from girls. Life was fun.

Aurora 7

On Thursday, May 24, we sent Scott Carpenter into orbit. "Deke" Slayton was supposed to be the pilot for this mission, but he was pulled from flight status because he supposedly had an irregularity in his heartbeat. After all the excruciating testing required of the Original Seven, one would think Slayton was as qualified to fly, physically, as the other six. But ultimately NASA said, "No." It was a tough rap for a great pilot like Slayton, a top-notch Air Force test pilot with a fantastic reputation at Edwards Air Force Base, where he had personally tested some of our hottest aircraft. Anyway, Slayton postured himself for a position of considerable power as head of the Astronaut Office as the program matured. And, eventually, Deke Slayton would get to fly in space.

But in 1962 Carpenter got the flight. His mission profile was basically a repeat of Glenn's, to confirm the integrity of the Mercury system in orbit. Additionally, Carpenter was responsible for a multitude of scientific experiments while in orbit. Really, I think they gave him too much to do.

We listened to the launch at school. As far as Mercury countdowns went, Carpenter's was relatively free of the anguishing holds that had plagued the previous flights. After the lift-off, I mentally prepared to watch coverage of the recovery portion of the flight at home that afternoon.

When I finally got in front of the TV, Carpenter had a serious fuel problem: as he manuevered *Aurora 7* about in orbit, he used too much of the peroxide fuel that controlled the spacecraft's attitude. So the spacecraft's attitude was incorrect during retro-fire, resulting in an overshoot of the targeted splashdown area of over 250 miles.

Walter Cronkite got choked up and said he feared we may have lost our first astronaut, because Carpenter, unable to communicate his position, had disappeared! I was shocked. Even Bob got upset.

In Connecticut, the agonizing wait to learn the outcome of Carpenter's flight was broken by another event.

Of all things, a *tornado* touched down in the nearby town of Wolcott, destroying a vast amount of property. The cracking noise we heard as we stood in front of our house was the sound of wood being ripped away from homes that were leveled by the funnel. Tornadoes are rare in New England, and the event was eerie. It was quite an afternoon.

Well, Carpenter finally showed up, bobbing next to *Aurora 7* in his life raft. Astronaut and spacecraft were safe, and you could almost hear sighs of relief from every house on our street.

After the flight of *Aurora 7*, the Mercury program reached a certain degree of maturity. Four astronauts had returned safely from space. The program moved toward more aggressive goals.

There were problems, but they were being corrected. One of the most serious problems was the excessive amount of fuel Carpenter used during his three orbits. The spacecraft was so small, there wasn't any room left for enlarged fuel tanks. And extra weight in fuel would rob the Atlas of performance needed to achieve orbit. Since a primary goal of Mercury was at least one long-duration flight of about eighteen orbits, NASA felt a mission was needed to demonstrate the adequacy of the fuel system as it was, before sending an astronaut up for the long mission.

Given the concerns over fuel depletion and some additional questions about the spacecraft cooling system, the automatic control system, and a list of less serious unknowns, NASA decided the next mission would consist of six orbits. The astronaut would be Wally Schirra, a sharp Navy pilot with the reputation of resident huckster among the Original Seven.

A lot happened, however, between Carpenter's flight in May and Schirra's, which took place in October.

On August 11, Khrushchev's boys scored another spectacular when a Soviet cosmonaut roared into orbit aboard *Vostok 3*. The next day, another Soviet cosmonaut achieved orbit aboard the *Vostok 4* spacecraft. *Vostok 3* remained in orbit for nearly four days. *Vostok 4* flew for nearly three days. Although the two Soviet craft could not rendezvous in orbit (neither *Vostok* was capable of changing—or translating—from one orbit to another), they were said to have come within sight of each other in space.

What could we say? The magnitude of those flights was overwhelming. Aside from technical success, the propaganda value of the combined flights of *Vostok 3* and *Vostok 4* was immense.

We regained the spotlight on August 27, when our own *Mariner 2* unmanned space probe pulled off a successful fly-by of the planet Venus. I didn't care what anyone said about the Russian circus shows in space, that Venus fly-by was a real work of art. We were in it for the duration; I just knew it.

By 1962, I was aware we had a racial problem of sorts in our country, but the problem wasn't very evident where we lived in Connecticut. Yes, there were blacks (we called them Negroes then, not blacks) in Connecticut, but there were hardly any in our town. We had one black street. The few we had lived there.

At school, there was but one black student, a girl. She was a year younger than I. Had there been such a thing as a special education class, she would have been in that program. She was what we now call a severely learning disabled child. We didn't refer to her problem in such dignified terms; to us, she was a "retard." Many believed part of her problem was simply her race: "They tend to be stupid, you know." We were the stupid ones for not recognizing her handicap.

President Kennedy actively campaigned for special classes for students like her and eventually passed critical legislation in support of special education and the mentally handicapped. The solution to the plight of the black American was vastly more complex.

Segregation and similar social inequalities were minor issues if you lived in Cheshire, Connecticut, in 1962. It just wasn't something you spent time worrying about until you watched the news on television.

In September, the governor of Mississippi tried to prevent a young black man from entering the University of Mississippi. There was an ugly demonstration and considerable violence over this issue, and President Kennedy went on national TV to talk about it. It took the National Guard and much intervention by President Kennedy and his brother Robert, who was attorney general of the United States, to finally get James Meredith, the black student applicant, admitted.

It was difficult to understand the mentality of the South. My parents tried to explain it, and certainly, we had studied about the Civil War, slavery, and related topics in school. But in 1962, when we were sending men into space and we had unbelievable technology like the *Telstar* satellite (there was a great recording by the Tornadoes in 1962 named "Telstar"), it was hard to believe such backward thinking still existed.

This was my indoctrination to the world of Freedom Riders, NAACP, and equality marches. It was the first time I worried about riots in our cities. I read about the Ku Klux Klan. It was confusing and sickening. You see, up to this point, black people were, well, just people. I didn't love them and I didn't hate them. Now I felt like I had to take sides. I took the obvious one. You couldn't treat people unequally just because of the color of their skin. I felt the governor of Mississippi didn't deserve the office, nor did anyone else who had such a narrow mind about other human beings. To me, Gov. Ross Barnett of Mississippi wasn't any better than old Khrushchev. They had no class.

Sigma 7

Wednesday, October 3, 1962, was a great day for NASA. Portable televisions were on in just about every classroom at school, and we watched astronaut Walter "Wally" Schirra bolt into orbit atop another thundering Atlas. Soon after lift-off, NASA monitored roll-rates (roll is one of three possible axes in flight), which were so high for the launch vehicle that flight controllers nearly aborted the flight. If they had done so, the escape rocket system would have pulled *Sigma 7* from the malfunctioning *Atlas D* and Schirra would have landed safely by parachute. Fortunately, the decision to abort was discarded and Schirra successfully flew six complete orbits, twice as long as Glenn or Carpenter. Even better, Schirra splashed down amazingly close to his recovery ship, with plenty of maneuvering fuel left. The astronaut learned his mission was nearly aborted after recovery.

By drifting in orbit and not worrying about aligning *Sigma 7* constantly, Schirra did a super job conserving his fuel. The flight of *Sigma 7* proved a Mercury spacecraft could remain aloft for a long-duration mission. It was exciting.

But October 1962 still harbored surprises. The simmering Cold War literally came to a boil. The incident that brought our nation and the Soviet Union to the brink of nuclear war involved, of all things, missiles, but not missiles with men riding on top of them.

On October 16, experts confirmed to President Kennedy that the Soviet Union was shipping missiles to Cuba, just ninety miles off the coast of Florida. With those missiles, warheads could be launched against a staggering number of American cities and against other key sites in the western hemisphere. High-altitude reconaissance flights conducted in U-2 aircraft (like the one the Soviets shot down in 1960) confirmed that missile sites on Cuba were indeed intact and ready to become operational.

This was President Kennedy's greatest test while he was in office. It also was his most stunning victory.

We heard nothing of the Soviet missile buildup in Cuba from the White House, on TV, or in the newspapers on the sixteenth. In fact, Kennedy kept what we now call the Cuban Missile Crisis an absolute secret until Monday, October 22, when he went on national television to explain that the United States was going to blockade ("quarantine" was term used) Cuba, to prevent further missile shipments from the Soviet Union.

The president stated that any missiles launched from Cuba against any point in the western hemisphere would be interpreted by the United States as a full-fledged attack upon the United States and that the United States would retaliate immediately. Remember the movie *War Games*? Well, this was real, live war games. The result may well have been global thermonuclear war.

We all watched President Kennedy on television that night. My mother cried. My father, who rarely showed emotion, went downstairs to our cellar with a grave look on his face, to check on the boxes of old Army C rations he's saved up. We checked the batteries in all of our flashlights, and my mother filled plastic bottles with water, in case we were attacked. Since we lived between New York and Boston, we speculated that we might survive an attack, but that all electricity would cease and there would be no food.

We were wrong. An all-out attack upon New York, Boston, or both cities would probably have been fatal to most Connecticut residents. The devastation of nuclear fallout was not fully understood in 1962. Many believed nuclear fallout was survivable by simply ducking under a desk or using a newspaper to protect the face.

Kennedy's plan was daring and shrewd. There are several excellent books about the Cuban Missile Crisis offering details on Kennedy's handling of the event. So if you are intrigued by the sheer intensity of this episode, when nuclear war was just the push of a button away, I heartily recommend them. Robert Kennedy's *Thirteen Days* is perhaps the best account of the crisis. His role in its resolution was crucial, and his book makes for thrilling reading.

On Sunday, October 28, the Soviets backed down. They agreed to cease shipments of missiles, and they further agreed to dismantle the sites already in place on Cuba. There was no war and President Kennedy emerged a hero.

Christmas of 1962 was a joyful, happy occasion at home in Connecticut. Santa brought me three books about the space program and a Gilbert chemistry set, which I never really used. My mother still had hopes I'd become a medical doctor someday, so I also got a model of the human eye. Models of hearts, eyes, and bodies were big that year. The dawn of the manned space program caused a scientific renaissance of sorts, and everyone was into some sort of scientific venture.

Even Bob got a neat scientific present. It was called a "Jimmy Jet"—essentially a replica of a fighter jet cockpit, complete with joystick, gun sights, and thrust levers. Of course, I had to fill young Bob in on proper usage of his new toy. I wore out his first set of batteries flying heavy combat missions.

My favorite Christmas present that year was a beautiful telescope fully equipped with an expensive metal tripod. I sat outside in −14 F. degree air, trying to find Polaris. I loved it. I could see space.

The perceived U.S. victory in the Cuban missile affair served as a positive transition into 1963 for President Kennedy. His popularity was climbing steadily, and memories of the miserable Bay of Pigs incident were fading. Our teachers spoke of the president in almost loving terms. There was a big Mercury mission coming up. The year 1963 looked like it was going to be fantastic.

Since I was such a fan of the president, I never failed to watch his State of the Union addresses, which took place in January of each year. My parents explained to me at a very early age how important it was to understand current events, and what the president of the United States said on television certainly fell into that category.

President Kennedy delivered his 1963 State of the Union address to a joint session of Congress on Monday, January 14. In his speech, he discussed a situation in a tiny country on the other side of the world. The country was called Vietnam. I darted into my room and located Vietnam on my globe. It was really close to Laos, another country the president had talked about on television.

My father explained that communists were trying to take over the government of Vietnam and that was bad. There were American soldiers in Vietnam helping the free Vietnamese people fight against the communist bad guys, who were known as the Vietcong. But the Americans who were there were volunteers. They were called advisors. There was no real American army in Vietnam, only the advisors. And President Kennedy was against sending regular American ground troops into Vietnam.

At the time, Vietnam was not an important topic in discussions with my family and friends. Like so many Cold War situations, it was just another nuisance to most of us who did not occupy positions of national power. What could I do about it? I was confident President Kennedy would handle the situation and that, in time, it would go away.

I was correct. In time, Vietnam would "go away." But it did a lot of haunting in between. From that day in 1963 Vietnam went on to wield tremendous influence on my life and upon the lives of millions. We grew up with the space program, all right. We also grew up with Vietnam. In fact, the American nightmare in Vietnam would take over twelve years beyond President Kennedy's 1963 State of the Union address to officially go away. Unofficially, I think it will never go away.

Springtime of 1963 was as beautiful as ever up in Connecticut. Vietnam was far away, and few really cared about it. President Kennedy made overtures to Chairman Khrushchev about a treaty between the United States and the Soviet Union that would ban testing of nuclear weapons in the atmosphere. And it looked like Khrushchev was interested.

At Cape Canaveral and at the new manned space center in Houston, Texas, NASA decided against more than one more Mercury mission. A new program, Project Gemini, had been approved a year earlier, and NASA was anxious to get on with it. Gemini sounded exciting: two astronauts (*Gemini* meant "twins") would fly instead of one, and a typical Gemini mission would be packed with exciting firsts, designed to give us the experience needed to fly to the moon.

A second group of astronauts had been selected, and

there was news of still another group. Astronauts from these groups would land on the moon someday, and that day was getting closer.

If you wrote NASA for information on the space program, they responded promptly. Naturally I did just that, and by the springtime of 1963 I was receiving regular mail from NASA. It was terribly exciting to get off the school bus, race to the mailbox, and find a big important-looking envelope from NASA there, with my name on it. Inside the envelope there were usually gobs of data. For instance, one package contained a beautiful booklet titled *John Glenn Orbits the Earth for America*. I brought that book straight to school and showed it off to everyone, including the principal.

Faith 7

'Although there was only one Mercury mission left, Mercury went out in style. Astronaut Gordon Cooper was scheduled to fly his Mercury spacecraft, *Faith 7*, for twenty-two orbits: a mission that would take over twenty-four hours!

Wednesday, May 15, was Cooper's day to fly. Once again, the television sets were tuned in and everyone at school was pumped up about such a daring mission.

The lift-off was spectacular. This was the final Mercury mission. A significant chapter in history was coming to a close. I knew I would miss Mercury and the primal excitement a Mercury mission evoked. But at the time, I didn't pause for a whole lot of reflection. There was too much going on. It was like there would be no end to the excitement of exploring space.

Cooper's mission was problem-free until the very last moment, when *Faith 7*'s electrical system went berserk on

Cooper and, literally, dropped most of his systems off line. Cooper aligned *Faith 7* manually for retro-fire . . . and scored a near bull's-eye splashdown.

After a speech to a joint session of Congress and a huge parade, Cooper became a superhero of near–John Glenn proportions. While I thought the world of Glenn (and the rest of the Original Seven), Gordon Cooper really got my attention. He was what the military pilots called a "hot stick." He was my kind of pilot. I began dreaming about flying lessons.

Did you notice there were certain times in your life when you were very aware of the fact that you were growing up? The summer of 1963 was one of those times for me. Things that weren't important before became important.

Take eating out, for example. Going to a restaurant was typically an inconvenience, as far as I was concerned. It meant putting down the space book or letting the model rocket sit for hours while my parents took forever just to drink a damn cup of coffee. And I usually had to get all dressed up just to watch.

Suddenly, I didn't mind going out so much. I didn't mind because when you went out someplace, there were usually girls to watch when you got to where you were going. And that wasn't all bad.

The bottom line was, girls were getting better looking every day. Jacqueline Kennedy was gorgeous beyond belief. Even the girls at school started looking better. I talked to my brother Bob about this, but he still didn't care. He was logging serious time in his Jimmy Jet.

By the fall of 1963, I had taken my first airplane ride. That, aside from seeing Ann Margaret in *Bye Bye Birdie*, was the absolute highlight of the summer, which hadn't been a bad summer at all. They wouldn't let me take flying lessons yet, so I just paid three dollars for a twenty-minute ride. But they did let me sit in the copilot's seat, and that was better than looking at *Playboys* with my friends.

The Soviets had staged their usual summer space spectacular; this time it was a boy/girl act, with *Vostok 5* flying for five days with a male cosmonaut aboard and *Vostok 6* joining him in orbit for over two days with the world's first female in space, Soviet cosmonaut Valentina Tereshkova.

I was elected class president again that fall. That made it three years in a row. The female vote made the difference. I loved them. Elvis sang "Little Sister" and Leslie Gore sang "It's My Party." I really started to like what my parents called pop music, although they said it was garbage.

There was a lot of speculation about the upcoming presidential election in 1964. Everyone expected President Kennedy to beat Sen. Barry Goldwater, the most probable Republican contender, by a landslide. Nixon, Kennedy's rival in 1960, was out of the picture. In 1962, Nixon ran for the governor's job in California and lost. He went on television and said the newspapers wouldn't have him to "kick around" anymore. I didn't really care. Next to Kennedy, Nixon was a wooden nickel.

President Kennedy had had a hell of a summer. His popularity increased to the point where there were even kiddie records about him. Bob got one, which he played faithfully at least a dozen times a day on his kiddie record player. The record was called "Sing a Song of Presidents." It had a song about George Washington on one side and a song about John F. Kennedy on the other. When was the last time you bought a record praising the president?

Kennedy also went to Berlin and viewed the Berlin Wall in person. The Germans went crazy over Kennedy; they loved him. He met with black leaders as they staged an enormous peaceful march upon Washington, D.C., as part of their quest for equal rights. The Equal Rights Bill was introduced, but it got snarled up in the red tape so typical of Capitol Hill. And the nuclear test ban treaty with the Soviets was signed. That was all good.

The saddest part of that summer was when President and Mrs. Kennedy had a premature baby boy named Patrick. The baby's lungs didn't function properly, and he died shortly after he was born. It was all on TV, just like everything else. And my mother cried her eyes out. Even though men weren't supposed to cry, I cried, too, in my room where no one could see.

I hated sad things and I looked forward to some good news about Gemini and Apollo and to a neat fall season. Football in New England was always great.

Walter Cronkite interviewed President Kennedy on television, and one of the topics was Vietnam. The President was determined to keep American forces out of there.

In late October, an American adviser got killed in Vietnam. The president announced our intentions to call back every American adviser from Vietnam, even the helicopter pilots, by late 1965. The thought of Americans dying there sickened Kennedy, and I didn't hear anyone in Connecticut disagree with the president's logic. Kennedy scheduled a series of meetings with key advisers regarding Vietnam and his concerns over American involvement there, to be held immediately after taking a couple of politically oriented trips about the country.

On a Friday afternoon just before Thanksgiving, I was sitting in Mr. Black's math class admiring this girl who sat next to me, Karen. She had a great face and fantastic legs. Mr. Black was a tough guy. He'd snap his fingers in front of your face when you couldn't get an answer quickly.

If he caught you talking during class, he usually threw a blackboard eraser at you. And he aimed right for your head.

Someone out in the hallway obviously got Mr. Black's attention, and he left the class in kind of a hurry, giving us some problems to keep us busy for a few minutes. I remember thinking, *Great, now I can talk with Karen and maybe get her phone number.* Calling a girl was proof of utter courage.

Well, Karen and I were having a terrific conversation when it became obvious that old Mr. Black had been gone for some time. He never left us alone that long; he was too scared we would do something sinister like have fun.

What happened next was the kind of thing you remember for the rest of your life. It was a nightmare.

Mr. Black finally came back into the classroom, but when he did, we immediately saw that he was *crying*. That's right! Tough old Mr. Black was so upset, he could hardly talk. Then he told us why.

All he said was, "President Kennedy's been shot. He was riding in his car in Dallas, Texas. That's all we know right now. Close your books and stay silent, please." His voice was soft. He was pleading with us to stay calm. He went back out into the hallway.

Karen started to cry. So did most of the girls. The guys, stupefied, attempted to comfort the girls. On November 22, 1963, I tried my best to help my friends Karen, Mary Jane, and Elizabeth. I was fighting back the tears myself, hoping if President Kennedy had indeed been shot that his wound was minor and he would be okay. But why would someone shoot him? What kind of moron would do such a thing?

A few minutes later Mr. Black came back into the room, sobbing openly. "He's dead," was all our teacher said. They let us out of school early. On the bus, typically a site of semiperverted pranks and humorous atrocities, no one spoke. It was the most silent school bus ride of my entire life. Girls were crying like crazy. The guys just stared out the windows. One guy did cry. He was the bus driver. He was black.

I went in the front door and heard my mother sobbing. She was just sitting there in front of the television. They were showing a rerun of Walter Cronkite an hour or so before I arrived home, when he announced that President Kennedy had died. Cronkite was so choked up he could hardly speak. My mother had been watching a soap opera called "As the World Turns" when the first special bulletin interrupted the program. Ever since that Friday, every time I'm watching television and regular programming stops and they say those all too familiar words, "We interrupt our program to bring you this special news bulletin," I shudder a little bit because that's exactly how they said it when President Kennedy got killed. It's never good news like, "We are overjoyed to announce a cure for cancer has just been discovered," or, "The Soviet Union and the United States have just agreed to dismantle every nuclear warhead in their arsenals. There will be no bullshit negotiations for the next ten years to decide who can break the terms of the agreement first."

My world collapsed. For the life of me I could not figure out why someone would kill a man like John F. Kennedy. If you disagreed with him, fine. But kill him? *Why?!* I was raised believing that ours was a kind, compassionate nation and that things like assassinating the president had ceased around the turn of the century, when a frustrated moron killed President McKinley. But in 1963 it was insanity.

Don't get me wrong. At a very tender age I had learned

to accept death. The night before Easter in 1957, my grand-mother (the same one who had given me that beautiful DC-7 model the previous Easter) died right in front of me in her living room. She was supposed to be baby-sitting for me while my parents were out. I called the police and the ambulance for her, and even though I had rehearsed all of this (she was pretty sickly and my parents had been concerned that something might happen to her) before and had reacted rapidly, it still wasn't good enough. She died anyway.

I cried for weeks over losing her because I loved her very much. She used to sing to me in German (both my grandmother and my mother were born in Germany, immigrating to the United States with my grandfather when my mother was about five years old), and she listened to my nonstop chatter about airplanes and rockets even when no one else would listen. But eventually I accepted her death.

I had a much harder time accepting President Kennedy's death because he wasn't even sick. He was only forty-six years old. His oldest child, Caroline, was only six. His little boy, John, was barely three. His beautiful wife was young and strong. My grandmother died because her body ceased to function properly. It was mechanical failure, of sorts, and I understood that. But with President Kennedy it was different. Some bastard blew his brains out, right in front of thousands of people. He murdered him. It was so brutal, I couldn't comprehend it. . . .

Vice President Lyndon Johnson was sworn in as the thirty-sixth president of the United States aboard *Air Force One*, the beautiful, specially modified Boeing 707 in which President Kennedy had arrived, as the aircraft sat on the sweltering ramp at Dallas Love Field. Beside the new president stood Mrs. Kennedy, her pink suit and stockings stained with caked blood from her murdered husband.

The world lost something special that Friday. Our country suffered a terrible wound.

The unimaginable didn't end with one assassination. Two days after President Kennedy was killed, his accused assassin, Lee Harvey Oswald (a well-documented social deadbeat), was shot and killed. The event was shown live, on national television, as Oswald was being transferred from one jail to another in Dallas. Oswald's killer, Jack Ruby, owned a sleazy club in downtown Dallas. And it all happened as President Kennedy's flag-draped casket stood in honor in the Capitol.

Earlier I mentioned the fact that millions of words have been written attempting to describe what made President Kennedy so special. Even more has been written in speculation, attempting to describe what would or would not have happened had President Kennedy lived. I have my opinions.

No, I don't think President Kennedy would have eliminated war and disease from the face of the earth. The world would not have become a mecca of love had Kennedy faced Goldwater in 1964 and won. Like anyone, President Kennedy was human, and he had many faults. His list of mistakes was as long as yours or mine. But he cared about things other presidents don't seem to care about. He was a compassionate man. He was a decent man.

Had Kennedy lived, I believe we would not have been involved in the tragedy we eventually created in Vietnam. More advisers would have died, and President Kennedy would have pulled out of a quagmire he knew we couldn't win. Our prestige would have been preserved, fifty-five thousand American servicemen would have lived, and the decade following that perverted weekend in 1963 would have been a more pleasant time in which to live.

Had Kennedy lived, I believe blacks would have achieved more equality sooner and the plight of the poor in this nation would not have been quite so desperate. I'd be willing to bet those "long, hot summers" of the later sixties would have been cooler.

And finally, had Kennedy lived, the degeneration of NASA, which began soon after his death, would have at least been postponed. Our space program would probably not be in the shambles it is in today, mired in bureaucratic garbage and scraping the bottom of the barrel for dollars to fund the noblest cause man ever assumed.

My words are strong, but so are my convictions. You can read all about the weekend of November 22–24, 1963, in books like *The Death of a President*, by William Manchester. It will move you. It will make you sick to think it even really happened.

The loss of President Kennedy affected all of us, but I think it had an especially profound affect upon those of my generation. A piece of our dreams wound up on the street in Dealey Plaza, along with the president's brain tissue. In a way, we all died a little bit.

I lived in the Dallas area for several years. It's a nice place, even though I always wished there were some trees and hills. The only thing I truly detest about Dallas is that part of town where it happened. It's a strange place. I remember the first time I stood there, I wasn't quite sure what I was looking at. Somehow all those pictures of Dealey Plaza and the Schoolbook Depository Building I saw in books and magazines made the area look like it would stand right out and slap you in the face. That's not what it's like. All of a sudden, you're there. It makes you sick to see how close the president was to the end of his motorcade. Just a hundred yards or so, and he would have been safe.

So 1963 ended on a tragic note. Christmas just didn't seem as joyful. There were pictures of President Kennedy everywhere—in classrooms, restaurants, libraries, barber shops. The flags in our classrooms had black bunting over them. Outside, flags flew at half-mast.

I forgot all about Leslie Gore and the Safaris and the Beach Boys. "The Beverly Hillbillies" wasn't as funny. Nothing was funny for quite some time. I'll bet even Gordo Cooper was disgusted.

1964

The year 1964 wasn't a big one for our space program. As I will outline in the next chapter, 1964 was really a transition year for us, as we got ready to fly the bigger, more complicated Gemini spacecraft.

Although President Kennedy was gone, his leadership checks and balances followed Lyndon Johnson into office, and at least for a while they remained intact. At NASA, safety and quality still reigned supreme, and that is why we spent 1964 preparing for the new program. I'm sure we could have flown a manned Gemini or two in 1964. Instead, we launched unmanned tests before we put men atop the powerful *Titan II*. And that was the right way to do it.

The year 1964 was the year of the British invasion, beginning with the Beatles' premier on "The Ed Sullivan Show" in February. They were followed by the Dave Clark Five, the Searchers, Gerry and the Pacemakers, the Rolling Stones, the Animals, Manfred Mann, the Honeycombs, Billy J. Kramer and the Dakotas, and many, many more. These happy, scruffy-looking musicians from England took away some of the pain we felt over President Kennedy. Maybe that's one reason why they did so well with the

American youth. We were looking for something to be happy about again, and the British were there, electric guitars and all.

I bought records like I never had before, and I thoroughly enjoyed listening to them. By July, when our unmanned *Ranger 7* sent back thousands of close-up pictures of the moon, a great deal of my anguish over the Kennedy assassination had left and I was ready to have some fun again. Even the Gulf of Tonkin incident in August failed to stun my feeling of optimism. But the memory of November 22, 1963, and what it meant would never disappear.

Gemini: Pride When Pride Was Scarce

As NASA prepared for our first manned venture in space since Mercury, I entered that magical stage of life known as adolescence. An assumption concerning adolescents during the sixties was their love of rock and roll music. That assumption was quite correct, and I was no exception. I listened to Top 40 music prior to the Gemini days, but it did not become terribly important until 1964, when the Beatles made their debut in the United States. After watching the Beatles on "Ed Sullivan" that fateful Sunday night in February 1964, I listened to the Top 40 with a fervor that would have impressed Billy Graham.

Top 40 music served several purposes. Aside from the sheer delight derived from the pained expressions on my parents' faces whenever I listened to it, pop music became my mental calendar of space program events. It was easy to associate particular hits with particular missions.

So my recollections of missions flown are closely associated with Top 40 hits I heard on the radio around the time each flight took place. For example, everytime I hear a "Baby Boomers, this was your life" station play "Back in My Arms Again" by the Supremes, I think of *Gemini 4*, because "Back in My Arms Again" was high on the charts the week *Gemini 4* flew. It's like a musical history book of the space program.

Unfortunately, I also associate the music of those years with the war in Vietnam, so it's like having a musical history book of Vietnam, too.

WDRC and WPOP in Hartford were the most popular rock and roll stations in the area. At the time Gemini began operations, both stations were broadcasting in AM. FM and FM stereo broadcasts were still scarce in 1965. Today WPOP is a news-only station and WDRC, which affords AM/FM and FM stereo programming, features—you guessed it—hits of the fifties, sixties, and early seventies. In Connecticut it is eerie hearing the same music on WDRC to which I listened so many years ago. Age will do that to you.

So, for thrills, I will refer to popular hits of this period as we recall Gemini and move on to Apollo. For readers who were in their teens during this time or for the parents of those who were teenagers during Gemini this might help you to recall what you were doing back then. Perhaps you may not want to recall any of it. I understand. Your choice.

Adolescence is a confusing stage of life. But to have been an adolescent in 1965 was something beyond confusing. Being a teenager during the midsixties was a unique—and not necessarily pleasant—experience. You could play it conservative like Beaver Cleaver, or you could opt for the dark side of things like Mick Jagger. It was like an equation. The Beatles, the Doors, and Vietnam were on one side and Mom and Dad, the lingering memory of President Kennedy, and the astronauts on the other.

The social deterioriation spawned by assassinations and the war in Vietnam was just beginning. In Cheshire, it had not yet reared its ugly head. Astronauts were still considered "in" in 1965. Heroes still existed. In Wally Cleaver-ese, for example, John Glenn was a "neat" guy, which meant Glenn was very special. My concept of our astronauts even went beyond "neat." *Gods* better defined it.

President Kennedy, our grandest hero, was gone. But he left us the astronauts. And in that time of vanishing heroes we embraced them.

I told you I was a great fan of the space program during the Mercury days. By the time Gemini approached, I was a space fanatic. Model rockets dominated my room. I could recite the date, pilot, and flight duration of each Mercury mission. I knew how much thrust the *Atlas D* generated. And I was thoroughly familiar with the new manned program, Gemini.

Spring of 1965 was an interesting time. To better understand the situation, let's do some history.

Although Project Gemini was created in 1961, its progress was overshadowed by Project Mercury and the Soviet successes from 1961 to 1963. Gemini received little public attention until 1964, when the U.S. program was in transition from Mercury to Gemini.

Project Gemini represented a process of maturation. Gemini was designed to afford us the experience we would need for Apollo, the lunar landing program. During Gemini, our astronauts would stay aloft for up to two weeks at a time. They would learn how to manuever outside the spacecraft, with a pressure suit as their only protection against the vacuum of space. The astronauts would practice rendezvous and docking procedures, a task required in the Apollo scenario. In the process, the U.S. would gain thousands of manned hours in orbit.

Gemini was a huge improvement over Mercury. It was built for two astronauts instead of one. It had the ability to change, or translate, from one orbit to another. This gave Gemini the unique capability to rendezvous and dock with other objects. Because Gemini was to remain aloft for long periods of time, the spacecraft utilized fuel cell technology, replacing the older storage batteries upon which Mercury depended for its primary source of electrical power.

One of Gemini's greatest assets was its modular design. While the Gemini spacecraft looked like a big Mercury vehicle on the outside, it was very different inside. Gemini was built to be easily repaired. When a major component in the Gemini system failed, it was replaced with relative ease. In Mercury, the replacement of even the simplest system often meant delay for weeks. Gemini was built to meet a demanding launch schedule safely and efficiently.

The *Titan II* booster rocket for Gemini was less complex than the Atlas booster used for the Mercury orbital missions. Since the fuel in the Titan required no special ignition system, launch procedures were much easier. Additionally, the *Titan* didn't require the supercold liquid oxygen the Atlas demanded. So special refrigeration requirements were eliminated.

Gemini flew two unmanned tests during 1964. I followed the tests closely, while the Beatles and the Dave Clark Five battled for our record dollars. After the second test, it was determined that the Gemini-Titan system was ready for manned flight. In NASA-ese, the system was man-rated.

In October 1964, the Soviets surprised us with another achievement: the orbiting of three cosmonauts in one vehicle. Named *Voskhod I*, the Soviet spacecraft was basically a Vostok that had been modified to accommodate more than one cosmonaut. This flight was encouraged by Chairman Khrushchev, who was still smarting politically from the Cuban missile debacle and anxious for another Soviet space "first." *Voskhod I* was indeed a success. It is ironic that during the flight of *Voskhod I* Nikita Khrushchev fell from power and was replaced by Leonid Breshnev.

As *Voskhod I* stole the headlines, WDRC and WPOP were busy playing hits like "Things We Said Today" by the

Beatles and "Leader of the Pack" by The Shangri-las. With the approach of the 1964 presidential election, it was entertaining to watch "Patty Duke" and television ads for Barry Goldwater, the Republican senator from Arizona who had the guts to oppose President Johnson that year. Goldwater stressed "peace through strength." The Goldwater campaign motto was "In your heart you know he's right!" In hindsight, I think he was.

Gemini followed, but not until yet another Soviet achievement: the first "walk" in space by Alexei Leonov during the flight of *Voskhod II*, on March 18, 1965. The last of the Voskhod series, *Voskhod II* nearly ended in disaster when Leonov was initially unable to reenter his spacecraft following the completion of his EVA (Extra Vehicular Activity, a NASA term for astronaut activities outside the spacecraft). After Leonov rejoined flight commander Pavel Belyayev aboard *Voskhod II*, the cosmonauts made an inaccurate reentry, which resulted in a landing far beyond the planned area. After landing in a snow-covered forest, Belyayev and Leonov spent a frigid night aboard the spacecraft. Outside, a pack of wolves howled at them.

While Leonov and Belyayev worried about wolves, I listened to smash hits like "You've Lost That Lovin' Feeling," by the incomparable Righteous Brothers. "You've Lost That Lovin' Feeling" was so popular, it remained strong on the charts from Christmas 1964 through March 1965. For all who saw *Top Gun* and thought "You've Lost That Lovin' Feeling" was something new, sorry. It's over twenty-four years old.

Gemini 3

Soon after *Voskhod II* flew, on March 23, 1965, Gemini made its debut. As in the days of Mercury, we listened to the launch in our classroom. I felt like a hotshot. Knowing more about the space program than our teachers, I was afforded the opportunity to comment about the flight as the mission progressed.

Gus Grissom was the command pilot of *Gemini 3*. He was a veteran of the second Mercury mission. Grissom and his pilot (really, the "pilot" of a Gemini mission was the copilot, and he occupied the right cockpit seat while the "command pilot" occupied the left seat), John Young, jokingly named their spacecraft the *Molly Brown*. You will recall it was Grissom's Mercury spacecraft, *Liberty Bell 7*, that sank after returning from space. "Molly Brown," of *Titanic* lore, was an appropriate name indeed for Grissom's next spacecraft; it was said Molly Brown was unsinkable. After *Gemini 3*, NASA discouraged personalized names for Gemini spacecraft by their crews.

Grissom and Young managed a nearly flawless mission. Although the flight lasted only as long as the Mercury missions of John Glenn and Scott Carpenter three years earlier—three orbits— the crew proved the quality of the Gemini system in flight. *Gemini 3* also performed for the first time orbital manuevers that would be necessary on future flights involving rendezvous and docking. After nearly two years, the U.S. was back in the manned spaceflight business. There was a sense of confidence not evident during Mercury. It was delightful.

When I got home from school the day *Gemini 3* soared into space, I tuned in WDRC and heard Petula Clark, a pretty girl from Wales, singing her big hit, "Downtown." Later, Walter Cronkite recapped *Gemini 3* on "The CBS Evening News." With *Gemini 3* safely recovered, I was able to watch "Combat" (remember Vic Morrow?) in peace.

March 1965 held other developments, too. In March, we went to war. It was unclear to me exactly why we were involved in this "police action" in Southeast Asia. But President Johnson was a strong leader, and initially, at least, I trusted his judgment.

Gemini 4

Ninety days after the first U.S. Marine Corps line companies arrived in Da Nang, South Vietnam, we prepared for the launch of *Gemini 4*. I often wondered what those marines thought about *Gemini 4*.

Aside from John Glenn's orbital mission in 1962, *Gemini 4* was the most daring manned spaceflight ever attempted by the U.S. Not only was *Gemini 4* scheduled to remain in orbit for four whole days; the pilot was to take the first American EVA. It was a double-header.

Gemini 4 lifted off on June 3, 1965. We listened to the lift-off at school, and afterward I watched Walter Cronkite's coverage of the flight on CBS. By this time, watching Cronkite's mission play-by-play was a tradition.

During the third orbit, Edward H. White performed his EVA. James McDivitt, the command pilot, took spectacular pictures of White as he manuevered outside the spacecraft. We thrilled to the in-flight transmissions. White had such a good time during his EVA that he was reluctant to get back into the cramped Gemini cockpit. NASA pleaded with him to "get back inside." God, I admired those guys.

Following White's walk in space, the flight progressed smoothly and, about ninety-eight hours later, *Gemini 4* successfully splashed down. Finally, the United States was in the big league of space achievement.

While *Gemini 4* made history, Herman's Hermits, another highly successful British group with hits like "Mrs. Brown, You've Got a Lovely Daughter" and "Something

Good" scored another. It was a remake of "Wonderful World." And the Motown sound of The Supremes reigned number one with "Back in My Arms Again."

Gemini 4 had such impact during the summer of 1965 that it found its way into the lyrics of a Top 40 hit that remained on the charts clear through August. Many will easily recall it. It was titled "Eve of Destruction" and recorded by Barry McGuire.

McGuire was upset about things taking place around the time of *Gemini 4.* His song addressed a compendium of woes: fears of communism (hatred in Red China), the continuing struggle of the blacks for equality (racial rioting in Selma, Alabama), and then came his reference to *Gemini 4*:

> Now you may leave here
> For four days in space,
> But when you return
> It's the same old place.*

My parents criticized all the offerings on the Top 40 stations, and they frequently discussed their hatred of rock and roll music during dinnertime, which was an open forum at our house. For example, my brother and I were often called upon to discuss current events. Then my parents would offer their opinions. Well, "Eve of Destruction" received a particularly harsh parental review, because it was too "radical."

Whether my parents hated "Eve of Destruction" or

not, according to "The CBS Evening News" and the headlines of the New Haven *Register*, the maladies McGuire
sung about were true! In the Deep South, blacks were
clubbed by the police and attacked by guard dogs. When
the cops and the dogs were through attacking them, the
cops sprayed the blacks with high-pressure fire hoses, just
to make sure.

In Vietnam, U.S. Marines charged with protection of
the airfield at Da Nang were getting killed by an enemy
who refused to even show himself so we could kill him. So
we sent more combat troops, just to make sure.

Accordingly, dinnertime conflict frequently centered
upon topics like those raised by McGuire in his tune. A
typical conversation went something like this:

Me: God, Dad, how come we have such a great space program and all this other crap has to happen?
Mom: Is that all you know how to say lately? Foul words
like *crap*?
Dad: It's all because of those damned *Beatles*!

I disagreed. So, in protest, I turned the volume up a little
louder each time the WDRC Good Guys played "Eve of
Destruction," just to make sure.

My folks weren't wealthy in 1965, but we were certainly
comfortable. I was very proud of my father. He had a good
job, and he worked smart. He brought home shiny, new
company cars often, and his income afforded some damn
pleasant summer vacations. The standard of living he made
possible for us in 1965 on about twenty-five thousand dollars annually would be difficult to beat today with a dual-in-
come family earning one hundred thousand dollars. That's
discouraging.

In 1965, we drove to Florida for summer vacation, since the car was a freebie and my father had earned lots of vacation time. We had gone to Florida before, but this trip was more special than previous vacations. The surge of the space program enveloped me emotionally. Spaceflight and astronauts dominated my thoughts.

The flight of *Gemini 4* was fresh in my mind. During the long, boring ride south, I daydreamed about the beautiful *Titan II*, its peculiar orange shaft of flame lofting McDivitt and White into orbit. I could almost hear White's breathing inside the pressure suit as he left the safety of the spacecraft. I envisioned White's lifeline tether curling behind him with a sea of clouds passing far below. And I could almost see Jim McDivitt's smile through the tiny spacecraft window.

Since I insisted on listening to as many Top 40 stations as possible during our ride to Sarasota that year, my memory is flooded with the sounds of the summer of 1965. Great stuff was on the air! There was "Down in the Boondocks" by Billy Joe Royal, "Unchained Melody" by the Righteous Brothers, "California Girls" by the Beach Boys, "I've Got You, Babe" by Sonny and Cher, "Wooly Bully" by Sam the Sham and the Pharaohs, and so many, many more.

Sarasota was a wonderful place to be that summer. Our apartment was practically right on the beach, so the girls were easy to spot. And there were plenty of them. But when we arrived in Sarasota, there was something else besides the girls to attract my attention: preparations for the upcoming launch of *Gemini 5*.

Gemini 5

Although we had already completed the second Gemini mission, most of the astronaut "favorites" among school kids were still the Original Seven Mercury pilots. Mine was "Gordo" Cooper, veteran of that fantastic final Mercury mission. Leroy Gordon Cooper was the ultimate pilot, the type of guy Tom Wolfe wrote about in his book *The Right Stuff*.

Cooper was selected to fly as the command pilot on the *Gemini 5* mission, so the flight was especially interesting. Along with Cooper was Pete Conrad, a slick Navy-trained pilot. Conrad would fill the right seat, as pilot.

During the drive home to Connecticut that summer, I read continuously about the upcoming mission. *Gemini 5* was the first in the series to utilize the new fuel cells NASA required as primary electrical source for long-duration flights. *Gemini 4* had used conventional storage batteries during its four-day flight. But *Gemini 5* was slated to remain aloft for *eight days*, an unheard-of duration in 1965.

Remember, one of the main objectives of Gemini was to test the pilots and spacecraft systems for periods equivalent to those we would experience during the Apollo lunar landing flights. *Gemini 4* represented the first mission in a ramp-up series of flights that would culminate in a mission lasting around two weeks. Since the longer flights would require more electrical power and conventional batteries were heavy and took up a great deal of space, using them for the duration missions following *Gemini 4* was not an option. Thus the ingenious fuel cells converted liquids and gases into not only electrical power, but also water (unfortunately which, aboard Gemini, was not potable; on Apollo, fuel cell water was fit for consumption).

Gemini 5 thundered aloft on August 21, 1965. Despite serious problems with the newfangled fuel cells, Cooper and Conrad flew the entire eight-day mission and returned safely. *Gemini 5* did not feature any daredeveil EVAs, but its success was no less significant than that of *Gemini 4*. Our program had demonstrated that we could keep two pilots in orbit and healthy for eight long days and that the systems that sustained them worked.

It was time for school to resume. The summer of 1965 was a terrific experience for space program fanatics. I put aside images of Ku Klux Klan demonstrators we had seen in Georgia and the images on TV of wounded marines and other soldiers being hoisted aboard MedEvac helicopters in Vietnam. Sometime during that summer I decided I would learn to fly. In many ways, some subtle and some more obvious, I was reaping benefits from the space program. We all were.

As school began in September of 1965, "Get Off My Cloud" by the Rolling Stones represented great listening. "Let's Hang On" by the Four Seasons and "Do You Believe in Magic?" by the Lovin' Spoonful were also hits. On TV, there was a new prime-time show, "Lost in Space." "Lost in Space" may have been fictitious, but it was worth watching not only for Marta Kristen (a goddess!) but for the great NASA film clips it occasionally featured.

As I evaluated the girls in the hallways of Dodd Junior High School that fall, the prospect of another Gemini mission was never far from my mind. We guys who had similar interests in the space program carried on about it at lunch, during phys ed, or even as we were whispering about the girl with the nonstop body who sat in front in homeroom.

We had a "book fair" shortly after school began. I bought a book called *We Seven*. This volume was written—at least in part—by the Original Seven astronauts. I read and reread the book, imagining how Glenn felt when he learned his heat shield might have deployed while still in orbit and how Carpenter felt when he realized he had used up all of his manuevering fuel. *We Seven* was terrific insulation against things like art class. It gave new meaning to study hall. It also served as a bridge over which communication with my parents was still possible. They thought I was getting "too damned rebellious." They didn't realize that in a world full of young rebels in 1965, the only thing their oldest son protested in public was the celery in the tuna salad served in the school cafeteria.

Gemini 6

When October rolled around, veteran Mercury astronaut Wally Schirra and his copilot, Tom Stafford, attempted the first rendezvous and docking with an Agena target vehicle. The key to success in this mission was launching two vehicles on an utterly precise schedule. Even in late 1965, with a fair amount of launch experience under our belts, there was plenty of room for mishaps. Throughout the orbital mission phase of Mercury, the mighty *Atlas D* booster performed flawlessly, sending Glenn, Carpenter, Schirra, and Cooper safely into orbit. But the Atlas had its share of problems. In fact, there had been much concern over using the Atlas for Mercury because so many Atlases had seriously malfunctioned in the days of our space program.

Gremlins struck the *Gemini 6* Atlas/Agena on October 25, 1965. An Atlas was supposed to boost the Agena target vehicle into orbit prior to the launch of *Gemini 6*. Schirra and Stafford would then catch up with their Agena—actually a small rocket itself with a special collar designed to faciliate physical docking—rendezvous, and dock with it.

Following launch, the second-stage Agena failed to attain orbit and was destroyed. Schirra and Stafford did not get to fly on October 25. But their day was coming.

Gemini 7 . . . and Gemini 6

What a disappointment! We got the bad news just prior to the "afternoon announcements" in our homeroom. One of the teachers stuck her head inside our classroom door and told our teacher, "It blew up." It blew up! What blew up? The Atlas/Agena or, even worse, the Gemini/Titan?

Aware of the Atlas and its history, I assumed Schirra and Stafford were alive and that their Agena simply went away. When I arrived home in a near-panic, Walter Cronkite confirmed my assumption.

Somehow *Gemini 6* had yet to fly. In a magnificent demonstration of resourcefulness, NASA decided to launch *Gemini 7* first, then launch *Gemini 6*, with the goal of performing an orbital rendezvous between the two manned spacecraft. The launch of *Gemini 7* was scheduled for December 4, to be followed by the launch of *Gemini 6* on December 12. What a way to end the year! It would be a Christmas double-header!

Gemini 7 was the crème de la crème of the long-duration missions. In the command pilot's seat was Frank Borman, and in the pilot's seat was Jim Lovell. Borman and Lovell were to spend *fourteen days* in orbit, the longest planned Gemini mission. Fourteen days was longer than the lunar landing missions were to last. *Gemini 7*, if successful, would prove our systems and our pilots could take it.

December 4, 1965, was a Saturday. My parents were out shopping, and they had taken my brother with them. With the whole house happily to myself, I sat before the TV and watched *Gemini 7* lift off. I recall wondering if President Kennedy knew all this was happening.

When Borman and Lovell were walking out of the transfer van en route to the pad, they wore new, specially designed lightweight pressure suits. Their appearance was eerie. I had a premonition of how the first lunar landing crew might look like on their way to the pad. The anticipation was immense.

Eight days later, *Gemini 6* sat on the pad, again ready to boost into orbit. The countdown proceeded normally, right down to the point where engine ignition took place and the commentator actually announced lift-off. But there was no lift-off. The Titan's engines had shut down, victims of a misplaced electrical plug.

The engine shutdown sequence placed Schirra and Stafford in a difficult predicament. For an instant, no one was sure whether the vehicle had physically left the pad or not. Schirra and Stafford made an immediate decision, electing to remain inside the spacecraft. Remember that since the Gemini did not use an escape tower system for a launch abort as in the Mercury (and, later, in the Apollo) series, fighter-style ejection seats were installed. While this arrangement did provide a safe crew abort system, use of the ejection system would destroy the interior of the spacecraft. The crew of *Gemini 6*, by remaining calm during a potentially hazardous situation, saved the spacecraft and the mission.

Shortly thereafter, on December 15, 1965, *Gemini 6* finally made it into orbit and performed a spectacular series of rendezvous passes with the orbiting *Gemini 7*. The pictures taken by the two Gemini crews remain to this day absolutely dazzling. Next to *Apollo 11* footage, the shots taken by *Gemini 6* and *Gemini 7* are perhaps the most inspiring of our entire manned space effort.

Gemini 6 reentered the earth's atmosphere safely on December 16, 1965, and was followed by *Gemini 7* two days later. Borman and Lovell won the endurance record for time in orbit, and Schirra and Stafford proved that rendezvous was not only possible but was, in Schirra's own words, "a piece of cake."

In December, the Byrds (we'll hear more from them later) had a number one hit called "Turn, Turn, Turn." They sang:

> "A time for love
> A time for hate,
> A time for peace,
> I swear it's not too late."*

"Turn, Turn, Turn" was an early "peace" tune, inspired by growing discontent with U.S. policy in Vietnam. It signaled the end of an era, the era of "happy rock." After late 1965, pop music underwent a vast change. Rock became unhappy music.

In Vietnam, a Marine lieutenant fresh out of college named Phillip Caputo was leading a rifle platoon west of Da Nang. Caputo's platoon was no different from others in Marine Corps line companies. With the exception of his platoon sergeant, most of the enlisted marines Caputo led through the stinking Vietnamese heat were kids in their teens and early twenties. Many of them were killed. In Vietnam, Gemini and the race for the moon were abstract things.

1966

The year 1966 represented the second half of the Gemini program. Already a smashing success, five Gemini crews had boosted safely into orbit during 1965. Each mission sought—and achieved—impressive goals. The missions of *Gemini 6* and *Gemini 7* demonstrated more flexibil-

---

*"Turn, Turn, Turn (To Everything There Is a Season)" Words from the Book of Ecclesiastes. Adaptation and Music by Pete Seeger. TRO—© copyright 1962 by Melody Trails, Inc., New York, N.Y. Used by permission.

ity than the public expected from NASA. It was refreshing. As 1966 approached, confidence of a lunar landing flight in 1967 grew.

Turbulent times were on the rise, but these were exciting times for the space program. Despite concerns over Vietnam, racial upheaval, and other ills in early 1966, there was excitement in the air for the space program. Everyone talked about it. We were going to the moon, and we were going to do it soon. You could say what you wanted about Southeast Asia, inequality, and all the rest, but I was damned proud to be an American in 1966. Many of my friends were not.

Under President Kennedy, Lyndon Johnson nurtured our fledgling efforts in space. Now, as president, Johnson was faced with the complexities of waging war while maintaining astronomical growth on the homefront. The president brought his awesome political power to bear upon the space program. He needed a shining star. And NASA was there to help.

Life at home was getting complicated—not as complicated as Lyndon Johnson's, but complicated nevertheless. Parents were fearful of the effects of rock music on their sons and daughters during the sixties. The long hair and mod fashions worn by pop groups seemed an insult to their generation. With the dawn of the antiwar movement in the sixties, the World War II generation found themselves torn between a sense of nationalism that was earned the hard way—by fighting—and the trauma of watching sons and daughters depart for a war they couldn't understand. The result: confusion and frustration.

As in most households, in mine there was nagging about the length of hair and the loud music that was so heavily favored. Were we all bums? Were we all to look like Mick Jagger? Those horrors were on the minds of parents everywhere.

At school, the discipline was so strict we felt more like prisoners than students. Dress code rules were severe, and they were harshly enforced. Teachers harassed boys whose hair even touched their ears. And girls were forced to kneel on the floor to test the length of their skirts. If you were suspected of wearing pants that were too tight, a golf ball was dropped down one leg. If it failed to drop out the bottom, you went home with a note. And God help you if you went home with a note.

Lunchtime at Dodd Junior High was frequently spent under "no talking" punishment, because when we talked, we made noise—and that was very bad. When lunch was over, we had to stand up upon command and march out of the cafeteria area in neat little lines without talking because, as I said, talking was bad.

Despite the discipline, I had a good time at Dodd Junior High School. I liked my teachers and they liked me. But I was a "Dick Decent." I was president of the Student Council. Playing ball, politically, was the key to success. If you made waves, things were not as pleasant. Our teachers and our folks expressed genuine concern over the prospect of a mass revolt in the schools. Can you imagine a couple of hundred thirteen and fourteen-year-olds taking over an entire town?

Gemini 8

In Connecticut, winter lasts a long time. It helped to have *Gemini 8* scheduled for March, because the time always seemed to fly in anticipation of another mission.

Gemini 8 was to accomplish what *Gemini 6* could not: actual docking with an Agena target vehicle. This meant another attempt to launch two vehicles into orbit within a short amount of time.

On Wednesday, March 16, 1966, it worked. Courtesy of another faithful *Titan II* booster, Neil Armstrong and Dave Scott rode *Gemini 8* into orbit in a flawless launch performance. *Agena 8* had ready boosted successfully into orbit atop an Atlas.

Like Mercury, Gemini was still too small for on-board television cameras, so those of us stuck on earth during a Gemini mission could only hear excerpts from voice communications and see coverage of launch or recovery operations. Although coverage had improved dramatically over the Mercury days, we still had to imagine what things looked like in orbit during a particular mission and wait for the Hasselblad photos in *Life* or *Time*.

During Gemini, the major networks employed various forms of simulation as a substitute for live, in-flight television. For instance, if EVA was scheduled, a guy in a full-scale Gemini pressure suit maneuvered outside a mock-up of the Gemini spacecraft, hanging from a contraption designed to simulate zero gravity. I remember the gent who did the simulation appearances for CBS, Leo Krupp. Krupp was employed by McDonnell Aircraft (now McDonnell Douglas), the spacecraft manufacturer. That poor man got to swing from his zero-G device, live, on national TV while the real astronauts performed in space. The simulation people had to listen to the real voice transmission from orbit, then make it look like they were doing what the astronauts said they were doing. When voice transmissions from the real crew were scarce or the real spacecraft was temporarily out of range, the only guidance the simulation folks had was the mission profile provided them by NASA prior to the launch. This afforded some exquisite entertainment in itself because, invariably, no maneuver *ever* went exactly according to plan and, invariably, the simulation guy was usually left hanging—literally. This made for terrific locker-room conversation during phys ed or while using the can after track practice.

No EVA took place during *Gemini 8*. However, there was a lot of simulation to show the viewers how the docking scenario looked in orbit. CBS showed a simulation of *Gemini 8* approaching *Agena 8* for docking. It was an excellent simulation when one compared it to actual photos taken by Armstrong and Scott. It was much better than the EVA simulations shown during *Gemini 4*.

Armstrong and Scott performed a letter-perfect docking with their Agena. Then the real fun began. Until *Gemini 8*, there were tense moments during our missions, but no dire emergencies. Even Glenn's heat shield problem turned out to be an erroneous event signal.

But shortly after Armstrong announced the docking ("We are docked"), the Gemini/Agena configuation began to tumble. Soon the two vehicles were gyrating out of control and the rate at which they tumbled was increasing—to over one revolution *per second*.

Neil Armstrong remained calm. His experience testing the X-15 rocket plane for NASA prior to selection as an astronaut was evident. When *Gemini 8* went berserk, Armstrong immediately undocked the two spacecraft. The Gemini only tumbled faster. Armstrong and Scott could barely read their instruments. But they were professionals. They were used to abnormal situations, and they knew how to handle them. That's why NASA chose test pilots.

The crew of *Gemini 8* shut down their primary maneuvering system and brought into play their only backup, the system to be utilized during reentry. The oscillations ceased, placing blame for the event squarely upon a thruster in the primary system.

There was a hard rule in Gemini that said if for any reason you ate into fuel intended for control during reentry, you aborted the mission. *Gemini 8* was no exception. For the first time in our manned space program a mission was terminated early. *Gemini 8* splashed down in a secondary recovery area.

After *Gemini 8* was recovered, a short circuit was found to be the culprit. It had caused a main manuevering thruster to become stuck in the ON position. The thruster, operating uncontrolled, caused the severe oscillations. Considering the violence of the event, the fact that the Gemini and Agena were "hard" docked when the thruster began to run wild, and the fact that this was only the first time we performed a docking manuever, Armstrong and Scott performed brilliantly. Whenever I think of *Gemini 8*, my admiration for those two pilots grows immensely.

Around the time of *Gemini 8*, rock groups began singing about drugs. One tune of the times is recalled with particular distinction. This lovely little ballad titled "Eight Miles High" was performed by the Byrds. Remember them? They sang "Turn, Turn, Turn" during the *Gemini 6* and *Gemini 7* spectacular.

The Byrds had found fame during *Gemini 4*, with a Bob Dylan classic, "Mr. Tambourine Man." "Mr. Tambourine Man" was harmless, full of twanging twelve-string guitar.

In 1965, on prime-time TV shows like "Shindig" ("Shindig" aired just before "Patty Duke" on Wednesday nights), the Byrds introduced a famous gimmick of the sixties—granny glasses. But the Byrds of 1966, like so many other groups (especially the Beatles), were in the process of change.

The first time I heard "Eight Miles High," I thought they were singing about fighter pilots. My kind of music! Not so, gang. "Eight Miles High" was a "drug hit." It described a drug flight, not a test flight.

Back in 1961, I learned how to play the drums. The education came courtesy of a fife and drum corps unit. In

New England, these eighteenth-century-style marching units were immensely popular. The music was shrill, war-like, and romantic. Weekends were filled with competitions and parades, from fourth grade right into junior high school. It was lots of fun.

When the Beatles made their splash in 1964, anyone who knew how to play the drums or guitar was a celebrity at school. Let's face it; it was a great way to meet girls.

I could hold my own on the drums. I had been playing serious martial music for years, had won numerous competitions, and was qualified as an instructor. It didn't take long to acquire the first set of drums (my dad helped me get them), and it didn't take much longer to start a group of my own. I spent about three years and several sets of drums playing with groups in the area, ending with enough talent to actually make a record (it never went further than a demonstration disk.)

The direction rock music took by the late sixties was nauseating, so I quit. It didn't fit lofty astronaut dreams. That made my parents happy. But in 1966 I was still playing the drums, caught between two goals: rock artist or astronaut. Maybe I could play the drums in orbit.

Although we nearly lost *Gemini 8*, the skill of the crew (for bringing the spacecraft back in one piece) and close scrutiny by the folks at McDonnell Aircraft revealed no fatal flaw with the Gemini system. The circuit problem that caused the thruster to malfunction was corrected, and Gemini was ready to fly again in about ninety days. That in itself was sensational.

Folks, this was 1966. We had only been in the manned spaceflight business for five years—and we were good enough by 1966 to let fly a Gemini at the rate of almost one every other month! And the only injuries suffered by a NASA astronaut were the skinned knuckles John Glenn received during recovery operations following his mission in 1962. That's impressive.

On the threshold of the summer of 1966, we prepared again for vacation. Having saved some money from mowing lawns and odd jobs, I planned on taking flying lessons in Sarasota. In 1966, you could get an "introductory" flying lesson in a Cessna 150 for five dollars. Cessna advertised this offer in *Life* Magazine. All you had to do was clip out the little coupon from the Cessna ad and bring it along with your five bucks to the airport. You got a real flight instructor and about twenty minutes at the controls. It was better than sex. Almost.

The Beatles were silent. The silence was intentional. They were trendsetters and they knew it. In keeping with the times, the Beatles were off recording music, not at all like the 1964–1965 Top 40 classics that had won them their initial fame. Their summertime releases were surprising.

Scores of new sounds from new artists dominated the charts. The Vietnam conflict escalated daily, and we had our first (and one of very few) patriotic Vietnam hits, "The Ballad of the Green Berets," by Army Staff Sergeant Barry Saddler. His words dealt with pride, not politics. Remember them?

> Fighting soldiers from the sky,
> Fearless men who jump and die,
> Men who mean just what they say,
> These are men of the Green Berets.

Just like the real thing, the song ended with a Green Beret getting killed, leaving his wife to ensure their son carried on the tradition:

Put silver wings
On my son's chest,
Make him one
Of America's best . . .*

Today "The Ballad of the Green Berets" could play with heartfelt sentiment. In 1966, its impact was one of confusion. I thought it was inspiring; others at school thought it was stupid. After all, Vietnam wasn't even a "real" war. They had a point.

Another tune from the *Gemini 8* period was "Along Comes Mary" by a group called the Association. "Along Comes Mary" was a drug hit. Other hits of the time were "Mother's Little Helper" by our friends the Rolling Stones (it was so bad, WDRC wouldn't even play it) and "Lightning Strikes" by Lou Christie, and Old Blue Eyes scored with "Strangers in the Night," which reeked of class.

With summer so close, the news focused on the upcoming missions of *Gemini 9* and *Gemini 10*. Both missions would feature multiple docking manuevers and EVA spectaculars of increasing duration. It made sense. Gemini proved itself in long-duration flight. The name of the game, by the summer of 1966, was to prove our philosophy of rendezvous and docking. (The docking during *Gemini 8* was all too brief.) Also, there was much work to do in the EVA department. Ed White's "spacewalk" during *Gemini 4* was adventuresome, but it did not prove we could do useful work outside the spacecraft. If we expected to fly to the moon, let a couple of guys out on the surface, and fire up for earth again—all within a couple of years—the time had come to let as many Gemini pilots as possible leave the cockpit, do some meaningful work outside, and return

*© 1963, 1964, 1966 Music, Music, Music, Inc.

safely. To accomplish all of this, the remaining Gemini flights were extremely demanding.

Gemini 9

After the startling successes of 1965, Gemini had its share of problems in the first half. of 1966. *Gemini 8* was dicey. We nearly lost that mission. *Gemini 9* wasn't off to a great start either.

Since Alan Shepard's flight in 1961, NASA had employed backup crews for each mission. For example, if Shepard had not been able to fly on May 5, 1961, John Glenn, his backup pilot, would have made the first Mercury flight.

Gemini 9's primary flight crew was Elliot See and Charlie Bassett, two fine pilots. They didn't live to fly *Gemini 9*. They were killed when their NASA jet (a T-38 Talon) crashed on approach to St. Louis.

Even the backup crew of Tom Stafford (Schirra's right seat on *Gemini 6*) as command pilot and Gene Cernan as pilot had a terrible time trying to get off the ground. *Gemini 9* was a rendezvous-and-docking mission, with a complex EVA thrown in for extra measure. To have a docking mission you had to get an Agena into orbit first. *Gemini 6* never got to dock because their Atlas/Agena failed to attain orbit. *Gemini 8* did dock, but not for long. Now, with the pressure on to pull off a successful docking mission, *Gemini 9*'s Agena fell into the ocean!

In a resourceful maneuver, NASA quickly boosted an alternate vehicle into orbit. They called this vehicle an ATDA (for Augmented Target Docking Adapter), and it was smaller than the Agena. Nevertheless, ATDA had a docking collar on it, like the Agena, which meant *Gemini 9* could still perform an actual "hard" dock.

Then the mission was scrubbed again for technical reasons. It was June 3, 1966 (exactly one year after the launch of *Gemini 4*), when *Gemini 9* finally got off the pad. Then Stafford and Cernan got another unpleasant surprise. ATDA, the savior of the docking mission, failed to shed its launch shroud. The photos in *Life* showed the ATDA in flight above a beautiful earth, its launch shroud dangling from its nose like, as Stafford called it, "an angry alligator."

All Stafford and Cernan could do was rendezvous with the ATDA. There was talk of Cernan going EVA and trying to free the shroud from the vehicle, but that idea was rejected. What the hell, there was still the planned EVA.

But gremlins haunted the EVA, too. Cernan was tasked with trying out the first version of the manuevering unit today's shuttle crews use for propulsion while outside the spacecraft, kind of like a "Buck Rogers" backpack. Called the AMU (for Astronaut Maneuvering Unit), this nifty device was located in the equipment module section of the spacecraft. It was stowed there because there wasn't enough room for it in the tiny Gemini cockpit. To reach it, Cernan had to go EVA, making his way aft along the retro and equipment modules to the nook where the AMU was stored. He was then to don the unit and evaluate its performance.

The EVA turned out to be more taxing than anticipated. Gene Cernan found himself so physically spent after trying to strap on the AMU that his faceplate was completely fogged! The guy couldn't see, and he was hanging out there, in orbit.

Stafford ordered Cernan back into the spacecraft, which in itself was a difficult maneuver for the nearly blinded astronaut. With the docking portion a disappointment and Cernan's EVA problems to boot, *Gemini 9* returned to earth on June 6, 1966. NASA was clearly hard pressed to get a good docking mission into orbit, and now, on top of that problem, there was the mystery of Cernan's fatigue during EVA. It appeared that doing meaningful work in zero-g was going to be a much larger problem than anticipated.

In the meantime, we went to Florida. Sarasota was beautiful as ever, and the girls were, well, spectacular. I met a few particularly good-looking young ladies from Mississippi on the beach. They were all cousins or something. Their southern accents were so strong I could hardly understand them. One of them kept saying she wanted to go poo. I felt sorry for her and suggested the ladies' room near the beach clubhouse. It was only then I realized she wanted to go swimming. She wanted to go to the *pool.*

I impressed those fine examples of southern womanhood by explaining about my imminent appointment with high adventure, in the form of my first flying lesson. I then enhanced the discussion by pointing out the importance of the space program. God only knows what they thought by the time I finished telling the lovely cousins all about Khrushchev and Kennedy and Gagarin and Shepard and why *Gemini 10* had better pull off a good dock and a decent EVA or we were up shit creek. But I succeeded in acquiring their addresses and phone numbers in Mississippi, just in case.

Gemini 10 was scheduled for July. The radio stations blasted some interesting music as the launch approached, which brings us, again, to the Beatles.

Like the space program, the Beatles had a significant effect on those of us who were growing up during the sixties. By 1966, everything the Beatles did was amplified out of proportion by the media. When a Beatle made a comment, it was sifted, analyzed, and reanalyzed in search of a deep, hidden meaning. You can imagine, then, the hype surrounding the first Beatle album released in the U.S. since *Rubber Soul* in late 1965.

In the summer of 1966, *Revolver* demonstrated the Beatles' changing image from "hip" to "hippie." With selections like "She Said She Said" and "Tomorrow Never Knows" it was obvious the Beatles were leading us into a new era in pop music. The era of heightened awareness had begun.

Others contributed, too. The Lovin' Spoonful rose to the top of the charts with "Summer in the City," appropriate for listening in the heat of July on Florida's gulf coast. And Donovan offered "Sunshine Superman," a song I equate with Vietnam because it seemed it was always played before the news and the news was always filled with how many Vietcong we'd killed that week and how many American soldiers we'd lost while killing them.

The jingle that best recalls the days of *Gemini 10* was offered, again, by the masters of mayhem, the Rolling Stones. It was called "Paint It, Black" and it was about drugs, drugs, and mainly drugs. It represented all kinds of things—and they were all negative.

Gemini 10

On Monday, July 18, 1966, *Gemini 10* lifted off from the Pad 19 complex at Cape Kennedy. Riding atop the Titan was *Gemini 3* veteran John Young in the command pilot's seat, with Mike Collins aboard as pilot. What a mission they had! First Young and Collins were to rendezvous and dock with their own *Agena 10*, already in orbit. Next, while in a docked condition with *Agena 10*, plans called for the firing of *Agena 10*'s engine. (Agena had a rocket engine

of its own, rated at sixteen thousand pounds of thrust.)
The acceleration into a higher orbit than that of any manned mission. Following that event, *Gemini 10* would translate back to a lower orbit and rendezvous with *Agena 8*,
inert and in orbit since its brief encounter with *Gemini 8*
in March. To top off the mission, Collins was slated to go
EVA and retrieve a unit of experiments still attached to
Agena 8.

To accomplish all of that in seven days would have
required great skill. *Gemini 10* was afforded slightly less
than four days to pull off the whole shooting match!

And they did it. The only negative aspect of the flight
occurred, once again, during EVA. Mike Collins struggled
to do his retrieval work on *Agena 8*. In fact, Collins was so
busy just keeping himself oriented, he lost his Hasselblad
camera.

Gemini 10 slammed home through the atmosphere on
July 21, 1966, the fifth anniversary of Gus Grissom's suborbital Mercury mission.

On August 9, 1966, I arrived at the Sarasota-Braden-
ton airport flight school carrying my five dollars and my
Life Magazine coupon. I savored the moment.

On that day, according to my oldest pilot logbook, I
flew a Cessna 150 aircraft for thirty-six minutes. That first
flying lesson was fun—but painful. You see, after *Gemini
10* I logged a great deal of time on the beach, seeking and
identifying targets of opportunity (girls). And I received
a brutal sunburn. So when the day arrived for the cloud
captain from Connecticut to show his stuff at the controls,
there was much preparation, placing pads and ointment
on arms, legs, and back—all of which were covered with
blisters. My mother tried to convince me to postpone the
flying lesson, but that, of course, was never considered as
an option. Real pilots don't worry about a little sunburn.

Following the lesson, I better understood the drug problem. I knew what it meant to be hooked. I was hooked on flying.

Home in Connecticut, the remainder of summer of '66 was spent with fellow aviation enthusiasts, launching model rockets with mice in them. Not one mouse perished in flight.

Gemini 11

September 1966. *Gemini 11* flew on Monday, the twelfth. Pete Conrad, who flew right seat with Gordon Cooper aboard *Gemini 5*, picked up the command pilot slot for this mission. With him was Dick Gordon, in the pilot's position.

It was a hell of a mission, with a precision-launch scenario allowing *Gemini 11* to achieve a spectacular first-orbit rendezvous with *Agena 11*. Then, in a maneuver similar to that performed by *Gemini 10*, the crew fired up the Agena and soared to a new orbital altitude record of 850 miles. Later Gordon attached a tether to the Agena and, undocked, *Gemini 11* and *Agena 11* rotated in space together, creating a weak field of artificial gravity.

Dick Gordon's EVA was a painful reminder of the fatigue problems faced by Cernan and Collins during the two preceding missions. Gordon wasn't outside the spacecraft very long when he informed Conrad he was overtaxed with fatigue.

When *Gemini 11* splashed down on September 15, the evening news reported that the largest remaining problem was the EVA situation: if we could not perform useful work outside the spacecraft, the lunar landing plans would have to be postponed.

The pressure was on *Gemini 12*. *Gemini 12* was the last of the proud Gemini series—if the EVA worries could be addressed and corrected during that mission. For those aching to see an Apollo fly, anticipation of *Gemini 12*'s success was intense.

Autumn of 1966 was unusually chilly. I had severe tonsillitis. That meant lots of time out of school, in bed with a high fever. The only good part about it was reading books about airplanes and space.

One of the major television networks tried to get the Beatles to do a weekly series that fall. The Beatles said no. Instead, we got the Monkees. There's nostalgia for the Monkees today (they improved with time), but they were considered poor substitutes for the real thing in 1966. Their recordings gave meaning to the term *teenie-bopper music*.

Nonetheless, the Monkees scored with "Last Train to Clarksville." The Top 40 stations played it too often. "Cherish," by the Association, was more appealing. "Poor Side of Town" by Johnny Rivers and "Under My Skin" by Frankie Vali were also favorites from the *Gemini 11–Gemini 12* period. When I hear them, I think of lying in my room in Connecticut with a sore throat, dreaming of flying airplanes and of flying in space.

Flying Magazine did a cover story that fall titled "The Air War in Vietnam." I read it dozens of times between sore throats. Although the news from Saigon was grim, I imagined I was flying sorties off carriers in support of our ground troops. It was a stupid daydream, a Walter Mitty classic. I had much to learn about Vietnam.

Gemini 12

It was freezing cold on Friday, November 11, 1966, when *Gemini 12* boosted into orbit from the Cape. Where was I? That's right! I was at home in bed with a sore throat and a high fever. But I watched the launch without interruption—it was worth the discomfort.

Gemini 12 was a great ending to a great program. As was common in the later Gemini missions, an astronaut who had previously flown as pilot took the commander's seat on the left. On *Gemini 12*, it was Jim Lovell's turn. Lovell spent two weeks aloft with Frank Borman in *Gemini 7*. Lovell's pilot for *Gemini 12* was Buzz (first name: Edwin) Aldrin. We'd hear from him again during Apollo.

Aldrin's EVA during *Gemini 12* was close to perfection. A great deal of modification work had been done to assist Aldrin, including the addition of Velcro straps and handholds to his suit and the spacecraft. Aldrin's pre-EVA training was also intense, including hours under water, in full pressure suit, to simulate zero-g.

When Lovell and Aldrin splashed down on November 15, the Gemini program came to a close.

Gemini was something special at a time when special things were growing scarce. The magic of the Kennedy era was gone. The nation was worried over Vietnam. Too many U.S. servicemen were coming back in boxes. At home, there were race riots in the cities and drugs on the college campuses.

Gemini was a source of inspiration through this rough period. Each mission was something to admire, something of which to be proud. Not one Soviet cosmonaut flew during the entire Gemini program. We sent ten Gemini crews into space, and they accumulated over nineteen hundred hours in orbit. There were no casualties.

That's an impressive record, one that represented keen preoccupation with quality and safety. If the shuttle program had been tied to Gemini standards, *Challenger* would still be flying and the seven we lost aboard her would be alive, bucking for that next mission.

Agony: '67 and '68

Christmas of 1966, a time of confusion. Remember the term *freaked out*? That's what a lot of my friends were. In 1966 I thought a good time was smoking cigarettes in the old cow pasture with the guys or imagining what it would be like to slip the old hand under Suzy's bra for a heavenly feel.

That was kid's stuff. The people at school were into other things. There were lots of parties, held when someone's parents went away for a few days. It wasn't sex, cigarettes, or a few beers that made those wing-dings happenings. It was drugs. And that was scary! Pilots didn't fool around with drugs! It was against astronaut standards!

My "straight" stance on drugs cost me some popularity. So what? There were plenty of airplane magazines, plenty of unbuilt model rockets, and Apollo to keep me busy. I had no time for fruitcakes and their dope.

While Christmastime 1966 may have been confusing socially, it was an exciting time for the space program. Gemini was over and Apollo was ready for action. And everyone knew that during Apollo we would land on the moon.

Like its predecessors, Apollo was scheduled to walk before it ran. Apollo was infinitely more complex. Instead of one or two astronauts, Apollo housed three. Instead of flying safely into and out of earth orbit, Apollo was designed to fly to the moon and back. This required several components.

Apollo was comprised of a command module, a service module, and, for lunar landing missions, a lunar module. Each component was critical to the success of a particular mission. Each component was critical to the safety of the astronauts.

The command module was a cone-shaped affair, much larger than Gemini, but crowded inside nonetheless when three men occupied it. It was designed to accommodate its crew during launch, travel to and from the moon, reentry, and splashdown. At the end of an Apollo mission, the command module was the sole remnant of the giant vehicle that left the pad upon launch.

Attached to the rear of the command module was the service module, a cylindrical extension that housed, among other systems, most of the spacecraft consumables (water, oxygen, et cetera), the fuel cells, and a reusable rocket, designed to get the spacecraft into and out of lunar orbit. The failure of the rocket to function during a lunar mission would spell death to the crew; Apollo would remain in some kind of cockeyed lunar orbit forever.

The third component was the lunar module. When President Kennedy set the course for manned missions to the moon, this component was called the LEM (Lunar Excursion Module). But as Gemini wound down, NASA began referring to it as simply the LM (lunar module).

The lunar module was stored inside the uppermost stage of the massive *Saturn V*, the S-IVB, during launch. After the Apollo configuration was on its way to the moon on a lunar landing mission (following TLI, or Trans-Lunar Injection), the command/service module rendezvoused with the lunar module, pulling it out of its shroud atop the spent S-IVB and docking so the lunar module was attached to the nose of the command module. In this configuration, the combined command/service module and lunar module coasted to the moon.

The lunar module was designed for two pilots, and it utilized a concept called LOR (Lunar Orbit Rendezvous). In LOR, once the spacecraft was in orbit around the moon, the commander and the lunar module pilot climbed through a small tunnel into the lunar module, separated from the command module, and went down to the surface of the moon. The command module pilot remained aloft in the command module. After exploring the surface, the commander and the LM pilot would fire up the ascent engine on the LM and boost back into lunar orbit. There the lunar module would rendezvous with the command module and dock. The two lunar explorers would climb back into the command module, where the command module pilot awaited them, and jettison the lunar module.

After firing the command module's rocket, the spacecraft would accelerate enough to escape lunar orbit and head on a predetermined trajectory for earth, splashing down after a fiery twenty-five thousand mph reentry, faster than any experienced during return from earth orbit.

LOR was the reason rendezvous and docking were so important during Gemini. Without the rendezvous and docking experience, there was no realistic procedure for returning the astronauts to earth.

There were several unmanned tests of various Apollo configurations. The first manned missions were planned for earth orbit, as tests of the three spacecraft components in flights lasting as long as a typical lunar landing mission.

The earth orbital missions without a lunar module were launched atop the beautiful *Saturn 1B* booster. *Saturn 1B* was a smaller rocket than the gigantic *Saturn V*, the booster for the lunar missions. But *Saturn 1B* was still gigantic, standing over two hundred feet tall when topped by an Apollo spacecraft. It was one hundred feet taller than Gemini-Titan. And instead of Titan's 430,000 pounds of thrust (which was considerable), *Saturn 1B* packed more than 1 million pounds of brute thrust.

Next, the lunar missions. It took 7.5 million pounds of thrust to get a moonbound Apollo system, complete with lunar module, off the ground. Then it took 1.2 million pounds of thrust to get the Apollo configuration into low earth orbit. And two hundred thousand pounds of thrust from a reusable rocket to achieve LOI, the kick from earth orbit to a trajectory aimed at the moon. All of this incredible power was provided by Wernher von Braun's *Saturn V*, the most powerful booster ever launched. The record remains.

An Apollo spacecraft poised gracefully atop a *Saturn V* rocket was an emotional sight. It stood 363 feet tall. The NASA artist's renditions of it were chilling. The jump from the seventy-eight thousand pounds of thrust Alan Shepard's Redstone provided to the *Saturn V's* unbelievable total of 8.2 million pounds of thrust was almost too great to comprehend. Our nation had performed magic! What a magnificent machine!

According to NASA at Christmastime 1966, it would only be another month or so before we heard the roar of the first manned mission to be launched atop a Saturn-series rocket, *Apollo 1*.

Apollo 1

Thursday, January 26, 1967, was my fourteenth birthday. The best present: a subscription renewal to *Flying* Magazine, which I read like a clergyman reads the Bible. *Flying* and *NASA Facts* were gospel.

It was bitter cold, typical for January in Connecticut. It was comforting to sit in the house and hear the old oil burner humming away, especially at night. In 1967, no one even dreamed of such a silly thing as an "energy crisis." There was no energy crisis, so the heat could run all night. With a window cracked, it was great sleeping weather!

The Rolling Stones had two smash hits. One was called "Ruby Tuesday." The other hit was so sexually suggestive that most stations either censored it or refused to play it entirely. The censored version sounded like a broken record. This song was called "Let's Spend The Night Together." Parents detested it with a vengeance. I bought it and played it loudly at every possible opportunity.

Donovan had a hit called "Mellow Yellow." It was strange and strange kids liked it. There was "Music to Watch Girls By" by the Bob Crewe Generation and "I'm a Man" by the Spencer Davis Group. And among many others there was "Strawberry Fields" by the Beatles, which sounded depressing. At the end of "Strawberry Fields" there were a lot of sound gimmicks, including John Lennon moaning, "I buried Paul." Hysteria! All of the radio stations fueled rumors that Paul McCartney, beloved Beatle bass guitarist and composer, was really dead. There were *contests* about it. McCartney turned up alive and well shortly after it all started.

Friday, January 27, 1967. Another week of school completed. *Apollo 1* was scheduled for launch soon. I drew a picture of an Apollo spacecraft during study hall. It kept company with the Mercury and Gemini spacecraft already inked into the brown paper bag book cover on my Spanish book. Beneath the drawing I printed:

APOLLO 1

Grissom/White/Chaffee

2/67

Friday nights were good TV nights. "Hogan's Heroes," "Get Smart," and a movie rounded off the lineup. It was shortly after dinner . . .

"We interrupt our regular programming to bring you this special report. . . ." This time, the bad news wasn't from Dallas. President Johnson was apparently okay. Instead, the word came from Cape Kennedy. There was a fire aboard *Apollo 1* during a routine ground test. Astronauts Grissom, White, and Chaffee were aboard the spacecraft, fully suited, for a simulated countdown drill. Among other items, the simulation included switching of spacecraft electrical power from external sources to internal spacecraft power.

The test began at 1:00 P.M. There were numerous glitches. To simulate prelaunch conditions, the spacecraft was pressurized with pure oxygen. Grissom smelled something strange, but nothing abnormal was found. Then the voice communications link misbehaved.

By 6:30 P.M., the astronauts were tired. The test was almost over.

Fifteen minutes later, they were dead. A flash fire swept through the spacecraft, and they were asphyxiated. *Apollo 1* was gone.

What happened? The question remains. Intensive investigation only led to conjecture; the best answer embraced a short circuit in faulty wiring somewhere beneath Grissom's seat. In the highly pressurized cabin, the spark that resulted caused the fatal fire.

Our magnificent space program, the one set into motion toward the moon by President Kennedy, the one that never, ever compromised safety, had somehow deteriorated while the Apollo hardware was manufactured.

The spacecraft for *Apollo 1* was a "Block I" design. Improved "Block II" spacecraft would follow after the first earth orbital missions. It didn't make sense. Why send a crew up in *anything* but the very best?

The *Apollo 1* spacecraft had a long list of maladies. The life-support systems functioned so poorly that they had to be replaced. Grissom eventually hung a lemon on the spacecraft to show his digust. How could NASA even consider using a spacecraft with such serious problems? It was unthinkable.

The cabin was not equipped with fire-retardant materials. The volatile pure oxygen environment was not taken into appropriate consideration. Any spark beckoned catastrophe.

The astronauts cried for assistance as the cockpit burned. They struggled to get the hatch open. The hatch was designed so poorly that it took at least ninety seconds to open it under ideal conditions. A hatch designed to open simply and quickly would have given the crew a chance for survival.

Most pathetic of all, there were no doctors or emergency crews available near the spacecraft during the test because the test was assumed to be "safe"; there was no fuel in the big *Saturn 1B* rocket below the spacecraft. Assuming the safety of *any* operation where complex machinery and energy are involved represents the same kind of thinking that made the *Titanic* and the *Hindenburg* disasters so pointless. Add *Apollo 1* to the list.

There is much information on the *Apollo 1* disaster. I recommend John Noble Wilford's account of the event and its aftermath in his outstanding book *We Reach the Moon*.

Opinion: The real cause of the *Apollo 1* fire was plain, simple bureaucratic crap, poor communications between the manufacturer and the end user, and total disregard for crew safety.

We accept certain risks. Pilots certainly accept them. In the matter of flying in space, astronauts accept even greater risk, but with the assurance that every facet of safety will be considered. That standard was set during Mercury and Gemini. It is our responsibility. In that responsibility, we sorely disappointed Grissom, White, and Chaffee, three fine pilots who trusted their team.

The year 1967 was off to a rotten start. If you were a Soviet space program fan, 1967 was not the year to pick either.

On April 23, the Soviets launched their first manned mission since *Voskhod II* in 1965. They introduced a new breed of spacecraft on this mission, called Soyuz. Although information on Soviet space operations was scarce, it was assumed Soyuz was very large—probably larger than Apollo. It was also assumed Soyuz had the ability to change orbits—translate—like Gemini and Apollo. Speculation was high. Was this new craft capable of a lunar voyage? Could Soyuz beat Apollo to the Moon?

Col. Vladimir Komarov was the sole occupant of *Soyuz 1*. No rookie, Komarov was a veteran of the *Voskhod I* mission in October 1964.

A day after achieving orbit, Komarov initiated reentry procedures and *Soyuz 1* appeared to be headed for an uneventful return to earth. Until the chute system got snarled. *Soyuz 1* smashed into Soviet soil, killing cosmonaut Komarov. Komarov was the world's first in-flight space fatality. Like Grissom, White, and Chaffee, Komarov was an outstanding pilot and a brave man. Rival or not, his loss was our loss.

The American and Soviet space programs were in a state of disarray. Manned spaceflight ceased. Pilots had died and investigations abounded. Typically, there were questions in the media concerning the value of sending men into space. As in the *Challenger* aftermath, it is always easier to say, "We shouldn't have done it in the first place."

The summer of 1967 was a time of social change. In the absence of a manned space mission—out of the question with Apollo and Soyuz down—it was interesting enough just to watch the people here on earth during the "summer of love." The "hippie" movement took to the streets. Who were the hippies? Hippies were people who were against things. I was not among them. But I must admit in 1967 there were plenty of things to be against.

"Vietnam was the first rock-and-roll war, a weird mix of sex, drugs, music, violence and idealism that was the dark mirror of the sixties," wrote William Broyles, Jr., of the conflict. And American involvement in Vietnam was out of control. On the news there was always a general or State Department official declaring victory in Southeast Asia. But American servicemen kept getting slaughtered.

It was perplexing. What was wrong? The United States earned victory on two fronts in World War II. For some reason, we couldn't control a tiny piece of real estate in Southeast Asia.

There was no plan to win; that's what was wrong. The techniques of "graduated response" Lyndon Johnson insisted upon from our combat units in Southeast Asia was ineffective against an enemy who had all the time in the world to fight. Fear of escalation caused our policy makers to avoid the very strategic targets in North Vietnam that would have brought the war to a quick end.

Consider: (1) War stinks. Don't go to war. Negotiate. That way, everyone gets to play again. (2) If you're dumb enough to go to war, it is suicidal to fight a war in which there exists no plan to clobber the bad guys. In Vietnam, for reasons of varying complexity, we were too stubborn—

or too stupid— to get out when it was obvious we didn't intend to win.

In American cities, the blacks were rioting, tired of being treated like second-class citizens. The freedom marches and peaceful demonstrations of the early sixties had produced few results. So the blacks got angry. Places like Watts, a suburb of Los Angeles, looked a lot like the combat zones in Vietnam they showed on TV every night.

Ironically, the "summer of love" was like a war movie double feature. First, there was the body count from the rice paddies on one side of the globe. Then, as an extra-special treat, there was color footage of combat at home. It was terrific.

A lot of people didn't like what they saw. So they revolted. In disgust, they sported long hair, wore sandals a lot, smoked pot, and dropped hard drugs. For outdoor entertainment, they enjoyed sit-ins, love-ins, and peaceful(?) demonstrations. They had a tendency to overtake things, like college campuses. These individuals were known as hippies.

A few of the hippies' basic beliefs were noble. They were against war, greed, racial discrimination, and things unfair. But the hippie culture defeated the purpose of their existence.

Music was essential to understanding the hippies. And there was lots of it in the summer of 1967. One of the Top 20 hits was a tune written by John Phillips (of the Mamas and the Papas) and recorded by Scott McKenzie titled "San Francisco (Be Sure to Wear Some Flowers in Your Hair)." Remember it?

> All across the nation
> Such a strange vibration,
> People in motion. . . .

There's a whole generation
With a new explanation,
People in motion,
People in motion.

For those who come
To San Francisco,
Be sure to wear
Some flowers in your hair.

If you're going
To San Francisco.
Summertime
Will be a love-in
There.*

Hippie or not, "San Francisco" was a beautiful song. It was sung with conviction. Its warmth defied the anger of the times.

Then there was acid rock. A new group called the Jefferson Airplane hit the charts with a whopper called "Somebody to Love." "Somebody to Love" made its debut on an album called *Surealistic Pillow*, crammed full of exciting drug hits. It was an angry record.

Others followed. The Grateful Dead. The Jimi Hendrix Experience. The Who. Tons of 'em. And . . . the Doors.

One song dominated the summer of 1967, and it was recorded by a new group, the Doors. It was called "Light

*"San Francisco (Be Sure To Wear Some Flowers in Your Hair)" Words and music by John Phillips © copyright 1967 by MCA Music Publishing, a division of MCA, Inc. and Honest John Music. Rights administered by MCA Music Publishing, a division of MCA, Inc., New York, N.Y. 10019. Used by permission. All rights reserved.

My Fire." I watched the Doors on Ed Sullivan. They were chilling. The music was chilling. The Doors stood somewhere between life and death.*

The Doors depicted the tone of that summer. Their music set the stage for the years to follow. It was scary. Everyone was angry! What was happening? Where was President Kennedy? What happened to Wally Cleaver? And Eddie Haskel?

The Doors depicted the tone of summer '67, but the Beatles set the tone. The Beatles completed their change from the innocent "Fab Four" to the ordained leaders of hippiedom with the release of their album *Sgt. Pepper's Lonely Hearts Club Band*. The recording earned the Beatles a cover story in *Time* Magazine. It was a magnificent piece of entertainment. But it was more than just a record. It was a way of life. An entire generation held *Sgt. Pepper* to its breast. *Sgt. Pepper's Lonely Hearts Club Band* remained the number one album in the United States for more than a year.

Along beautiful Crescent Beach on Siesta Key in Sarasota, Florida, the air was filled with the sounds of many, many transistor radios—one radio blared "Lucy in the Sky with Diamonds" from the *Sgt. Pepper* album, another played the more soothing sounds of the Tremeloes' "Silence Is Golden," and from yet another were the haunting strains of "Light My Fire." The memories linger.

I saved some money I earned mowing lawns and doing other jobs. By the time we returned to Connecticut, I was able to take more flying lessons. It was obvious after several hours of dual instruction (when you fly in the left seat with an instructor in the right seat) that cash was going to be a problem. Flying was expensive! At twelve dollars per hour

*The Doors took their name from the book *Doors of Perceptions*, by Aldous Huxley, about the author's experience with hallucinogens.

(today it's more like eighty dollars per hour), I sorely lacked the cash necessary to schedule flying lessons in succession, which is exactly what it takes to retain anything from previous lessons.

There had to be another way. After school resumed, some friends and I formed an Aviation Explorer Scouts branch. With the assistance of the chief pilot at New Haven Airport, we negotiated reduced rates on flying lessons. With the reduced rates, I could schedule a flying lesson almost every other weekend.

Flying lessons made school seem easier. Those Saturdays were special when my instructor and I flew Piper Cherokees over the Long Island Sound for maneuvers. And waiting for the space program to resume Apollo operations was easier with flying lessons to take up the slack.

Fall, 1967. The Doors sang "Strange Days," and the Union Gap sang "Woman, Woman." General Westmoreland said the enemy was licked in Vietnam; we just needed a few hundred thousand more troops to clean up the mess. I was elected to represent the freshman class at Cheshire High School. And NASA hinted at flying Apollo sometime in late 1968.

On November 9, NASA launched the first mighty *Saturn V*. Dubbed *Apollo 4*,* the Saturn flew with a full-scale Apollo command/service and lunar module. The mission was a total success. The program was recovering, but there was much work to be done before men could fly in Apollo with confidence.

Christmas, 1967. I spent a lot of time talking about

**Apollos 1* through *3* were unmanned tests flown atop the *Saturn 1B* rocket. This is a source of confusion, since we now call the Grissom-White-Chaffee mission *Apollo 1*. It was actually known as *Apollo 204* before the fire.

space with my girl friend, Candi. She at least acted interested. Flying lessons continued, but only on a monthy
basis: cash was short.

The year was one of personal development and disappointment. Vietnam, the riots, and the drugs were depressing. The *Apollo 1* and *Soyuz 1* disasters were sobering.
Perhaps 1968 would yield more positive results.

'68

It began with a song. Remember the Monkees? They
were more advanced since "Last Train to Clarksville" aired
in the fall of '66. They were, by 1968, more creative and
more popular outside the "teenie-bopper" crowd.

The lead guitarist, Michael Nesmith, was a talented
composer. He penned many of the Monkees' tunes. During
the fall of 1967, the Monkees released a new album, *Pisces,
Capricorn & Jones, Ltd.* Bob, who was doing some growing
up himself, bought the record. "Love Is Only Sleeping," a
Nesmith creation, was one of Bob's favorites.

Early in 1968, a song Nesmith wrote went to the top
of the charts. But it wasn't performed by Nesmith or the
Monkees. A new female artist, Linda Ronstadt, recorded
Nesmith's "Different Drum" with her group, the Stone
Ponies. "Different Drum" reminded me of the freedom of
flying, so I liked it. The Monkees may have been dorks of
sorts, but Nesmith won my respect with "Different Drum."
"Different Drum" will always be a reminder that (in addition to *Apollo* 7 and *Apollo* 8) at least something good came
out of 1968.

The year was terrible. Continued U.S. involvement in
Vietnam divided the nation. Lyndon Johnson's Democratic
party was in shambles, and the president's popularity hit
an all-time low. The tension between those who supported

the war and those who opposed it was dramatic.

In January, furious fighting in Vietnam erupted. The evening news was filled with coverage of our marines defending a remote base in Khe San, where they were opposed by perhaps thirty thousand North Vietnamese troops under Gen. Vo Nguyen Giap. Giap was the North Vietnamese military mastermind. The scene was ghastly. Then the North Vietnamese launched their bloody Tet offensive, which demonstrated the sheer determination of the enemy to prevail. Despite all the bombing and the awesome mechanization of American combat forces in Vietnam, the Hanoi regime established a supply network that extended deep into South Vietnam. And the South Vietnamese peasants frequently aided Giap's troops. We were in no way "winning" the war that had dragged on for nearly three years.

What a setting for an election year! In February, as the Tet mess unfolded, Johnson's candidacy seemed assured. Other Democrats like Sen. Eugene McCarthy commanded tremendous popularity with antiwar factions, like the hippies. The president faced bitter competition. In New Hampshire, the primary held in March saw McCarthy nearly tie with the president, who, while unofficially in the race, still retained considerable political strength. McCarthy's showing in New Hampshire underscored the surprising political strength of the antiwar movement. With the national mood deteriorating daily, an antiwar candidate had a great chance of becoming the next president of the United States.

Hovering in the background, like a ghost of better times gone by, was the junior U.S. senator from New York. Robert F. Kennedy, former attorney general, and brother of the beloved slain president inherited the much-publicized "Kennedy legacy" on November 22, 1963. Since that fateful day, millions of Americans wondered when Robert—whose resemblance to the late president was haunting—would make a run for the White House.

There was talk of a Kennedy candidacy for months. Robert Kennedy, like the late president, was immensely popular in Connecticut. Kennedy criticized U.S. policy in Vietnam as early as 1966, a year after his brother's plan—had he lived to enforce it—would have removed all U.S. military personnel from Southeast Asia. Many saw Kennedy as Lyndon Johnson's ultimate rival for the Democratic nomination.

Another possible antiwar candidate was Sen. George McGovern, a respected liberal also opposed to our Vietnam policy. So the antiwar supporters had McCarthy, Kennedy, and McGovern as the best antiwar candidates, although officially Kennedy and McGovern had not yet declared their candidacies.

One rumor followed another concerning Kennedy's decision to run. Speculation ceased on Saturday, March 16, 1968, when Robert F. Kennedy declared he was a candidate for the Democratic nomination for president. It was a moment of sublime political drama—history was repeating itself. Eight years earlier, John F. Kennedy declared his candidacy in the very same Senate caucus room. At the time of their respective announcements, John F. Kennedy and Robert F. Kennedy were forty-two years old.

Robert Kennedy's candidacy was like the resurrection of a dream. There was magic in it. We lost John F. Kennedy. Perhaps, in Robert Kennedy, there was a second chance for visionary leadership when it was needed most. I wanted Robert Kennedy to succeed as badly as I wanted to see Apollo land on the moon. It seemed like our only hope to end the fighting and heal the nation.

The year 1968 was also a year of surprises. Big news happened almost nonstop. On March 31, only fifteen days after Robert Kennedy declared his candidacy, Lyndon Johnson—the incumbent Kennedy was determined to defeat—removed himself from the race in a speech on nationwide television. The famous Sunday night speech was originally positioned as an "important announcement" regarding our policy in Vietnam. His announcement not to seek a full second term as president came as a total surprise at the very end of the speech.

Johnson wasn't running! That was mighty big news, not only to folks like Richard Nixon, the Republican candidate most likely to be nominated, and Hubert Humphrey, vice president of the United States and most likely Johnson's choice for the Democratic nomination, but to Eugene McCarthy and Robert Kennedy, who were firmly against the administration's handling of our Vietnam policy. Now McCarthy and Kennedy had to battle it out. And the result of a successful Kennedy campaign: Richard Nixon would face a second Kennedy in the general election!

The plight of the blacks was a crucial topic during the 1968 campaigns. Every candidate had to address the problem and propose solutions. Of all the candidates, Robert Kennedy appeared the favored runner. This was partially because he was President Kennedy's brother and partially because Robert Kennedy commanded substantial credibility in the civil rights arena because of his work as attorney general and as a senator.

Kennedy enjoyed a close relationship with Dr. Martin Luther King, who headed the civil rights movement. It was John F. Kennedy who came to assist King when he was jailed during the 1960 campaign. Now, in 1968, Robert Kennedy championed the blacks. His primary pluralities included tremendous turnouts from the black population.

Thursday, April 4, 1968: "We interrupt our regular programming to bring you this special news bulletin. . . . " The news was typical. The news was bad. The news was insane. Some idiot shot Martin Luther King at a motel in Memphis. Head wound. Killed him.

The whole country seemed out of control. If you stood for something worthwhile, you stood an excellent chance of getting shot. Why kill these men? There were no answers.

Having heard the bad news as he campaigned in Indiana, Robert Kennedy gave a moving impromptu speech to a crowd assembled in the slum district of Indianapolis. Kennedy appealed to the crowd, which was mostly black, to use restraint and not seek revenge because a white man killed King.

Kennedy said, "For those of you who are black and are tempted to be filled with hatred and distrust at the injustice of such an act, against all white people, I can only say that I feel in my own heart the same kind of feeling." He continued, "I had a member of my family killed, but he was killed by a white man. But we have to make an effort in the United States; we have to make an effort to understand, to go beyond these rather difficult times."

Kennedy marched alongside national black leaders through the streets of Atlanta during King's funeral. The sight of the coffin, the lowered heads, the speeches seemed too familiar.

In Washington, there was grave concern over the black population's reaction to the Martin Luther King assassination. Would the riots start early this season? Would there be another civil war? Our teachers pondered these points with us in school. What kind of country were we living in anyway? In 1968, one had doubts.

The campaigns continued. In Florida, we launched *Apollo 6*. (*Apollo 5*, which flew in January, was a test of the lunar module atop a *Saturn 1B*.) This second unmanned test of the giant *Saturn V* was not as successful as the first. Booster engines either shut down prematurely or completely failed to ignite. But NASA determined the cause of the problem—severe vibrations—quickly. The problems were fixed and *Saturn V* was given a "green light" to boost people into space. Now all we needed was a green light for the redesigned command module.

Spring 1968. There were no manned space flights to think about. NASA was uncertain about resumption of manned Apollo operations. Considering the herculean overhaul being performed on the command module to correct the problems uncovered during the fire inquiry, I assumed flights would not resume until 1969. Happily, I was wrong.

The psychedelic counterculture was firmly embedded in the music of the spring of 1968. Rock bands bearing weird names surfaced by the dozens. For instance, there was Vanilla Fudge, who hippieized a Motown favorite previously recorded by the Supremes titled "You Keep Me Hanging On." Blue Cheer sang another oldie in revitalized hippie fashion, "Summertime Blues." In more traditional fashion, the Classics IV released "Spooky." And Richard Harris (the actor) sang "MacArthur Park."

On television the best show, by far, was "Rowan and Martin's Laugh-In." "Laugh-In" was very daring for its time. The phrase "sock it to me" was promoted to the hilt on this show. They even got Richard Nixon to say, "Sock it to me" on the air. For the first time, antiwar humor hit television and bureaucrats gasped when it was suggested on "Laugh-In" that our adventures in Vietnam were wrong.

These were the final years of cigarette advertising on television. The cigarette commercials were fantastic. In addition to "Marlboro Country" and other advertising standards of the tobacco industry, "gimmick" cigarettes appeared in 1968. For example, Silva Thins 100s were copiously advertised, introducing the "long cigarette." It was a new way to kill yourself and appear suave in the process. Remember the Silva Thins man? He moved cautiously through a smoke-filled lounge, surrounded by intrigued miniskirted bombshells who were, the scene suggested, trying to get the attention of this unique gentleman. If you smoked Silva Thins, you could be just like him.

My parents bought one of those big Magnavox console stereos during the spring of 1968. Console stereos were very popular. Components were still terribly expensive, complicated, and somewhat unreliable. I pushed for the console because all of my friends had them and I was embarrassed to think we still depended upon the old monaural hi-fi set for sound entertainment. And the sound the consoles reproduced was glorious—not only from records, but from FM stereo radio. I took a lot of crap off my father for wanting it. He didn't want to spend the money, and besides, what could he get out of it? His hearing was as bad as ever. But he got it for us anyway. And I played the hell out of the thing. WDRC was broadcasting in FM stereo—and that was "big time."

The school year was almost over. Perhaps 1968 could be salvaged by a great summer vacation. My attention turned to resumption of space flights, the airport, and girls—the keys to existence.

Tuesday, June 4, 1968. As usual, I got up around 6:00 A.M. and rushed for the bathroom. Gaining the bathroom first was key. We had a nice house, but it only had one bathroom. That made mornings a real challenge, with everyone trying to perform morning rituals in time to depart for work or school. To command "first tour" in the bathroom was efficiency personified.

I had a General Electric transistor radio my mother gave me when I entered junior high school in 1965. The radio accompanied me faithfully into the bathroom each morning so I could hear WDRC (AM) while performing the morning ritual. On June 4, the the weather report for southern New England was great.

The view from the bathroom window confirmed the weather report. June 4 was going to be a beautiful day in Connecticut. The trees were green. It was warm outside, indicating summer's approach. I decided to wear some good warm weather gear—a yellow oxford-cloth button-down shirt (long sleeves rolled up), cotton patch-madras pants (with cuffs), a cordovan belt, Bass Weejuns, and no socks. Lisa Birnbach (who, years later, wrote *The Official Preppy Manual*) would have loved me. This favored regalia was permissible between Memorial Day and Labor Day in Connecticut. If you weren't a hippie and you lived in Cheshire, you dressed like this. The statement made by such attire indicated you liked to have fun but you were normal.

It was a good day. There was this girl in my English class, Lydia. She was pretty. On June 4, she wore a dynamite new spring outfit, a short dress with yellow stockings and white high-heels. She had long, dark hair, and it looked smashing with her clothes. Since she sat near me in class, I made a special effort to joke around with her—and her responses were encouraging.

There was no space flight to think about on that day, but there was the California primary. It was exciting to anticipate the primary returns that evening. Robert Kennedy won in every primary he entered except Oregon. McCarthy beat him there. It was a tough loss for Kennedy. In California, speculation was high to see if Kennedy would beat McCarthy. The California primary was the last primary before the Democratic convention, to be held in Chicago during the summer. A Kennedy victory in California would mean Kennedy had a good chance for the nomination—and there were many who wanted a Kennedy victory badly. Millions.

Election coverage had matured significantly since the 1960 and 1964 campaigns. Each major network had a battery of computers to provide more accurate "vote projections." (CBS called their system "Vote Profile Analysis," and they advertised this technological capability frequently as the 1968 campaign progressed.) Via computer analysis the networks could judge, with reasonable accuracy, the winner of a particular race, based on only a small percentage of vote results. It was fascinating.

After dinner, Walter Cronkite, assisted by Roger Mudd and a host of others, began the evening's lengthy coverage of the California turnout. It was only 4:00 P.M. in Los Angeles (7:00 P.M. on the east coast), where Kennedy had his campaign headquarters at the Ambassador Hotel. Some folks in California had yet to vote. But there was confidence of a Kennedy victory.

The vast population of Mexican-Americans and blacks in the cities of California voted heavily for Kennedy that day. They believed in him. Additionally, Kennedy's magnetic appeal with young white-collar voters in California was translated into scores of ballots for the senator.

I went to bed at 11:30 P.M. (8:30 P.M. in Los Angeles). According to CBS, Kennedy had already won the South Dakota primary, also held that day. This was especially good news because South Dakota was Hubert Humphrey's native state. If Kennedy could win there, his credibility against Humphrey increased significantly. CBS also predicted Kennedy would win in California. Since I believed almost anything Walter Cronkite said, I closed my bedroom door feeling smug about a Kennedy win.

The radio volume was low, as I typically kept it before going to sleep. This was an expensive habit, because the radio usually stayed on all night. I went through batteries like the *Saturn V* went through rocket fuel. WDRC played "Be My Baby," an oldie recorded by the Ronettes in 1963. *Those days may live again*, I thought, *when Robert Kennedy gets elected.* My last thoughts before falling asleep were of how great the inauguration of President Robert F. Kennedy would be.

My mother is a very sentimental person. She cries easily. So when I woke up early on Wednesday, June 5, 1968, I wasn't very surprised to hear her crying. She did it all the time. I decided she probably saw something on TV about some poor kids or something and it made her cry.

But her tears weren't the result of some sad, silly thing. It had happened again: "We interrupt our regular programming to bring you this special bulletin from CBS News. . . ."

Insanity. Your worst nightmare come true. Shortly after midnight LA time, another social zero (the jerk truly fits the description) shot Robert Kennedy, shortly after he claimed his victory in California. Kennedy was walking through a corridor full of well-wishers, and this dope pulled out a cheap pistol and shot Kennedy. In the head.

I sat before the television, numb. Medgar Evers. President Kennedy. Martin Luther King. And now Robert Kennedy. This and Vietnam too. I was no prophet of peace in 1968, but this was too much.

The assassination of Robert Kennedy represented a sick crescendo of bloodletting and violence. It had a devastating effect, especially on young people. What was that effect? Sadness. Sadness because we couldn't control what happened. Lee Harvey Oswald is dead and we'll never even be sure he was President Kennedy's murderer. The guy who killed Martin Luther King turned out to be a typical mental midget. And Sirhan Sirhan, Robert Kennedy's murderer, sits in jail under heavy protection, a madman in madman's quarters. Who would have suspected him? Where did we get people like Sirhan Sirhan?

By June 1968, television funerals for assassinated leaders were rather common. Bob was used to it, too. He even commented on the differences between Martin Luther King's funeral in April and Robert Kennedy's, which was Friday, June 7. Bob was eight years old. I thought it pathetic that my little brother was already an expert on the funerals of murdered American heroes.

Those who remember well the violence of 1968 don't walk the earth today in a trance of eternal sorrow. Time heals—and the damage done during that awful spring has been tempered by wisdom. But the emotional pain of June 5, 1968, when Robert Kennedy died of a massive gunshot wound to the head, is easily recalled. The feeling was similar to that of November 22, 1963, but it was more intense. I was only ten years old when President Kennedy was killed, so the issues he addressed in 1963 seemed rather abstract. In contrast, five years later, the issues Robert Kennedy addressed were utterly relevant. Guys I knew were being drafted. And they were going to Vietnam. I could see the poverty-stricken in New York every time I went into that embattled city. And in school the peace movement was everywhere.

Robert Kennedy addressed the world in which I lived. His dreams for the nation would have favorably touched my life and the lives of millions. When he died, so did the dreams.

In 1969, Jack Newfield published a book titled *Robert Kennedy: A Memoir* His recollections following the events of June 1968 sum up the emotional tone of the times better than most. Newfield wrote:

> Now I realized what makes our generation unique, what defines us apart from those who came before the hopeful winter of 1961, and those who came after the murderous spring of 1968. We are the first generation that learned from experience, in our innocent twenties, that things were not really getting better, that we shall NOT overcome. We felt, by the time we reached thirty, that we had already glimpsed the most compassionate leaders our nation could produce, and that they had all been assassinated. And from this time forward, things would get worse: our best political leaders were part of memory now, not hope.

Sad comments indeed. But after Robert Kennedy's death, it was easy to feel that way.

Summer vacation was like a recovery program. I can't remember anyone being very happy about anything, not even my parents. The assassinations moved them, too. It was painful to watch a strong, opinionated person like my father attempt to make any sense out of the killing at home or in Vietnam. He felt as badly as I.

The trip did have a healing effect. When I got back to Connecticut, I decided to take some positve action in order to get back into the air. I won my first real job. I repaired apple crates at a local apple orchard for $1.25 an hour. It was big time.

Really, it was interesting work. When it wasn't raining, there was work to do outside. There was WDRC on the transistor radio. My boss left me alone most of the time, so I set my own pace. It was a very private time, a time for reflection. So we kept each other company, history and I, sitting there in the sun of late July and August, sweating and listening to the music and news of the turbulent summer of 1968.

The conventions came and went. The Democratic convention was like a combat zone, with armed police beating up the protesters outside the convention center in Chicago. One night, Dan Rather, then an ambitious CBS correspondent, was mugged right on the convention floor by an angry mob. Everyone was angry. Everyone.

The Democrats selected Hubert Humphrey and Edmund Muskie as their presidential and vice presidential nominees. The Republicans chose Richard Nixon and Spiro Agnew. Nixon and Humphrey were respectable candidates, but after the soaring hope of Robert Kennedy's ill-fated campaign, those standard politicians lacked substance.

Strong stuff was playing on the radio. A real all-American bunch of guys who called themselves Steppenwolf did a number titled "Born to Be Wild." And you're right; my parents hated every note. (I'm being facetious when I say Steppenwolf was "All-American." They looked more like hard-core criminals who had crashed on their last acid trip.) So I bought the album, which was called simply, *Steppenwolf*. It had lots of nice songs on it like "The Pusher." Remember "The Pusher"? It had eloquent lyrics:

> Well, I've smoked a lot of grass.
> Oh, Lord, I've popped a lot of pills,
> But I never took nothin'
> My spirit could kill.
>
> You know I've seen lots of people
> Walkin' round with tombstones
> In their eyes,
>
> But the pusher don't care
> If you live or if you die.

God damn the pusher . . .*

Or, even better, how about the spiritually lifting words of "The Ostrich"?

We'll call you when you're six years old,
And drive you off to the factory . . .

But then you're free,
And for forty years you waste
To chase the dollar sign,

So that you may die
In Florida

At the pleasant age
Of sixty-nine . . .**

Steppenwolf music was like "tunes to commit suicide by" because most of it enshrined the hopelessness of the times. Things weren't really bad enough to warrant suicide. Nothing is worth taking life. But in 1968, many exercised that option.

Another big hit of the summer of '68 was by a group called Cream. I thought they were great, even if they were more obscene than Mick Jagger and the Rolling Stones themselves (who scored with an evil hit titled "Sympathy for the Devil" at about the same time). The name of the hit was "Sunshine of Your Love." It went right to number one. I bought it.

The "dirty movie" of the summer was *The Graduate,*

* Words and music by Hoyt Axton © Lady Jane Music, BMI. Used by permission.
**"The Ostrich" Words and music by John Kay © copyright 1967 by Duchess Music Corporation. Rights administered by MCA Music Publishing, a division of MCA, Inc., New York, N.Y. 10019. Used by permission. All rights reserved.

featuring Dustin Hoffman and Anne Bancroft. It was even better than *Bonnie and Clyde*, because no one got killed. I was sick of killing. Sex was much better. And in 1968 *The Graduate* was sexually daring. It was the kind of movie your parents didn't want you to see but you saw anyway.

When school began, NASA was ready to get back into business. The command module had been pronounced healthy and ready to fly. The first scheduled for flight since the *Apollo 1* disaster was recycled and named *Apollo 7*. Wally Schirra, who flew in Mercury and Gemini, would command *Apollo 7*. With him would be command module pilot Donn Eisele and lunar module pilot (although there would be no LM for this mission) Walter Cunningham.

While the command module was ready to fly, problems remained with the LM. It was too heavy. NASA decided there would be no sacrifice in safety to proceed with missions that tested the capabilities of the command module while the LM problems were corrected. It was a good decision, and it indicated that safety once again reigned supreme at NASA.

Apollo 7

On October 11, a beautiful *Saturn 1B* booster lofted Schirra, Eisele, and Cunningham into earth orbit. *Apollo 7*'s systems were tested to the hilt; this was a classic "shakedown" mission. The most-publicized problems aboard *Apollo 7* were the head colds the crew developed during the flight. (Wally Schirra still does Actifed commercials on TV, in testimonial to the product's effectiveness aboard *Apollo 7*.)

The big service module engine was fired and refired with precision. In lunar orbit, any malfunction of the service engine would be catastrophic. It had to work, or else.

Apollo 7 completed 163 orbits in eleven days. It was a memorable mission for many reasons—but the most obvious was television coverage direct from the spacecraft. For the first time, an American spacecraft was large enough to accommodate television equipment. It was a thrill to see "The Wally, Walt, and Donn Show," as the crew dubbed their broadcasts from orbit.

On October 22, 1968, *Apollo 7* made a successful reentry and splashdown. The mission was considered 101 percent successful by NASA. In fact, *Apollo 7* flew so well that additions were made to the flight plan even as the spacecraft was in orbit!

Even better, *Apollo 8* mission simulations took place while Schirra, Eisele, and Cunningham flew. Originally, *Apollo 8* was supposed to be the first to fly with the LM. Atop a *Saturn V*, *Apollo 8* would soar to an apogee of several thousand miles. The command module would dock and separate from the LM, and the LM would get a workout in earth orbit. Not long before *Apollo 7* lifted off, NASA announced that *Apollo 8* would have to fly without an LM; the lander still had problems. So speculation surrounding *Apollo 8* increased dramatically. Would *Apollo 8* become a serious earth orbital test featuring the *Saturn V*? Or were there even more fantastic ideas for *Apollo 8*?

The final flight plan for *Apollo 8* went far beyond our wildest dreams.

NASA determined that the flight of *Apollo 7* had gone so well that Apollo was ready for something more advanced. In November, NASA announced the new target for *Apollo 8*: lunar orbit! *Apollo 8* would fly sometime just before Christmas.

Apollo 7 flew during a typically beautiful New England autumn. I resumed flying lessons at New Haven Airport and savored every minute aloft. On the way to the airport,

"Hush," by Deep Purple, could be heard on any of the Top 40 stations. Other memorable hits of the period were "Hey Jude" by the Beatles and "Magic Carpet Ride" by Steppenwolf.

Apollo 8

With the upcoming mission of *Apollo 8*, the last two months of 1968 were more interesting—and less violent. The pride derived from NASA's recovery detracted from the war, the assassinations, the ugly conventions, the drugs, and the riots. Just the image of NASA professionals in crisp white shirts in Houston and Cape Kennedy was reassuring. Even in 1968, there were still people doing things worth thinking about.

Bad weather and low funds precluded more flying until the new year. I was ready to solo. I only needed to maintain proficiency for that event. But even maintaining proficiency was expensive. Colder weather ended the apple orchard job, which was still available on weekends before frost set in. I only had to wait until January, when I would turn sixteen and could get a better part-time job. In the interim, there was *Apollo 8* to dream about.

Our homecoming dance was interesting, complete with an impressive acid-rock band. They kicked off the evening with a hit from *Surrealistic Pillow*: "She Has Funny Cars." For special effect, the lights were turned off and the band switched on its own special strobe light system. It was the first time this gimmick was used at Cheshire High School. It was impressive and fun.

Our chaperone teachers thought differently. They demanded either the lights go back on or the band had to leave. I wasn't an antiestablishment type of student by a long shot, but some of the stuff our teachers handed out was real crap. They were so scared someone might have a good time. In 1968, everyone was paranoid.

There'd been so much sorrow in 1968 that more traditional folk singers, reminiscent of the days of JFK, reappeared. Peter, Paul and Mary, who were great favorites of mine, released, "I Dig Rock and Roll Music." Judy Collins scored with "Both Sides Now." Her album, *Wild Flowers*, was sadly appealing in those late days of 1968. Dion, an artist from the early sixties, released "Abraham, Martin and John," a tribute to Lincoln, Martin Luther King, and John and Robert Kennedy. When Dion sang it on "The Smothers Brothers Comedy Hour" (which was eventually canceled by CBS because Tom and Dicky Smothers said too many bad things about what we were doing in Vietnam), there were images of the fallen leaders in the background. It hurt to watch that kind of stuff.

In December, the Beatles emerged with their most successful album since *Sgt. Pepper's Lonely Hearts Club Band.* It was known simply as "The White Album." Imprinted on the front was "The Beatles." Nothing more. There were two records in "The White Album." The offerings were widely varied.

There was evil, in the form of songs like "Helter Skelter" (which would acquire a morbidity of its own soon enough) and "Happiness Is a Warm Gun." There was deep emotion, in songs like "Julia" and "I Will." And there was the ridiculous, in "O Bla Di, O Bla Da" and "Piggies."

Everybody bought "The White Album." *Everybody* played it religiously. Knowing the words and reading meaning into them was a favorite pastime. The girls were especially serious about it. In the sacred halls of Cheshire High School between classes a girl would call to a friend, "Did you listen to 'Julia' again? I know what it *means*!" And then you'd hear a guy yell out from somewhere, "Who gives a fuck?" And everyone would die laughing, girls included.

With the flight of *Apollo 8*, our nation stood upon a new threshold. The dream of Americans on the moon by 1969 that President Kennedy had inspired was suddenly upon us as the magnitude of *Apollo 8*'s mission set in. Bob and I sat up late on many cold evenings early in December, trying to define the meaning the upcoming circumlunar navigation by a manned spacecraft. Would the world seem different after the flight? Would the fighting end in Vietnam because politicians on both sides were mentally paralyzed by the feat?

Bob was only nine, but he understood what was about to happen. My brother had always been highly intelligent.

Saturday, December 21, 1968. On that first day of Christmas vacation, I was up early to watch *Apollo 8* begin its journey to the moon. The television image of the awesome Saturn, poised to carry its fragile payload of human beings to another world, was inspirational, haunting, and beautiful. Every launch of a manned mission was news, but the launch of *Apollo 8* was big news. For example, CBS had author Arthur C. Clarke, who penned *2001: A Space Odyssey*, on hand to comment on the launch.

There was an overwhelming sense of pride and admiration for the crew of *Apollo 8*: Frank Borman, the commander, who had flown as command pilot on *Gemini 7* back in December of 1965; Jim Lovell, riding as command module pilot, who had flown with Borman as pilot on *Gemini 7*; and Bill Anders, flying as lunar module pilot, a rookie astronaut with an impressive set of credentials.

The emotion attached to the launch of *Apollo 8* paralleled or exceeded the frenzied atmosphere that surrounded the flights of Alan Shepard or John Glenn. Aside from the actual lunar landing, no mission could have been more exciting.

People have the power to invent awful things, like nuclear bombs and wars in which to use them. But on December 21, 1968, there was proof that the human race, which was doing rather poorly in 1968, could still produce magnificent things. *Apollo 8* was one of them.

At 7:51 A.M. (EST), *Apollo 8* lifted off Pad 39 at Cape Kennedy. *Saturn V* didn't produce the roar that was so familiar from Redstone, Atlas, Titan, or even *Saturn 1B*. Instead, initially there was something strange: silence. The network audio equipment, almost three miles distant from the pad, was so far away from the Saturn that *Apollo 8* seemed to rise silently on a massive column of fire. Finally, when the sound equipment registered the violent pressure shock created by the ignition of 7.5 million pounds of thrust, the sound heard by the television audience (and by those actually witnessing the launch at the cape) was a deep, deafening crackle. At the cape, the ground trembled for miles. The incredible adventure began.

After two earth orbits, the S-IVB engine, which remained with *Apollo 8* after achieving orbit, was fired again to initiate TLI (Trans Lunar Injection). At a speed of over twenty-four thousand mph, *Apollo 8* blasted free of earth orbit and sped toward the moon.

On December 24, *Apollo 8* entered lunar orbit. The service engine worked perfectly, firing enough to slow the spacecraft down into a near-circular orbit that came within sixty-nine miles of the lunar surface at its lowest (perilune) point.

Apollo 8 orbited the moon ten times. On Christmas Eve, Borman, Lovell, and Anders sent back tremendous television pictures from lunar orbit. The astronauts read from the Bible. I'm not terribly religious, but the moment was deeply moving. The sight of our planet, so blue and bright in the middle of the infinite blackness of space, was spectacular.

On Christmas Eve, I always go for a walk. It's an annual meeting with myself. In 1968 it was bitter cold. I had plenty of wind, snow, and ice for company. As I recall, I walked for about a mile. The sky was velvet-black and crystal clear, with bright stars. The moon hung majestically overhead. There were astronauts up there! And I did something melodramatic: I said a little prayer. I still remember it. It went: "Dear God, please let everything be all right." It was a very appropriate request to make in 1968, and I thought, with Borman, Lovell and Anders up there, perhaps they could relay the message.

Apollo 8 returned safely to earth on December 27. The reception the astronauts received was unbelievable. Messages of congratulations arrived from everywhere, even from Soviet cosmonauts, who applauded the accomplishment. *Time* Magazine made Borman, Lovell, and Anders their "Men of the Year."

And with the hope of *Apollo 8* the terrible year ended.

The crew of *APOLLO 1*, from left to right, Astronauts, Virgil "Gus" Grissom, Edward White II, and Roger Chaffee prior to their scheduled launch early in 1967.

CHALLENGER prepares to make its second landing at Edwards Air Force Base in California following the successful completion of the STS-7 mission in June, 1983. Among the *Challenger* crew for STS-7 was astronaut Dr. Sally K. Ride, the first American woman to fly in space.

The crew of STS Mission 51-L (*Challenger*), left to right, front row; Astronauts Michael Smith, Francis "Dick" Scobee, and Ronald McNair. From left to right, standing in the back row, are Ellison Onizuka, Sharon Christa McAuliffe, Gregory Jarvis and Judith Resnik. McAuliffe and Jarvis were payload specialists, representing the Teacher in Space project and Hughes Aircraft, respectively. The crew is portrayed prior to their launch on Janaury 28, 1986.

America's first astronaut, Alan B. Shepard, is launched atop a Redstone rocket in the flight of *Freedom 7*, on May 5, 1961. President Kennedy announced our plans to go to the moon shortly after this historic flight.

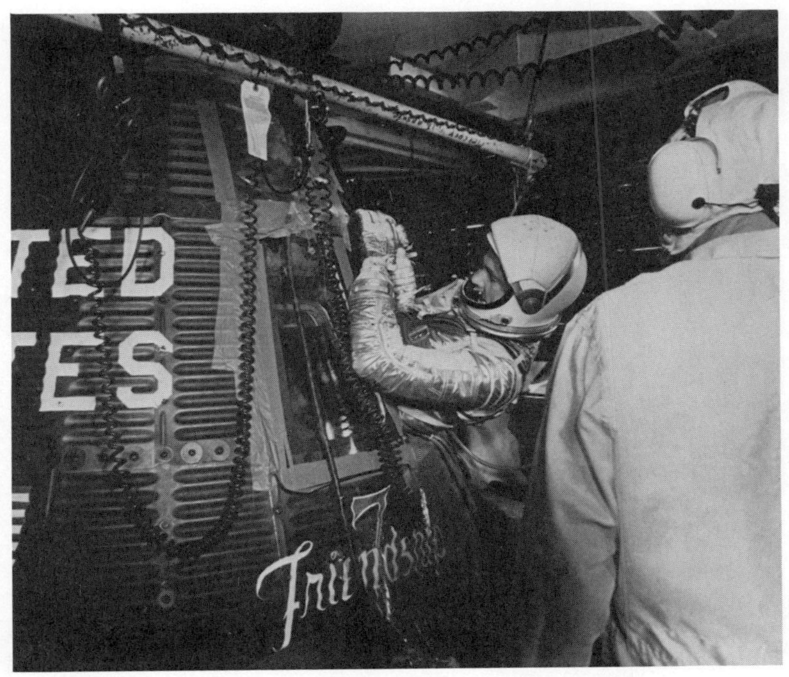

Project Mercury Astronaut John H. Glenn, Jr. enters *Freindship 7* during the final phase of the countdown on February 20, 1962. At 9:47 A.M., EST, a mighty *Atlas D* booster hurled Glenn into the first American manned orbital mission.

"President Kennedy accepts a model of an Apollo spacecraft command module presented to him as a gift by Dr. Robert R. Gilruth, center, Manned Spacecraft Center (MSC) Director, during the Chief Executive's visit to the MSC on September 12, 1962. Looking on was Vice President Lyndon B. Johnson. The space program was aggressively supported by both Kennedy and Johnson.

Astronaut Edward H. White II, pilot of the *Gemini 4* four-day earth orbital mission, floats in the zero gravity of space outside the *Gemini 4* spacecraft. White's "space walk" was the first time an American ventured outside the safety of a spacecraft. Astronaut James A. McDivitt, the command pilot of the mission, took this incredible photograph from inside the spacecraft, which is reflected on White's helmet visor, on June 3, 1965.

This photograph of a nearly full moon was taken from the *Apollo 8* spacecraft during its historic flight in December, 1968. In 1968, *Apollo 8* restored my faith that something good would come out of that horrible year.

Our fragile, beautiful earth as viewed from *Apollo 8* in December, 1968.

Bound for another world, all 363 feet of the magnificent vehicle that was *Apollo 11* thunder skyward on July 16, 1969 from pad A, Launch Complex 39, at the Kennedy Space Center in Florida.

Americans were the first humans to land on another celestial body, pictured here during activities outside the *Apollo 11* lunar module *EAGLE* on July 20, 1969. In this dramatic photo taken by *Apollo 11* commander Neil Armstrong, Astronaut Edwin Aldrin, kiddingly called "Dr. Rendezvous" by his peers for his acute knowledge of orbital mechanics, works on a Scientific Experiment Package on the lunar surface.

This photograph of the *Apollo 16* command module *CASPER* in flight above the desolate terrain of the far side of the moon was taken by the lunar landing crew of *Apollo 16* on April 20, 1972 from the *Apollo 16* lunar module *ORION*. The sense of pride and accomplishment afforded us by the Apollo lunar landing missions was immense.

The final lunar landing mission of the proud Apollo series was the flight of *Apollo 17*. The *Apollo 17* vehicle is pictured here on Pad A, Launch Complex 39, at the Kennedy Space Center prior to its majestic nighttime launch on December 7, 1972. Lack of leadership, the horrible cost of war in Vietnam, and other social maladies of the early seventies prevented additional Apollo voyages to the moon.

In reality, the first space station was NASA's Skylab, an S IV-B section from a giant *Saturn V* booster, modified to support astronauts during long-duration earth orbital missions. Here, the crew of *Skylab 4* caught the orbiting Skylab vehicle from their Apollo spacecraft prior to returning to earth on February 3, 1974.

Astronaut Rhea Seddon working aboard *Discovery* during the April 1985 STS Mission 51-D. Her contributions were vital in efforts to repair the malfunctioning *Syncom IV* satellite in earth orbit.

Pinnacle

In January 1969, lots of people simply took comfort in the fact that 1968 was over. Folks just plain wanted to wash their hands of that horrible year.

We raised our expectations. Change was at hand. Lyndon Johnson departed the White House a tired, beaten man. Vietnam ruined his presidency. And the war still raged. But we had a new leader.

Johnson's successor was Richard Nixon. From Nixon we expected action on the Vietnam mess. We wanted it to end, the sooner the better. Even though Nixon was a far cry from a "dove" (during the Vietnam years, people who were against the war were know as doves and people who were for the war were known as hawks) there was speculation that, since Nixon was considered to be "tough" on communism, he would at least attempt to either achieve a military success in Vietnam or unleash his new power on the stalled Paris Peace Talks, in an attempt to swiftly negotiate an end to the meaningless war.

In 1969 we were not aware of Richard Nixon's dislike for the space program. You see, the space program was President Kennedy's proudest technological showcase. And since Nixon despised anything with the name Kennedy on it, the space program under Nixon's watch was destined to begin a painful period of deterioriation even as we basked in the glory of *Apollo 8*.

It's not like Nixon simply canceled the program. Far from it. In fact, Nixon went on to support the program, at least publicly, more strongly than he originally had intended. So the impression one had in 1969 was that President Nixon loved Apollo almost as much as his predecessors had.

Not so. Quietly the NASA budget cuts began. When plans for the future beyond Apollo came up for a vote, it was Nixon who opted to cancel a U.S. manned mission to Mars, and he did so at a time when we were in a most advantageous position to take that next bold step.

The hardware was already there. We had Apollo technology upon which to expand. The Saturn series of boosters was performing well. It was possible to develop an even larger booster—one capable of delivering the thrust needed for a Mars venture—from the *Saturn V* design. The idea of a "Super Saturn" was not even new. Prior to the theory of Lunar Orbital Rendezvous, one of the options that received a great deal of attention in the early stages of the lunar landing program was called the direct ascent, which meant going directly to the moon, landing there, and boosting back for earth, without any rendezvous procedures. This would have required a rocket of gargantuan proportions and power.

The rocket we intended to use for direct ascent actually lived on the design engineer's drawing boards. It was called Nova. Nova was never produced because the time factor, our race with the clock to get Americans on the moon before 1970, did not allow for its development. *Saturn V* development was already proceeding, and the decision was made to go with the Saturn and a rendezvous scenario instead.

My philosophy on Nixon deserves more detail. It is true that he was not a fan of the space program, and it is true that under his leadership our space program faced its first series of debilitating budget cuts. But in all fairness to Nixon there were political factors of immense proportions facing him as he assumed office in 1969.

When Nixon took the oath of office in January, the nation was preparing for that supreme moment when Apollo astronauts would set foot on the moon. The political question was: after that event, what next? The American people were becoming increasingly occupied with the war in Vietnam, the deterioration of our ecological resources, disease, and hunger on our own planet. A typical phrase used by those against spending the hundreds of millions of dollars it took to keep Apollo alive and well was, "Why do we have to fly to the moon when we can't even feed our own people here on earth?" *Let's get the "moon things," over with*, they thought, *and get on with more important things*. And those sentiments multiplied after the flight of *Apollo 11*, when the national goal of putting men on the moon was achieved.

Now under John F. Kennedy or under Robert F. Kennedy you'd get an intelligent, visionary response, capable of squelching all but the most bitterly opposed to our efforts in space. JFK or RFK would point out that our future lies in what we learn from our exploration of space, that we cannot afford *not* to continue an aggressive manned space program.

But in 1969, that type of leadership did not exist. And there was a movement of increasing momentum to compare NASA with the militaristic type of thinking that got us stuck in Vietnam. So, to some, the talented people who were getting us to the moon were bad guys, just like anyone else over thirty who didn't protest things a lot. And the dissidents were voters and future voters.

Nixon went with the flow. After *Apollo 11* made its victorious return, Nixon capitalized on the success of the flight. His interest in the space program, Kennedys or no

Kennedys, increased. But later, when we should have been thinking strategically in terms of manned exploration beyond the moon, Nixon yielded to the rhythm of public interest, which in the post–*Apollo 11* days waned where the space program was concerned. It was a fatal error.

Speaking of opposition, there was a lot of antieverything philosophy from our own resident hippies at Cheshire High. And antieverything certainly included antispace.

I couldn't subscribe to the antieverything policy regarding the space program. I truly believed the war was wrong. But the space program was *right*. It represented brilliant planning. Its by-products were already making life easier, even for the normal jerk on the street.

For example, every time one of our great Cheshire-based hippies turned up his stereo to the the Grateful Dead, he was utilizing the miniaturized transistors that made the sound possible, invented as a result of the space program. Vietnam and the space program? They were two separate issues. Hearing ignorant people confuse them made me sick.

But even with concerns over the war, the ecology, and poverty at home, the space program in early 1969 appeared invigorated. This was largely due to the overwhelming successes of *Apollo 7* and *Apollo 8*. When *Apollo 8* returned from its Christmas lunar spectacular, I heard more people saying more good things about NASA than at any time since the flight of John Glenn.

Apollo 8 was a tough act to follow, but the plans for *Apollo 9* were extremely aggressive. *Apollo 9* was scheduled for lift-off on February 28, 1969. The mission called for the first *Saturn V* launch of all three Apollo components: the command/service module and the lunar module. In earth orbit, the crew of *Apollo 9* would test the lunar module in flight for the first time.

This was not only an exciting prospect; it was downright dangerous. Why? For starters, the lunar module (LM) would separate from the command/service module (CSM) in orbit. That meant the commander and the LM pilot flying in the LM would have to rendezvous and dock with the CSM to rejoin the CM pilot, who would fly alone in the CSM while the LM was being tested. They would simulate the same procedures to be utilized in lunar orbit during an actual lunar landing mission.

And there was one other little concern. The LM was designed to operate in a total vacuum. It was a spindly, nonaerodynamic contraption built to land astronauts on the moon and return them safely to the CSM, in orbit around the moon while the lunar exploration took place on the surface. The LM was in no way capable of reentering the earth's atmosphere. Lacking a heat shield, it would burn like paper.

The *Apollo 9* crew faced this challenge: if the LM failed to rejoin the CSM following its shakedown manuevers, the commander and the LM pilot were doomed. So while the mission profile for *Apollo 9* lacked the glory of *Apollo 8*'s translunar triumph, it was actually a more dangerous, daring flight.

Jim McDivitt, who had commanded that beautiful *Gemini 4* mission with Ed White in 1965, was selected to command *Apollo 9*. Neil Armstrong's *Gemini 8* copilot, Dave Scott, would fly as *Apollo 9*'s command module pilot. And Rusty Schweickart, a talented rookie, was chosen to fly as lunar module pilot. They were a strong crew for a tough mission.

As the February launch date approached, I got a job at a local pharmacy, where I worked for $1.75 an hour after school and on weekends. It was great, because it meant bucks for flying and for dates. (I had won my driver's license in January, and the deal my father cut with me was, I paid for the gas when I used either family car, my mom's Volkswagen or my father's newest company car, a '69 Plymouth Fury III.) It also beat repairing apple crates.

Even as I began working at the pharmacy, I had my sights set on a more aggressive target: a job at Hutton & Cook, the posh local men's store. Situated near the prestigious Cheshire Academy prep school (established in 1795, history fans), Hutton & Cook was the town's bastion of the Ivy look. The cream-of-the-crop high school guys worked there. Those privileged few wore Ivy blazers with rep ties and button-down shirts and were paid well to wear them. They stayed clean; dirt just wasn't part of the job. The gent who owned the store had a reputation for being a fine employer. And great-looking women shopped there. It was my kind of place! The place had class!

Remember the Zombies? They had recorded "She's Not There" and "Tell Her No" around the time Grissom and Young flew *Gemini 3* in 1965. They resurfaced with another recording early in 1969, titled "Time of the Season." It was a big hit because it demonstrated a great deal of artistic maturity. Clearly the Zombies were a breed apart from many of the less-talented recording groups of the sixties.

The first time I heard "Time of the Season" on WDRC, I was driving the Amity Pharmacy delivery car. This was an interesting part of my new job, because it got me out of the store and afforded the opportunity to "cruise." It was instant love. Whenever I hear "Time of the Season," I float back to the days of early '69, driving the Amity Pharmacy delivery car around Cheshire, daydreaming about astronauts, airplanes, and girls.

Apollo 9

Nothing happened on February 28, the scheduled date for *Apollo 9*'s journey to begin. McDivitt, Scott, and Schwickart were all sick with sore throats and colds. So NASA pushed the launch date back three days.

On Monday, March 3, at 11:00 A.M., the second magnificent *Saturn V* to propel American astronauts into space lofted *Apollo 9*. Sadly, the days of watching lift-offs at school had ended back during the final Gemini flights. Spaceflight was too commonplace (for some). More recently, news of *Apollo 7*'s successful launch was relayed to us at Cheshire High School via special announcement over the school PA system. *Apollo 8* flew while we were on Christmas vacation. Details concerning the launch of *Apollo 9* were announced on the school PA, as in the case of *Apollo 7*.

When *Apollo 9* boosted from the cape, I was in geometry class, reading a *NASA Facts* that was conveniently concealed within my geometry book. *NASA Facts, Flying, Plane & Pilot*, and *Playboy* were all essential life support elements. They were necessary for survival at Cheshire High. I used them well.

Apollo 9 went so smoothly that LM pilot Schweickart referred to his mission as "the Connoisseur's Flight." (Actually, it was somewhat less than perfect for Schweickart, who suffered from nausea during the flight.) On March 7, McDivitt and Schweickart separated from the CSM, which the crew had nicknamed *Gumdrop*, and they flew alone in the LM, which they called *Spider*. *Spider* performed well and rejoined *Gumdrop* after 6.5 hours of solo flight in earth orbit, having ventured as far as one hundred miles from *Gumdrop*.

When *Apollo 9* splashed down on March 13, we knew the three main Apollo components worked. The LM, our first "true" space vehicle, performed with precision. Now NASA was ready to send all three components to the moon.

There are good memories of the flight of *Apollo 9*. The only bad news I recall from the period was of the ceaseless slaughter that occurred daily in Vietnam. Vietnam just wouldn't go away. . . .

If there was one Top 40 hit I associate with *Apollo 9*, it is "Someday Soon" by Judy Collins. I heard "Someday Soon" for the first time while *Apollo 9* flew.

"Someday Soon" was a romantic little recording about a lonesome girl and her daredevil rodeo-rider boyfriend. In a different scenario, he could have been a football player, a downhill racer, a pilot, or . . . an astronaut. An astronaut! Imagine Judy Collins's irresistible voice singing about her daredevil astronaut boyfriend! That is exactly what I did every time I heard "Someday Soon."

My attachment to "Someday Soon" was steeped in boyish fantasy, but there was geniune emotion, too. Just imagine *Apollo 9* orbiting hundreds of miles above the earth, piloted by a trio of daring young men who each had at home a woman who awaited his return. Isn't there something emotionally provocative about that? Isn't that the kind of situation that causes artists like Judy Collins to write songs like "Someday Soon"? Couldn't "Someday Soon" emotionally merge the cold metal of the spacecraft with the warmth of a woman's voice?

If you can find a recording of "Someday Soon" and a quality picture of an Apollo spacecraft in flight, stare at the picture while you listen to the recording. Let your mind wander. There were human beings inside that shiny can of a spacecraft! People with feelings, spouses, and children! Try it. I think you'll see what I mean.

As *Apollo 9* orbited the earth, I also recall feeling fortunate to be around at the time when we had Apollo for inspiration. I was there to observe our space program as man's greatest adventure. Apollo was my personal counterbalance. It was there to offset all the negative crap. And I depended upon it as a constant source of positive reinforcement. Apollo was there for the asking.

Spring of 1969 was beautiful in Connecticut. The weather, which often remained chilly well into April, turned warm in March, shortly after *Apollo 9*'s highly successful flight. It was great weather for flying. My new job afforded the resumption of flying lessons, and although I was disappointed I could not afford to solo right on my sixteenth birthday, I was aiming for my first flight alone sometime during the summer.

Although I wasn't playing with a group anymore, I happily accepted an invitation from the senior class to do the drumming for their class play, *Bye Bye Birdie*, a favorite of mine. I enjoyed mastering the percussion score to *Bye Bye Birdie*. It was infinitely more demanding than banging away at rock music, and it was also much more rewarding.

Rehearsals began in March, leading up to the late April performance. Our band for the play consisted of a clarinet, a tenor sax, a guitar, an electric bass, a violin, and drums. It wasn't spectacular, but all the guys in the band, members of the sophomore, junior, and senior classes, were good friends of mine. We did a rather respectable job with the score.

When the Cheshire High School Class of 1969 performed *Bye Bye Birdie* (featuring yours truly on the drums) in April, the time for our next Apollo flight was just around the corner.

After *Apollo 9*'s flight, there was considerable talk about the next mission, *Apollo 10*. Since *Apollo 7*, *Apollo 8*, and *Apollo 9* had flown with such success, NASA entertained the idea of making *Apollo 10* the first lunar landing mission. At first, after *Apollo 8*, NASA intended to make *Apollo 11* the first lunar landing mission. This was logical, since the lunar modules for *Apollo 9* and *Apollo 10* were not fully equipped for the landing. The first LM equipped to make the landing was the LM assigned to *Apollo 11*.

But in the radiance of *Apollo 9* there was legitimate cause to reconsider. The flight plan for *Apollo 10* called for a full-blown dress rehearsal for the actual landing. *Apollo 10* would fly to the moon and make 31.5 orbits. While in orbit, the LM would separate from the CSM and descend to within fifty thousand feet of the lunar surface, taking pictures of the planned *Apollo 11* landing site in the Sea of Tranquility en route. The LM would then rejoin the CSM, just like it would following an actual landing. *Apollo 10* would then head back to earth, with everything but the lunar landing in the bag.

Why not let *Apollo 10* do the landing? Because we needed more practice, that's why, said NASA. I agreed. I am sure that *Apollo 10*, properly equipped with a landable LM, could have pulled off the lunar landing successfully. But NASA didn't want to gamble. There was little reason to gamble.

Like the United States, the Soviets had been back in the manned space business since the fall of 1968. *Soyuz 3* flew in October of that year, and *Soyuz 4* and *Soyuz 5* performed the first successful Soviet rendezvous and docking mission in January of 1969.

But details confirming a Soviet lunar landing effort were scarce and, at best, subject to much conjecture. By the time *Apollo 10* was ready to fly, the Soviet press informed their people that American astronauts would walk on the moon first. In a magnanimous tone, the Soviets praised NASA's efforts and the accomplishments of Apollo.

It is widely assumed the Soviets canceled plans for a lunar landing immediately after the flight of *Apollo 8*.

So the big race that began in October, 1957 was, essentially, already an American triumph by the spring of 1969.

In the end, NASA refused to take unnecessary chances. *Apollo 10* would fly the most daring mission yet, but it would not land on the surface of the moon. The first lunar landing would take place only after *Apollo 10* proved we were ready.

Apollo 10

On Sunday, May 18, *Apollo 10* began its historic flight. Riding atop the *Saturn V* in the command module were Tom Stafford, the commander, John Young, the CM pilot, and Gene Cernan, the LM pilot. This was an all-veteran crew. Stafford had flown as copilot on *Gemini 6* along with Wally Schirra and later commanded *Gemini 9*. Young had flown right seat with Gus Grissom on *Gemini 3*, and he later commanded *Gemini 10*. And Gene Cernan had flown as copilot on *Gemini 9* with Tom Stafford.

Stafford, Young, and Cernan relayed the first color television pictures from space during *Apollo 10*. They were spectacular.

On May 21, *Apollo 10*'s LM, *Snoopy*, separated from the CM, *Charlie Brown*. Inside *Snoopy*, Stafford and Cernan were at the controls. They flew *Snoopy* so close to the lunar surface that the landing radar bounced signals off the surface from an altitude of about fifty thousand feet. Fifty thousand feet (above the lunar surface) was a critical altitude for a lunar landing mission. At fifty thousand feet, the commander and the LM pilot would make their "go, no-go" decision concerning the final phase of the lunar landing. If they were convinced of a normal descent profile, they would command the descent engine to fire its final burn, easing the LM to the surface. If they had problems, they could refire the engine and climb back to the CM, circling at a higher orbit. Fifty thousand feet was also the lowest altitude possible for the CM to descend and make a rescue pass for the LM if there was a full emergency.

Aside from an incorrect switch position that resulted in some gyrations of the ascent stage of the LM during Snoopy's climb back to the CM, with John Young waiting inside, *Apollo 10* performed flawlessly in lunar orbit. Cernan swore a couple of times while Snoopy banged him and Stafford around, and this caused some thickheads back on earth, who obviously couldn't imagine what it must have been like, to complain to NASA about Cernan's foul language. It you ask me, Cernan deserved a medal for his cool handling of the LM during the flight. Gene Cernan is a great guy. Given the same situation, *my* language would have probably caused heart attacks back on the ground.

Apollo 10 made a perfect splashdown on Monday, May 26, 1969. There was a big press conference, and NASA announced that *Apollo 10*'s overwhelming success had paved the way for *Apollo 11* to make the first lunar landing flight. It was showtime.

On May 20, as *Apollo 10* streaked toward the moon, the vehicle that was *Apollo 11* left the mammoth Vehicle Assembly Building for the Pad 39 launch complex at Cape Kennedy. And the unofficial countdown for the lunar landing mission began.

Other snapshots of May 1969 come to mind. For instance, something happened around the time of *Apollo 10* that was extremely depressing and it didn't even happen in Vietnam. It happened right in Cheshire.

A couple of friends of mine were delivering flowers for Mother's Day. A guy in another car hit them at high speed, right down the street from our house. One of my friends was killed; the others were seriously injured.

Auto accidents aren't "big news." People are slaughtered daily on the highways by drunk drivers and others who are accidents waiting to happen when they get behind the wheel of a car or truck. To those who are un-affected by auto accidents, news of these mishaps is a nui-sance, the kind of press that makes page 10 in the local paper. On television, the networks only air roadway tragedies when there isn't enough bad news from elsewhere to fill the broadcast, which happens infrequently.

This wreck got personal. I mean, the guy who lost his life was on the track team. I had watched him run, and he was quite an athelete. Besides, he was a great guy. When he died, they ran the flag at our school down at half-mast and his girl friend went running out of the building in tears. It was quite a scene. They were supposed to be going to the junior prom together. A movie could have been made out of the incident. The experience was sobering. We were sending Apollo crews to the moon without inci-dent, but high school students were dying in ordinary car wrecks. Like the war in Vietnam, what a way to waste human life.

On a lighter note, although the Beatles released re-cords in 1970, 1969 was their last big year of recording as a group. In May of 1969, their hit "Get Back" was hot on the charts in Hartford. There was a television special in which the Beatles played "Get Back" on the rooftop of their recording studio in England. They looked quite bizarre; a far cry from the well-tailored foursome who had appeared on "Ed Sullivan" in 1964. In May 1969 those days in '64 seemed long past. So much had happened.

What was I doing for fun between *Apollo 10* and *Apollo 11*? Well, with that wonderful machine of personal free-dom—the car—now at my fingertips, dates became much more interesting. In 1969, I dated quite a bit. A typical date involved picking Candi up at her house (about a ten-minute drive from mine) and either going out to eat somewhere or going to the movies. Then we'd go back to her house, wait until everyone was asleep, and do some heavy petting and then I'd go home. We always had a pretty good time.

Another popular venture was the night out with the guys. This form of recreation usually involved cruising. (My father called this joy riding.) In serious cruising, there were two primary targets: women and burgers. We rarely consumed any alcohol, but we did smoke copious amounts of cigarettes or, ever better, cigars. The height of the evening arrived when we consumed Big Macs (as another historical footnote, the Big Mac first appeared at the Hamden McDonald's the previous fall, around the time of *Apollo* 7) at the Hamden McDonald's or Whoppers next door, at the Hamden Burger King. Then we'd see who would get sick first and take bets on which stalls had toilet paper and which did not.

It would have been much more convenient had there been, say, a McDonald's right in Cheshire, Hamden was a good twenty minutes away, even at the speeds we typically drove. But the folks in Cheshire didn't want a McDonald's there in 1969, because they feared us nasty teenagers would sell dope there and get their daughters pregnant while we waited in line for our double cheeseburgers. And we couldn't have that! The result: McDonald's finally built a restaurant in Cheshire many years later, when kids were "safe" again. We were just too damn rebellious, I guess.

I had belonged to a Rotary-sponsored service club at Cheshire High School since my freshman year. It was an interesting organization, and we had a great time sponsoring various activities that promoted good citizenship. A key benefit was, we got to know a lot of the town's business leaders. In the spring of 1969, I was elected president of the club and one of my buddies was elected vice president. We were often invited to the posh restaurant where the Rotarians held their regular dinners. The food was always good, and so was the company.

Those Rotary dinners were a blast. Typically attired in navy blazer, white button-down shirt, rep tie, gray flannels (with cuffs, of course), and wingtips, I frequently made after-dinner remarks to the Rotarians regarding the club's progress on various projects. Whether I joked around or talked seriously, they were always attentive.

I enjoyed speaking to the Rotarians immensely. The experience was a real confidence builder. The school hippies ridiculed organizations like the Rotary, but I didn't give a damn. The Rotarians were a fine bunch of guys. I learned a lot from them.

Shortly after school ended in June and summer vacation began, I got my big break. I won the job at Hutton & Cook, the men's clothing store I told you about earlier. This meant a financial raise and a clear boost in social status. I really thought I was big time!

So I kissed the pharmacy good-bye, put on my Weejuns, and started selling menswear. It was terrific to get paid $1.75 an hour for selling a few suits! You never got dirty! The place was air-conditioned! And you got *an hour* for lunch!

After only one week or two, I knew I could afford to fly often enough to solo before I went back to school. Life was sweet as the summer of '69 unfolded.

Apollo 11

I celebrated my new job with Candi by taking her out to dinner at the Yankee Silversmith Inn, a really nice place in nearby Wallingford. For a couple of high school kids, a dinner date at the Yankee Silversmith was top drawer. I think I blew about twenty-five dollars for that dinner, which represented quite an expensive evening out in 1969. But it was a beautiful, warm evening, I didn't drool on my tie (a major fear involved dropping one's scallops on one's tie while trying to impress a nice girl on a hot date), and Candi looked fantastic. We had a real good time.

On the way to the restaurant, we heard a new hippie group, Crosby, Stills and Nash (all were former members of other groups) doing their new hit, "Marakesh Express," on WDRC. They also played a new smash hit by Bob Dylan, "Lay Lady, Lay." That one played throughout the summer.

We were finalizing our plans for the usual Florida trip when my grandfather got sick. Since he lived alone, my mother didn't want to leave for three weeks. After tossing around options for a couple of days, we decided to stay in Connecticut and take a few weekend trips instead of going to Florida. I was disappointed, but not suicidal.

I had another trip in mind anyway. It was sort of an educational trip. I was now a junior in high school. In Cheshire, there was a great deal of pressure concerning going to college. You started hearing about it around fourth or fifth grade, and the pressure increased proportionately as one advanced through junior high school and into the big league, at Cheshire High.

From where did the pressure come? Everywhere! Parents spoke of it constantly: "If you keep bringing home these sorry grades, you'll *never get into college*! Teachers used it as the ultimate threat: "Unless you get five hundreds on your SATs, you'll *never get into college*! Your girl friend's parents spoke of it at every possible opportunity: "Now Candi's big brother, Andy, got into *Penn State* because of his *high grades* and Candi's big sister, Bambie, got into *Vassar* because of her *high grades*, and we have very, very high

172

hopes that Candi will enter *Yale* because of her *high grades*." One even heard about it from one's employer: "Our son, Stinky, got into *Harvard* on the strength of his *strong SAT scores*! If you don't do well from here until the day you die, you'll *never get into college*!"

It was like a little club. Everyone loved to talk about the big-name schools their kids or brothers or sisters got into—of course because of their *high grades*. I got so sick of hearing about it, I damn near puked whenever I heard one of those discussions beginning.

It's not that I ever considered *not* going to college. I wanted to go. *Pilots go to college.* Even the Original Seven had to have four-year degrees to fly in the Mercury program, and they came from an era when many military pilots did not have four-year degrees.

For the life of me I couldn't figure out the "going to college phobia" that prevailed while I went to school. Perhaps it's still there. I don't know. But I think it was wrong. There was too much pressure to do it and too few reasons why. One became obsessed with it.

I can remember having severe stomachaches and headaches from worrying about SAT scores and which big-name school I could attend so everyone would be impressed. You know what? In the end, it didn't matter very much. I found it helped to learn as much as possible from each subject, achieve a respectable grade (most of my grades were respectable: a few were not), and go on to the next course.

When it was time, I got into a fine school, not a super, big-name place, but a damn good school nonetheless. And I got in because I had a reasonable record and listened well and I sold myself to the admissions crew as a good candidate for a degree. Isn't that an appropriate reason for acceptance? Communication, fans, that's the key.

Anyway, since we decided against Florida for the summer of '69, I contacted an old friend who had moved to St. Louis. His father was a university professor and a very brilliant man. My friend invited me on a trip he was taking with his father to look at prospective colleges and universities. There'd be plenty of good talk, good food, and college women. It sounded like a great idea. I accepted immediately. We set the trip for August. Now I had *Apollo 11*, flying, and a trip of my own coming up. Summer was off to a good start.

Preparations for *Apollo 11* dominated the news on television and in the press during June. But even the upcoming manned lunar landing mission could not squelch Vietnam from the news.

The Tet offensive of 1969 killed over eleven hundred Americans. President Nixon resumed B-52 bombing raids on the North Vietnamese. In private, Nixon corresponded with the North Vietnamese leader Ho Chi Minh. They agreed to secret peace talks, above and beyond the ridiculous Paris Peace Talks. Already notorious in the press, the Paris Peace Talks were noted for less than stellar diplomatic triumphs, among them the consumption of more than seven months just to place those in attendance in an agreeable seating arrangement. How's that for bureaucracy in action?

The secret meetings were scheduled between Henry Kissinger, then national security adviser, and Le Duc Tho, a North Vietnamese Politburo member and chief negotiator. Their talks, structured to speed a negotiated end to the hostilities, began that summer. But they would take nearly four more years to yield tangible results.

On July 13, *Apollo 11* passed its countdown test, sort of a dress rehearsal for the actual countdown. A week later, the real countdown began as electrical power entered the Saturn. *Apollo 11* was alive.

The guys who flew as Apollo crews were impeccable professionals. To say the crew for *Apollo 11* was any better or worse than any other Apollo crew would be unfair; I believe any of the crews who flew during Apollo could have flown the first lunar landing mission with great success. But the *Apollo 11* crew was a very special team indeed.

The commander of *Apollo 11* would be the first human to set foot on another celestial body. His name would live in history, alongside names like Columbus, Magellan, Lindburgh, Gagarin, and Glenn. His qualifications as a pilot would have to be beyond reproach.

That's why Neil Armstrong was selected to command *Apollo 11*. Remember his close call during *Gemini 8*? Remember how his ice-cold control under pressure got him and Dave Scott safely back to earth? Remember his hours of hard flight experience in the X-15 program as a NASA test pilot? Armstrong's qualifications just couldn't be topped. His boot would make the first footprint on the moon. The guy earned it.

To fly as lunar module pilot, one needed brains. And that's why Edwin "Buzz" Aldrin got the slot. Aldrin would follow Armstrong out the hatch and onto the lunar surface to round out the first team on the moon. Aldrin would have been a real star in Cheshire because *he got very high grades*. In fact, as far as education goes, Aldrin maxed out. He already had a Ph.D. from MIT. In astronautics, no less. His EVA during *Gemini 12* was the longest and most successful of the entire Gemini program. And he knew so damn much about the navigational necessities of orbital mechanics his cohorts called him Dr. Rendezvous. Need I say more?

Flying as the *Apollo 11* command module pilot was one

of my favorite astronauts, Mike Collins. Collins did a great job on *Gemini 10*, when he and John Young performed the most complex mission of the series in record time. Surgery to remove a benign tumor from his neck bumped Collins from the *Apollo 8* crew to the Armstrong crew. Having mastered the inner workings of the command/service module from his *Apollo 8* training, Collins was a sure winner for the CM pilot slot on *Apollo 11*.

The suspense deepened. On July 13, the Soviets launched *Luna 15*, an unmanned probe, toward the moon. Was history repeating itself? Would the Soviet probe beat *Apollo 11* to the lunar surface and return to earth first with samples?

It was possible. Prior to Apollo, we sent our Surveyor unmanned probes to the lunar surface, where they scooped up samples of the lunar soil and transmitted important data about the samples back to earth. It was certainly feasible for the Soviets to have developed a vehicle like Surveyor, only capable of returning to earth with the goods, too. A manned landing it wasn't. But such a feat would rain all over *Apollo 11*'s parade. So, as the July 16 launch date for *Apollo 11* drew nearer, *Luna 15* suddenly added to the anxiety.

Preparations for *Apollo 11*'s return were in full swing long before the spacecraft ever left the ground. This was typical of any mission, but for *Apollo 11* there was something new. As Apollo developed, concerns grew over the possibility that astronauts returning from lunar landing missions might carry microorganisms back with them, germs that could cause uncontrollable disease on earth if the human immune system could not cope with such alien intruders. The possibility was remote, but it had to be considered.

To insulate such organisms from attacking the world's population, NASA developed the LRL (Lunar Receiving

Laboratory) near the Manned Spacecraft Center in Houston. The scenario called for the astronauts to don suits designed to prevent contact with the free air, called BIGs (Biological Isolation Garments), immediately upon recovery. They would then be transferred to Houston in a hermetically sealed trailer, equipped to provide the comforts of home to the returning voyagers. The astronauts would next enter the LRL for eighteen days while technicians and doctors monitored their conditions. If testing proved no biological invasion, the astronauts were free to leave their quarantine.

The quarantine measures for the *Apollo 11* crew added more to the mystique of the mission. God Almighty, those guys were going to *another world*! It was just like *2001*. But it was for real.

The countdown proceeded. The final days raced by. Armstrong, Aldrin, and Collins gave a last prelaunch press conference on the evening of July 14, 1969. I watched in amazement as the astronauts, already in quarantine to guard against colds like those experienced by the crews of *Apollo 7* and *Apollo 9*, spoke of their confidence in the mission. I recall telling Bob, who by this time was also a space program junkie, that if I could have stowed away on *Apollo 11*, I would have taken that chance. With enthusiasm.

I was working full-time at Hutton & Cook in the summer of 1969. That meant nine to six on Mondays and Tuesdays, with Wednesdays free (the store closed on Wednesdays during the summer), and Thursday through Saturday nine to six, except for Friday evenings, when the store stayed open until eight. I worked those Friday nights, too. In short, I worked my buns off.

While I got tired of having so little free time, I felt fortunate that *Apollo 11*'s launch date, July 16, was a Wednesday. That meant I could be right in front of the

TV for every minute of the launch coverage.

So on Wednesday I .watched *Apollo 11* rise from the pad on a column of fire so brillant it could have been supernatural. It was 9:32 A.M., EDST. My parents were at work. Bob and I just whooped. To say it was fantastic is an understatement. I still cannot describe the launch of *Apollo 11*.

The giant rocket streaked skyward. I have always been proud to be an American. But there has never been a time I was more proud than on July 16, 1969. There was so much to think about as the launch occurred. Former president Johnson and his wife, Lady Bird Johnson, were at the cape to watch the launch. I felt sorry for him; even though he screwed up badly in Vietnam, he cared deeply for the space program.

And I thought of John F. Kennedy. How I wished he could have been there to see his dream fly! But I think he was there anyway.

The launch of *Apollo 11* affected, though briefly, the national mood, which was rotten. Torn apart by the war, our country was in deep turmoil in the summer of 1969. Hippies were everywhere. Drugs were everywhere. On every newspaper page and on every news broadcast there were pictures of the protesters, thousands of them. Draft cards burned freely. College kids were living in communes to escape the evils of the over-thirty generation. Even college professors were "dropping out."

But *Apollo 11* drew favorable recognition from even the worst society had to offer. We referred to our hard-core town hippies as veggies because, crippled by drug abuse, they were essentially mental vegetables. By July of 1969, the hippies even had their own little section of town, where they had a head shop. The head shop was a place for them to focus on their efforts at doing nothing. Well, even our hard-core town veggies thought *Apollo 11* was "hip." Amen.

On Thursday I followed *Apollo 11*'s progress throughout the day on the radio at the store. That evening, I received a call from Candi's father. He and I got along real well, and I admired him quite a bit. He used to listen to my airplane and rocket bantering even when Candi got sick of it.

Candi's dad invited me to spend the weekend at their family's lake house in Lake Hopatcong, New Jersey. Candi and her mother, sister, and little brother were already at the lake. Her father commuted between Connecticut and the lake on weekends. It sounded like a great deal. My only question was, "Do you have a television so I can watch the *Apollo 11* coverage?"

Satisfied there was indeed an operating television on the premises at the lake and having cleared my plans with my parents and my boss (it was like having two bosses lots of times, my parents and the guy who owned the store), I left for Lake Hopatcong with Candi's dad directly from work, where he picked me up at about 5:00 P.M. on Friday, July 18.

I was in a hurry to get to the lake for two reasons. First, I wanted to get in front of the TV because there was going to be a televised tour of the LM from *Apollo 11* as it raced toward the moon. Second, I had the hots for Candi and I was anxious to see her.

It was a great weekend. We arrived at the lake around 8:30 P.M. All conversation centered on *Apollo 11*. The television transmission from the spacecraft was excellent. The Soviets told NASA *Luna 15* would in no way interfere with *Apollo 11*, and that was reassuring. Aside from worrying what *Luna 15* might accomplish on the lunar surface, there were concerns the two spacecraft might have an unpleasant meeting while in lunar orbit, since we knew nothing regarding *Luna 15*'s mission objectives or orbital data. A collision was highly unlikely, but there was always a chance.

On Saturday we spent most of the day on the water. The only embarrassment of the day was seeing, firsthand, that Candi was much better on water skis than I. Around lunchtime, *Apollo 11* went into orbit around the moon.

Sunday, July 20, 1969. It's funny how certain dates stand out from all the others. December 7, 1941. November 22, 1963. But July 20, 1969, was different from those places in history where terrible things happened. For once, something good, something *fantastic*, happened. And I'll never forget it. . . .

It didn't rain much at Lake Hopatcong that day, but it was cloudy and damp, not the best weather for water sports. It didn't matter. Television coverage of *Apollo 11* was on by noon. I sat there with Candi and her family, glued to the television. Outside, all was quiet. The lake was silent. No waterskiers, no boats. Everyone was indoors. Everyone was watching the events from space, over 230,000 miles away. *Eagle* separated from *Columbia* just before 1:00 P.M. The voyage to the lunar surface began.

It was a time of personal reflection. No one spoke. I knew we were all thinking the same things, that we were watching humans land on another world for the first time in history. It was the kind of event that leaves a lasting impression. The scene is still vivid.

I remember what I was wearing: a navy blue La Coste shirt with blue jeans and deck shoes. Candi was wearing a striped top with with bell-bottom jeans (remember bell-bottoms?), a canvas belt (tied, not buckled), and sandals. We were watching CBS, which, in Hopatcong, New Jersey, came directly from New York City on WCBS TV, Channel 2. Naturally, Walter Cronkite anchored the broadcast.

My mind spun backward, like flipping pages from the

back of a book to the beginning. I thought about all of the missions, from those days in 1961 when guys like Gagarin and Shepard rode their frail craft into space for the first time. There were recollections of *Gemini 7* and *Gemini 6*, just feet apart in earth orbit at Christmastime 1965. The faces of Grissom, White, and Chaffee were there, eager to fly the mission they'd never fly. And the image of *Apollo 8* at lift-off was there, gallantly frozen in time.

Had it been eight years? Was eight years a long time to accomplish this much? Or was eight years an acceptable period in which to go from a fifteen-minute suborbital lob to landing a team on the moon? Since there were no standards by which to judge, I could only reason that the accomplishment had been achieved in record time, that such a feat may have been impossible for others, and that the United States was the most wonderful place on earth to have created and flown *Apollo 11* to its current position, about to land on the moon.

And there were other things to consider, things aside from the raw science of the space program. Emotional things. It sounds screwy now, but I was overwhelmed! I was close to tears! There were so many feelings! *Apollo 11* was . . . beautiful! There should have been music! Were men allowed to have all these feelings? I knew men weren't supposed to cry. I thought only women got so emotional.

I had been dreaming about something like *Apollo 11* for most of my life. My God, I grew up with this thing! I learned to love it like a friend. Mercury and Gemini were more familiar than my own aunts and uncles. I discussed Apollo and women with equal enthusiasm. On July 20, 1969, I decided that I would fly in space. And if I didn't fly in space soon enough, I'd write about it until I could (okay, sports fans, I'm writing about it!)

At 4:17 P.M. EDT, *Eagle* landed safely on the moon.

There were some tense moments as Armstrong manually guided the LM across a field of boulders and craters, nearing the limit of the descent engine's fuel supply as he searched for the best spot to land. But all was well. Armstrong and Aldrin were safely down on the moon's Sea of Tranquility. ("Houston, Tranquility Base here, the *Eagle* has landed," were Armstrong's words confirming the landing.) On CBS, Walter Cronkite's eyes were brimming with tears. I hugged Candi. The emotion of the moment cannot be described.

That evening, we watched in amazement as Armstrong stepped off the ladder of the LM onto the surface, his footprints to remain there for ages in the sterile lunar vacuum where no wind, rain, or storm could disturb them. Aldrin followed Armstrong onto the surface shortly after. The quality of the television pictures from Tranquility Base was outstanding, but the images of Armstrong and Aldrin in their white EVA suits appeared ghostly nonetheless. There was something unreal about them. It was breathtaking. It took the transmissions just under two seconds to reach earth traveling at the speed of light. It wasn't much, but the miniscule delay served as a reminder that Armstrong and Aldrin were far, far away.

President Nixon was patched through the NASA relay network from the White House directly to Armstrong and Aldrin, who had just planted an American flag in the lunar dust. It was quite a scene. Nixon's message of congratulations was hearty, and I am sure it was sincere.

Reflecting back on the historic moment, I can't help but believe *Apollo 11* changed Nixon's mind, at least partially, regarding the space program. With such a massive success on his hands, the president could hardly downplay what NASA had accomplished. Nixon even used the flight of *Apollo 11* in speeches that summer, calling for international peace in the "spirit of Apollo." Nixon was no dummy. In the summer of '69, Apollo played well.

If the war in Vietnam hadn't sapped such a devastating amount of the nation's vitality by the time of Nixon's first term, I believe the president would have encouraged a more aggressive post-Apollo future for NASA. Congressional support would have been available. But the price of Vietnam was too staggering. And presidents like to be reelected.

In Vietnam, William Broyles, Jr., a Marine Corps platoon commander operating with his unit in the field, reflected on *Apollo 11*, too. He writes in his outstanding book, *Brothers in Arms*: "At night in the mountains, I would watch the track of satellites making their way around the earth. Other Americans were on the moon, sent there by the same American can-do spirit that had sent us to Vietnam, and using the same technology that was so useless there. Those astronauts were the first men to leave the earth for another celestial body, but they knew more about the moon than we knew about Vietnam." Sadly, Broyles is absolutely correct.

The lunar EVA ended without incident. Twenty-one and a half hours after landing, the ascent engine ignited flawlessly and *Eagle* departed from the moon to rejoin Mike Collins, orbiting overhead in *Columbia*. *Eagle* and *Columbia* docked at 5:35 P.M. on Monday, July 21. The crew of *Apollo 11* were together again. Following a successful main engine burn, the spacecraft headed for earth.

Mike Collins's role in the mission deserves additional comments. His contribution to the success of *Apollo 11* wasn't nearly as glorious as those of Armstrong or Aldrin, because he didn't get to walk on the moon. But his was every bit as important. Had there been a serious problem while *Eagle* descended or ascended, Collins would have been tasked with a rescue attempt, if one was feasible. In the event of utter catastrophe—the loss of the LM with Armstrong and Aldrin aboard—it was Collins's responsibility to get *Columbia* out of lunar orbit and back to earth by himself. And even in the event of a perfect mission profile (which was, fortunately, the case), with Armstrong and Aldrin returning to *Columbia* after a successful lunar landing, Collins still carried phenomenal responsibility for the mission's success in terms of navigation, rendezvous, docking, and maintenance of the awesome contraption better known as the command module. More salient, Collins, as CM pilot, drew the responsibility of flying alone in *Columbia* while his partners were on the surface. That meant losing contact with the human race for nearly half of the time he orbited the moon, while *Columbia* passed from line-of-sight communications as it traversed the far side. As NASA pointed out, after *Apollo 11* landed, Mike Collins experienced a form of loneliness no human had ever felt (with all due respect to John Young, CM pilot of *Apollo 10*, who flew alone while crewmates Stafford and Cernan descended to within fifty thousand feet of the lunar surface). And that took a certain amount of balls.

My weekend at the lake ended all too quickly, and on Monday afternoon I returned to work, where I listened to the radio as *Eagle* and *Columbia* docked. I was working downstairs, taking inventory on dress shirts. It was a perfect opportunity to reflect back on the events of the last few days and try to comprehend them.

The days of *Apollo 11* were filled with the sounds of the summer of 1969. There were hits like "A Boy Named Sue" by Johnny Cash, "The Theme from Romeo and Juliet" by Henry Mancini (which accompanied the 1969 Franco Zefferelli film of Shakespeare's famed play), "Hair" by the

Cowsills, "The Ballad of John and Yoko" by the Beatles, "Honky-Tonk Women" by the Rolling Stones, "2525" by Zaeger and Evans, and, ironically, "Bad Moon Rising" by Creedence Clearwater Revival. I sat in the basement at Hutton & Cook, counting shirts, the crazy lyrics to many of those songs banging around in my mind as I pictured Cronkite, overwhelmed with emotion when *Eagle* landed . . . Armstrong stepping out onto the lunar surface . . . and Candi's pretty smile. It was like a kaleidoscope. It was the weekend of the moon.

There were several television broadcasts from *Apollo 11* as it sped home toward earth. It was evident the astronauts were trying to cope with the magnitude of their accomplishment. There were renewed calls for world peace by the leaders of many nations. Politicians at all levels of government spoke eloquently of *Apollo 11*, attempting to merge the success of the flight with their own endeavors.

From the time *Apollo 11* left the vicinity of the moon on its return voyage, we all wrestled with the meaning of the flight. Realistically, nothing changed down here on earth. In Vietnam, the senseless killing continued. In our cities, the poverty-stricken didn't get any richer. People still argued over religion. Inflation continued its upward spiral. Friends of mine still buried themselves in drugs, angry at themselves, their parents, and the imperfect world they were about to inherit.

But something intangible had changed. Until *Apollo 11*, I often measured time in terms of "before President Kennedy" and "after President Kennedy." Now, with *Apollo 11* close to splashdown, man had walked on another world. We had ventured daringly from our own planet in search of knowledge. The human condition had skewed, mentally, from the surface of our planet outward. And it would never be the same again. So, as of July 20, 1969, there was a new measurement: "before *Apollo 11*" and "after *Apollo 11*.*" I needed that logic to help make sense of the whole thing. It did.

On Thursday, July 24, *Apollo 11* made a perfect reentry and splashdown. President Nixon was on the aircraft carrier *Hornet* to greet Armstrong, Aldrin, and Collins when they arrived. The president couldn't shake hands with the astronauts because they were biologically quarantined as of the moment the hatch on *Apollo 11* was opened. But Nixon spoke with them through the window of the special trailer that would carry the astronauts to the Lunar Receiving Laboratory in Houston. It was a touching moment, and the president was unusually joyous and relaxed.

Eighteen days later, Armstrong, Aldrin, and Collins were released from quarantine. There were no lunar germs. The world greeted them with open arms.

Apollo 11 was the pinnacle of our first era in space. The pride and accomplishment the mission represented was unparalleled in history.

Writing of *Apollo 11* in his book, *We Reach the Moon*, John Noble Wilford stated that Apollo "showed what remarkable achievements a society can accomplish, given adequate leadership, national resolve and personal courage."

Unfortunately, after *Apollo 11*, instead of reaching further, we retreated. A majority of Americans remained convinced a strong manned space program was a national necessity. There was certainly no lack of personal courage; an entire band of astronauts was prepared to carry manned exploration even further. But the "adequate leadership" of which Wilford wrote did not exist. And the funds that were so vital to additional manned space exploration were diverted elsewhere. The manned Mars mission was canceled. In fact, NASA was forced to cut back on the remaining number of Saturn boosters and, therefore, the number of remaining Apollo missions.

The immediate post-Apollo scenario, which called for use of Apollo technology in a program (once) called Apollo Applications, was watered down to a pitiful level. The political manuevering over the future of U.S. manned spaceflight, in efforts to keep the Nixon White House happy, was unbelievable.

It is saddening to think the proud NASA organization that made the lunar landing—an achievement man dreamed of since the beginning of time—possible was being financially and politically raped even as *Apollo 11*'s parachutes eased the spacecraft onto the water. There has been some excellent research on the matter of NASA's political downfall. One volume I recommend is Joseph and Susan Trento's *Prescription for Disaster*. Whether you love the space program or not, the mediocrity of the leadership that guided us past Apollo, as presented by Mr. and Mrs. Trento, will shock you. It did me.

As July 1969 melted into August, there was little discussion in Cheshire, Connecticut, about the downfall of NASA. NASA was riding a tremendous crest of popularity. For a little while, it seemed the aura of *Apollo 11* would never end.

Beyond Tranquility Base

In the aftermath of *Apollo 11* was an emotional letdown, the result of years waiting for the lunar landing mission only to have it take place and disappear into history. The feeling was similar to the depression children often experience after Santa has come and gone.

Apollo 11 represented the primary goal of Project Apollo. Not only was the mission the apex of Apollo; it represented the peak of the U.S. manned space program. Everything else flowed downhill after Armstrong, Aldrin, and Collins were safely aboard *Hornet* that July.

Personally, August 1969 was as eventful as July. On August 11, the weather was perfect for flying, "severe clear," according to my instructor.

Flight instruction that day was typical for a student pilot preparing to solo. At altitudes between two thousand and three thousand feet, we practiced stalls. (Contrary to what many nonaviation people may think, a "stall" might only be indirectly related to loss of thrust. Aerodynamic stall is created by exceeding the aircraft's critical angle of attack. Simply, the lifting surfaces of the aircraft quit flying because low airspeed limitations are exceeded in flight.) Then we headed back into the airport traffic pattern for "touch-and-go" landing practice.

A "touch-and-go" consists of taking off, climbing to pattern altitude (at New Haven, pattern altitude was eight hundred feet), flying downwind to the active runway, turning onto final approach, and landing the aircraft, followed by immediate application of full power and repetition of the entire drill. When you're doing well, touch-and-goes are a blast. When you can't seem to find the runway, much less land the airplane, touch-and-goes are a very frustrating experience, especially when there's an instructor seated closely to your right telling you what a lousy job you're doing.

After our third landing, my instructor said matter-of-factly, "Okay, Jack, pull over at the ramp and let me out. You take it around two or three times and come on back."

I damn near died! He was letting me loose! What a great guy!

I carefully taxied the Cherokee 140 out to the runway. After performing a thorough pretakeoff check of the engine and various systems, I lined that mother up with the centerline of the runway and added full power. What a feeling!

Just past 60 knots,* I lifted the nose; the aircraft rotated and flew off the runway. I was flying alone for the first time!

The aircraft made the same amount of noise (too much) it always had, but Roy's voice was conspicuously absent. The only human voice in the cockpit besides my own (talking to myself mainly) came from the radio, which was on the airport traffic advisory frequency known as "unicom."

At eight hundred feet I turned downwind, leveled off, and performed a midfield check of systems and fuel. The Cherokee was cruising at one hundred knots (115 mph).

---

*In aviation, airspeed is typically measured in knots, instead of miles per hour. This is done so aviators feel they know something special that other people can't figure out. A knot equals 1.15 miles per hour. So my lift-off speed that day was roughly sixty-five miles per hour.

It was like sex! In the airport traffic pattern, there's not a lot of time for sightseeing. Watching for other aircraft in the airport vicinity is paramount—more midair collisions take place in or near the airport traffic pattern than any-where else. But I stole a few glances out, where I could see Sleeping Giant Mountain to the north and across the water to the south was Long Island, shrouded in the haze of late summer. I dreamed of the next step, when I could take the plane out of the airport pattern and begin flying cross-country.

Each landing went well. I set the aircraft up in ap-proach configuration, added flaps as necessary, and flared the Cherokee at the proper height above the runway. I savored the familiar chirp as the wheels made contact on my third and final landing of the day.

After a hearty round of congratulations from other pilots and students, Roy wrote; "First Solo—OK!" in my logbook. I climbed into the Volkswagen and sped home to tell everyone. My family was thrilled. For days it was hard to think about anything else but those first precious mo-ments of solo flight.

That first solo flight in August 1969 was a catalyst for further aviation pursuits. By 1977 I had earned the private, commercial, multi-engine, and instrument certificates and ratings. I also went on to pass the Boeing 727 flight en-gineer written examination after active duty as a Marine Corps officer.

As the summer of 1969 drew to a close, there was a huge rock celebration in New York State, near the town of Woodstock. Lots of kids in Cheshire said they were going. I had no desire to go. Big crowds mean porta-potties. I detest porta-potties. There's too much pressure involved when you find yourself using a porta-pottie and there's a line of people banging on the door, wanting to get in.

The Woodstock concert turned out to be the biggest hippie music fling of the Vietnam era. It was like a giant antiwar rally, with music, drugs, and sex thrown in for good measure. Hundreds of thousands of kids went and lived in the mud and rain for a couple of days. In return, they saw some of the top protest and drug performers of the day. Jimi Hendrix was there. Santana did "Soul Sacrifice." The Who performed. And there were many others.

God, how my parents griped about Woodstock! They carried on about it for weeks, and I didn't even go! Remember dinnertime show-and-tell at my house? Well, it was as interesting as ever around the time of Woodstock:

Dad (*after watching reports of the Woodstock concert on TV*): *Bums!* You're all *bums!* I wouldn't have *thought* of looking like that when I was your age! You're all a bunch of cruddy, no-good, lazy *bums.* And those goddamn *Beatles* started all of this! I *forbid* that kind of behavior in *my* house! Do you understand! I *forbid it!*

Me: But, Dad, I'm not a bum or a hippie! I didn't invent the concert! I didn't even go! I was working at the goddamn store, remember?

Mom: You watch that filthy mouth of yours, young man!

Dad: If we *ever* catch you hanging around with trash like that you'll be grounded for the rest of your life! *Do you hear me??! For the rest of your life!!!!*

Sound familar?

After school resumed, my father checked the length of my hair at regular intervals to make sure it didn't touch the tops of my ears. If it did, I was in violation of the rules. And I knew the rules: if my hair touched my ears, the hair would permeate my brain, turning me into a Joe Cocker clone instantaneously. My father was sure of it.

Fall 1969. Hardly anyone gave a damn about anything.

To show you how low morale was that fall, I'll tell you about a club we had at school. You know what the name of the club was? The Give-A-Damn Club! That's right! We had a Give-A-Damn Club! And do you know why we had a Give-A-Damn Club? Right again! Because no one gave a crap about anything! Apathy was so rampant, the Give-A-Damn Club almost went out of business because none of the Give-A-Damn members would come to any of the Give-A-Damn meetings! It was an epidemic! The antiwar movement and the social ills it promoted became so embedded within the student body that its real purpose—to end the war—was a moot point.

It was no longer good enough to be simply against the war. You had to become a fruitcake, too. You had to care enough to *show* how much you didn't care about anything! You had to look, smell, and act like social zero. You had to embrace the whole hippie bill of rights to be one of the gang in the fall of 1969.

Unless you were a straight arrow.

There *were* still a few straight arrows. The kind of guys who still wore cuffed pants instead of bell-bottoms. And the kind of girls who took baths every night. Most of these traditional castaways from days gone by were against the war, too. But for complex reasons these people elected to appear normal. They expressed their discontent with U.S. foreign policy in ways that differed with the antieverything approach. This endangered species was my group. We embraced NASA. We liked things the hippies hated.

The antieverything faction hated money. Today people praise "business heroes." Not in '69! The hipsters made fun of people's fathers who earned high incomes. They sang songs mocking people who wore ties. Money didn't matter to them. Yet.

Apollo 12

At work, the boss insisted on listening to the "easy listening station." I hated it. It gave me a headache because they played bastardized versions of the popular hits WDRC played. No original performers. The announcer would say in this soothing tone something like, "And that was a wonderful medley of Jimi Hendrix love songs, sung for us by the Milk of Magnesia Chorale. Before that we heard a beautiful recording of Eleanor Rigby by the Sporadic Sperm Strings here on your stereo island, Hartford."

The boss usually left for the day around 4:00 or 4:30 P.M. We'd wait to see his car disappear around the corner, and then we'd change the station to WDRC or one of the peace-love-dope stations like WYBC (Yale's own station) or WHCN. (They used a peace sign for their advertising logo.) This was considered "sporting."

The World Series was really something special in 1969 because the New York Mets were in it, against the Baltimore Orioles. We were constantly changing the radio to an AM station to hear the series games, which were still played during the daylight hours on weekdays in 1969. The final game of the World Series ended, and the Miracle Mets beat the Orioles. The boss was gone. We put on WDRC

The DJ played Steam's new recording, "Na-Na, Hey-Hey, Kiss Him Goodbye." Then it was time for the news, with great information: after announcing the Mets' victory over Baltimore, they announced the launch date for *Apollo 12*, which was November 14. If the easy listening stuff had been playing, I would have missed the Steam hit and I would have missed the *Apollo 12* announcement, too. God I hated that easy listening stuff. In 1969.

Pete Conrad would command *Apollo 12*, along with

Dick Gordon as command module pilot and Al Bean as lunar module pilot. Conrad and Gordon had flown together on *Gemini 11* in 1966. Bean was a rookie. The mission scheduled *Apollo 12* for a lunar landing in the Ocean of Storms. There Conrad and Bean would inspect *Surveyor III*, our robot lunar lander that had touched down in the area in 1967. They would also set up a great deal of geophysical experiments, remaining on the lunar surface about three times longer that Armstrong and Aldrin did during *Apollo 11*.

President Nixon flew to the cape to watch the launch, which occurred during a rainstorm. Really, it occurred during a full-blown thunderstorm. And the spacecraft was struck by lightning during the boost phase. The lightning strike knocked all the spacecraft's vital electrical gear off line, forcing emergency batteries to pick up the electrical load.

Miraculously, the *Apollo 12* electrical systems were not damaged and full power was restored in the spacecraft while it flew in parking orbit around the earth. The mission went on to complete its lunar landing and the entire set of experiments.

The pictures and the rock samples *Apollo 12* brought back were fantastic. There is a picture of Pete Conrad inspecting *Surveyor III* that is unbelievable: man inspecting the equipment sent before him on another world.

Apollo 12 didn't seem as exciting to lots of people because *Apollo 11* had already accomplished the first lunar landing. That's too bad, because every lunar landing mission that flew after *Apollo 11* was more difficult and more daring. And each mission that flew after *Apollo 11* brought back vastly increased amounts of lunar samples and information that *Apollo 11* simply could not collect. And there is still so much we don't know about the moon. . . .

Apollo 12 splashed down on November 24, and it was the last U.S. mission to fly in 1969. In October, the Soviets orbited *Soyuz 6*, *Soyuz 7*, and *Soyuz 8*. No lunar landings, but impressive work nonetheless. The multiple Soyuz missions were launched one day apart, and they performed an orbital ballet in which the Soviet teams practiced rendezvous techniques they would need for their ambitious space station plans.

Christmas, 1969. The war in Vietnam was still with us, but according to the news, it was "winding down." Since President Nixon had announced his "Vietnamization" program, plans were set into motion beginning the first withdrawal of American troops. According to the plan, the South Vietnamese would pick up the responsibility of defending themselves. Sure thing.

Forty thousand U.S. servicemen had already lost their lives. Two hundred and sixty thousand had been wounded. Our involvement reached its peak in 1969, when 543,000 Americans were serving in Vietnam.

You didn't have to be a Rhodes scholar to figure out what Vietnamization really was—a way to make it look like we were somehow getting out of the mess. It was a way for Nixon to buy some time. And in that matter Vietnamization was also unsuccessful.

What about the guys who were still stuck there? How did they feel as 1969 drew to a close? There were few happy campers in Vietnam.

When our servicemen returned home after their twelve-month tours in Vietnam, few cheered. There were no parades. In fact, the hippies mocked them. They made fun of them!

When my father returned from World War II, he was offered drinks on the house when he visited a bar. Women cried with joy to see him and his buddies, fresh from combat in the Ardennes. Flags were waved and folks patted him on the back for a job well done.

Not so for the returning Vietnam veteran.

The result? Service in Vietnam became a terrible game of watching the clock, trying to make a year go by as fast as possible and still stay alive. There were no tangible results from the firefights. When villages were burned, there were no victory parties or local dignitaries on hand to welcome you as the "liberating force."

Our men died as bloody in Vietnam in 1965 as they died in 1969. The difference was, in 1965, there were at least some who thought they were in Vietnam to defend America's honor and to defend freedom. How could we expect our men and women in Vietnam to feel that way in 1969?

Most people think we lost in Vietnam in 1975. That is not actually the case. We lost it in 1969 when Vietnamization signaled our desire to lose. We would have been better off pulling out unilaterally in December 1965 after bombing the crap out of North Vietnam. Vietnamization would have failed just the same, but about forty-five thousand Americans lives would have been saved.

If we wanted a military victory badly enough, we could have achieved it. With the tremendous amount of firepower we put in the field in Southeast Asia and with the superiority of our air forces, the North Vietnamese campaign could have been halted within a few months of intensive, all-out combat. Instead, we read about "fire zones" and border restrictions. Our combat pilots flying missions in the north *were not allowed* to bomb key strategic targets until the last days of 1972!

This insanity was the flavor of war, particularly during the late sixties and early seventies. The aura of Tranquility Base shone less brightly every time an American serviceman felt the sting of shrapnel.

Ask the older citizens of Dresden, Germany, about "fire zones." When the Allied forces decided that Dresden needed bombing, it got bombed into obliteration. Or how about the French civilians living near Normandy? When we needed their beaches to land on, by God, we landed on them! It was war! And we were in it to win, while sacrificing the minimum amount of casualities.

I'll repeat: war sucks. The best bet is, don't play. But if you're dumb enough to play, play to win. Otherwise, what's the purpose? At Christmastime, 1969, no one knew if we had or ever did have a purpose in Vietnam. Not even the men and women who were getting killed there knew.

The Beatles released another albumn just before Christmas. It was called *Abbey Road*. Although they would release another album in 1970, *Abbey Road* was their last great album.

The record resembled *Sgt. Pepper* and "the White Album" more closely than recordings made before *Sgt. Pepper*. It featured few refreshing sounds, but it did well on the charts; all the pop stations and all the hippie underground stations played it constantly. My favorite track from *Abbey Road* was "Maxwell's Silver Hammer," a grotesque little song. I also liked "She's So Heavy" because my parents hated it.

Another group, called Led Zeppelin, had a hit album as *Abbey Road* climbed the charts. The album was simply named *Led Zeppelin II*. It drew rave reviews from the drug population because *Led Zeppelin* fit the filthy group genre they craved. But I liked it, too. It sort of "cocked the fist." And that is why my parents hated it. And that is why I bought it.

The hit track of the album was called "Whole Lotta Love." It had great lyrics:

Way, way
Down inside,
I'm gonna give you my love,
I'm gonna give you
Every inch of my love,
I'm gonna give you my love.

And then the resounding finale:

. . . Way down inside,
Woman,
You need . . .
Loooooooooovvvvvvvvvveeeeeee.*

"Whole Lotta Love" was the kind of tune that made fathers fear for their daughters. It was the kind of tune that made other fathers lecture their sons about other father's daughters. It was a genuine parent's nightmare on tape— and we bought it like it was worth its weight in gold.

On television, series were plentiful. "Hawaii Five-O" was among them, featuring Jack Lord as the daring Steve McGarrett. The best part was always at the end of each episode, when McGarrett, having snared the bad guy, turned to his partner and said, "Book 'em, Dan-O, murder one." Then he'd shove the crook, just to make sure.

Next, I smacked up my mother's car. I dropped one of my buddies off at his house following a cram session for an algebra test. Algebra was not my best subject, and I took all the help I could get. It was dark and bitter cold outside, with lots of snow and ice on the roads. Right in front of the Cheshire Police Station—a prime location for high drama—I hit a patch of ice and skidded into a parked car. I didn't get hurt, but the car sure did.

The reaction from my folks was as I expected. First, my mother's input:

Mom: You little hoodlum, you. Don't you know I have *spies* who see you speeding around town with your hoodlum friends? Well, young man, I happen to know you were out *joy riding* tonight and that you were *speeding* when you *lost control of the car! My car! Wait until your father gets a hold of you!*

Then my father came home from work. Again, the scenario played just as I expected:

Dad: This will serve you right for *joyriding* around town like a *bum*. As of this minute *you are grounded*!

Fortunately, Bob was there to witness the whole thing. Bob was beginning to realize that Mom and Dad occasionally went overboard—and that the psychology they employed during the Case of the Crashed Car was slightly flawed.

In the sixties, my parents tried to scare me into being a good guy without taking the time to see how hard I was trying to meet their standards. It wasn't easy for them or for me. Everyone was so confused and so angry! When I look back on those sick times, I can see why it was difficult for my parents. Their on-the-job training in the forties and fifties was not adequate for the turmoil of the sixties. They did their very best, and I am proud of them. I hope to do as well.

Bob and I retired to my room, where we discussed plans to escape. Escape was a favorite topic of ours during the late sixties and early seventies. We fantasized about ways we could not hear about things from our parents. In one dastardly plot, we constructed a concrete voiceproof room in our basement. This fictitious impenetrable shelter was complete with stereo, smut magazines, and beer—the vital components of survival—and we could escape into it via a secret tunnel in my bedroom, sealing a special hatch behind us. Over an elaborate monitoring system inspired by the space program we would listen to the enemy as they tried to find us.

So 1969—and the decade—ended as I sat in my room, much as I had throughout the sixties, thinking about girls, airplanes, and astronauts. Simple math indicated I had spent 62.5 percent of my life during that decade. That should qualify as cruel exposure to insanity.

I went to a New Year's Eve party of some sort with Candi. (We got a ride with friends, since I was temporarily out of the transportation business.) Everyone sat around and talked about . . . you guessed it! Vietnam, Woodstock, and drugs. What a waste of time! Even Candi was starting to talk like one of *them*. I'd had it. Where were the rockets and the astronauts? Where was John Glenn? And Gordon Cooper?

For the first time since 1957, there wasn't a glorious goal in space ahead. Although there were Apollo missions remaining, talks of budget cuts and apathy toward the space program filled the air. It was terribly depressing, because the space program had served as an inspiration to achieve for so long.

I can't blame all that was wrong in 1969 on Vietnam. But it was responsible for a hell of a lot. It sapped the vitality of our space program amd the spirit for which it stood. Where strategic planning for space exploration was concerned the awful cost of waging political war in Vietnam caused our leaders to focus on only the present, at the expense of the future.

In addition to the war in Vietnam, lack of strategic leadership for the space program following the Kennedy-Johnson years placed the remaining Apollo flights in a viselike grip, where bureaucrats attempted—and succeeded—in bleeding the funds necessary to maintain program direction from NASA.

Everyone lost something in the sixties. It might have been youth. It might have been standards, happiness, or heroes. Many lost their lives. I was lucky. At the end of 1969, I just felt much older than I thought I would feel on the threshold of my seventeenth birthday. So much had happened. . . .

The sixties did yield impressive benefits. The most positive events, by far, were the manned space missions flown by American astronauts and their counterparts from the Soviet Union. Despite the assassinations, war, riots, and social upheaval, we did manage to accomplish those incredible feats—and man was the benefactor.

I was ashamed of much that took place in our country and elsewhere in the world during the sixties. But the burning pride I felt for the space program never ebbed.

Statistics help tell the story of the U.S. manned space program after 1969. From the time we got into the manned spaceflight business with Project Mercury in 1961 to *Apollo 12*, which flew in 1969, the United States flew a total of twenty-two manned missions. That means, on the average, we flew 2.4 manned missions per year during the sixties.

Things were different in the seventies. Funding was scarce. And, given the poor strategic planning of the later Johnson years and the early Nixon years, no manned space program was in place to pick up where Apollo left us, midway through the new decade.

The result: From the flight of *Apollo 13* in 1970 to the ASTP (Apollo/Soyuz Test Program) mission in 1975, we flew ten manned missions. No American astronaut flew in space again until 1981. So the average for the seventies dropped to only one mission per year. That's pretty slim compared to the golden era of Mercury, Gemini, and Apollo in the 1960s, when more than twice as many missions flew in considerably less time (since manned flights began in 1961 instead of 1960.)

As the new decade began, the Nixon administration changed the course—and the nature—of our space program. From the urgent priority the program received in the early sixties, the program was "bumped" to a much lower priority in the seventies.

When Vice President Agnew presented President Nixon with a list of options for the space program in 1969, Nixon chose the option that essentially ended our manned efforts. Only a fraction of NASA's plans for a functioning space station survived. That fraction was a reusable shuttle craft.

NASA planners (including von Braun) saw the necessity for a shuttle craft within the space station scenario, where the vehicle would be needed for transportation and resupply.

In its effort to gain President Nixon's favor, NASA agreed to one budget cut after another, hoping to obtain the funding needed for the space station concept, complete with shuttle and a manned Mars landing program.

The Air Force already had a space station program called the Manned Orbiting Laboratory on the drawing boards. Nixon killed that program shortly after *Apollo 11* flew.

It was up to Nixon to decide the future of NASA. And NASA lost.

When it was obvious only the reusable shuttle was feasible, given the severe budget cuts afforded NASA, there wasn't enough money to build a scaled-down version of the craft to use for tests. Work on the shuttle vehicle got off to a slow start. The snail's pace toward the shuttle's first powered flight continued throughout the seventies. Problems were difficult to overcome with no money.

Funding for Apollo missions beyond *Apollo 17* was denied. Additional Saturn boosters would not be built. That was a terrible decision. A single *Saturn V* and a few *Saturn 1Bs* were all that was available for the Skylab program, the surviving entity of the Apollo Applications scenario.

So even while the advanced Apollo lunar landing missions flew, the vast machine that had made Apollo possible was disintegrating for lack of funds.

Apollo 13

April 1970. I remember the month well because, aside from *Apollo 13*, we had a solar eclipse and we had Earth Day.

What the hell was Earth Day? Well, remember when I told you about the growing concern over the earth's ecology? Ecology was another issue onto which millions of young people clung during the late sixties and early seventies. There was the war, ecology, people over thirty, money, greed, and hate to hate—if you cared enough to hate them (just ask a member of the Give-A-Damn Club!)

In a gesture of national concern over things terrestrial, a day was set aside for sit-ins, protests, and all the other visible forms of acute concern so typical of the era. Students were encouraged to walk to school instead of riding. Bell-bottom jeans and faded T-shirts with the ecology sign (we had peace signs and ecology signs to differentiate which cause you were for; since most students were against the war and for the ecology cause, we should have had a sign that combined the peace sign and the ecology sign, but no one thought of it) were the uniforms of the day.

So on Earth Day about two-thirds of Cheshire High School poured out onto the streets of old Cheshire to demonstrate concern for dirt.

Earth Day? Jesus Christ! You mean after doing LSD and pot and promoting communal living, those morons really understood the ecological problems of the planet? Bullshit!

I remember watching everyone walking to school that day singing "Give Peace a Chance" (a John Lennon hit from the previous summer). It was just another parade for the antieverything society. And as usual, they all looked like crap.

Opinion: Earth Day would have been more successful if everyone who participated, instead of wasting valuable time parading around like a bunch of idiots, wrote a well-worded letter to their legislators stating the need for increased awareness of the deterioration of our precious natural resources.

Then we had a solar eclipse. The eclipse occurred during spring vacation. Naturally, I worked full-time that week, trying to make a buck so I could go flying.

At Hutton & Cook, the boss was on vacation, too, so we had a little fun. We had an Eclipse Sidewalk Sale. This sale was held during the time when you weren't supposed to be looking at the sun. You'd be surprised at how many jerks showed up at the sale to buy stuff while we hid under the protection of our awnings. It was great fun.

Music, April 1970. A girl named Bobbi Martin had a

hit called "For the Love of Him." She sounded sexy, so I bought it. There was also a smash hit by the Ides of March titled "Vehicle." It soared to the number one slot in Hartford. And the Beatles' final album, *Let It Be*, was on the charts, too, with the title track becoming the most popular cut from the album. I didn't like the record. It lacked the power of a typical Beatle performance. It was the end of the Beatles, and everyone knew it. That was sad.

On Saturday, April 11, Jim Lovell, Fred Haise, and Jack Swigert blasted into space aboard *Apollo 13*. There was surprisingly little fanfare before the launch. All I knew was that *Apollo 13* was scheduled to land in the desolate Fra Mauro vicinity on the moon.

Lovell, veteran of *Gemini 7*, *Gemini 12*, and *Apollo 8*, had more time in space than any American astronaut. As commander of *Apollo 13*, Lovell would finally get to land on the moon. The command module pilot, Fred Haise, was a rookie, as was the lunar module pilot, Jack Swigert.

Swigert's participation on *Apollo 13* was by accident. The prime lunar module pilot for the mission, Ken Mattingly, found himself exposed to measles shortly before the flight was scheduled for lift-off. Two days before the event, Swigert was substituted for Mattingly, over fear Mattingly—and possibly the entire crew—would become ill during the flight.

The launch of an Apollo *Saturn V* never lost its magic. *Apollo 13* roared majestically from the Pad 39 complex on the third lunar landing mission of the program.

It was good to know an Apollo spacecraft with American astronauts aboard was again speeding toward the moon. And everything seemed to be playing correctly.

On the evening of the third day into the mission, I watched the *Apollo 13* crew do one of the best in-flight TV transmissions yet. Then I went out on an errand with Bob.

While we were out, WDRC interrupted its ("We interrupt our regular programming to bring you this special report from . . . ") regular music to announce that an "accident" had occurred aboard the spacecraft. "Explosion" would have better described the event. An entire oxygen tank within the service module section (located directly aft of the command module) blew up, victim of an electrical short circuit.

Apollo 13's oxygen and fuel cell systems were in shambles. The crew could see their oxygen supply venting into space through a gaping hole in the service module. It was a first-rate crisis in space.

In a tremendous demonstration of teamwork and professionalism, NASA and the crew of *Apollo 13* devised a "lifeboat" mode, utilizing the *Apollo 13* LM, which the crew had named *Aquarius. Aquarius* supplied emergency oxygen and power to *Odyssey*, the command module.

The spacecraft could not just simply turn around and head for home. *Apollo 13*'s trajectory was such that it was easier for the spacecraft to whip around the moon, using lunar gravity as a slingshot to send it earthward again.

The problem was one of time. Oxygen, water, and electrical power—all vital consumables—were available only in limited supply via *Aquarius*. The mathematical equation devised by NASA's computers said the supplies aboard *Aquarius* might be sufficient for the astronauts to survive the trip home, given dire conservation by the crew. The situation was desperate.

Apollo 13 represented scary coincidences. That the mission was the thirteenth of the series and the explosion on board took place on April 13 was mysterious enough to arouse even the least supertstitious.

As the crippled spacecraft sped around the moon and headed for earth, another coincidence came to mind—a coincidence between the mission as it actually unfolded and a new movie titled *Marooned*.

Marooned was about a fictitious long-duration mission in earth orbit, similar to missions planned for the upcoming Skylab program. After a prolonged stay in orbit, the crew of *Ironman One*, as the mission was named, departed their space station for a return to earth in an Apollo spacecraft, just like the one Lovell, Haise, and Swigert were flying.

Ironman One could not get out of orbit because of a faulty SPS engine, which served as the retro-grade rocket to slow the spacecraft from orbital velocity. The result: three astronauts stranded in space, awaiting either the depletion of their oxygen supply or a rescue mission, whichever came first. The story was eerily close to the predicament of Lovell, Haise, and Swigert aboard *Apollo 13*.

After the explosion, there was massive television coverage of the flight of *Apollo 13*. I recall thinking, *How sad that it took an out-and-out emergency to get everyone interested in this mission.* Children in elementary schools prayed for the crew.

Lovell, Haise, and Swigert were gutting it out. The temperature in the command module hovered near freezing. And it would be extremely difficult to align the command module computer for proper reentry without normal power in the command module. Whenever an Apollo smashed into the earth's atmosphere following a lunar mission, there was only one chance at reentry. If the angle of entry was too steep, the spacecraft simply incinerated. If the angle was to shallow, the spacecraft would "skip" off the thickening atmosphere and careen out into space . . . with no ability to return.

There was great relief all over when, on April 17, 1970, *Apollo 13* splashed down safely. I can't remember having more admiration for any crew than Lovell, Haise, and Swigert. They flew like thoroughbreds. They were tough. Their mission failed in that it didn't complete the lunar landing at Fra Mauro. But its success in the face of imminent disaster was a credit to the crew, the equipment, and everyone at NASA. There was no pride lost on *Apollo 13*.

On December 27, 1982, Jack Swigert, LM pilot on *Apollo 13*, died of bone cancer. His death occurred one week before he was to assume the seat in the U.S. House of Representatives that he had won that November.

The explosion aboard *Apollo 13* delayed plans for the flight of *Apollo 14* considerably. By the time investigations were completed and a redesign was engineered for the service module to prevent another explosion on future flights it was 1971.

There were no other American astronauts off the pad in 1970. The Soviets scored a duration record in June with their *Soyuz 9* mission. And then the Soviets landed a probe on the surface of Venus in August. That was a brillant accomplishment. Although it wasn't as exciting as landing men on the moon, its significance cannot be denied. When the U.S. should have been making vast plans for the next twenty-five years in space, at least the Soviets were engaged in long-range planning for their space efforts in 1970.

The worst thing that happened in 1970 was another fabulous by-product of the war in Vietnam. This event took place in the United States, on the campus of Kent State University.

In May, just before classes got out for the summer, a bunch of Ohio National Guardsmen who were sent onto the campus of that school to squelch an antiwar demonst-ration shot and killed several students. Two of the victims were girls. Eleven others were seriously wounded.

I've told you how I disliked the antieverything crowd,

and I've expressed negative feelings about the protesters of the times. But protesters or not, I couldn't accept what happened at Kent State. It was a tragedy in the first degree. As with the killings of President Kennedy, Martin Luther King, and Robert Kennedy, I asked the same question: what kind of moron(s) would do such a thing? How insane were we in this country anyway? Now we were stooping to killing college students. Who was next? Junior high students? Kindergartners? Where was the pride of Mercury? Or the "spirit of Apollo"? Why were we shooting our own when we could have been having a John Glenn Day?

The shootings at Kent State caused an uprising on the campuses of the United States that every bureaucrat in Washington feared. Now, to add fuel to the fire of the antiwar movement, the military was killing college kids who opposed the war.

Our nation had the Vietnam flu. In 1970, there was still no vaccine.

Back in 1965, around the time of the *Gemini 6/Gemini 7* rendezvous spectacular, a singing duo known as Simon and Garfunkel shot to the top of the charts with their hit "The Sounds of Silence" (which was later featured in the 1968 film *The Graduate*). Since "The Sounds of Silence," Simon and Garfunkel had been immensely successful with their familiar folk rock sound. Simon and Garfunkel had the knack of capitalizing on things negative like no others from the era, Bob Dylan included.

Simon and Garfunkel released hit after hit as the sixties wore on. Frequently their recordings dealt with the losers, those who were down and out. Even worse, Simon and Garfunkel frequently zeroed in on those who were considering suicide as the logical alternative.

Simon and Garfunkel's lyrics typified the depression that permeated the youth of our nation as Vietnam, assassinations, and riots "outclassed" the space program and became commonplace. Because depression was a condition with which they could easily identify, the kids at school sucked up Simon and Garfunkel like it was free pot. We all felt badly. Simon and Garfunkel made lots of money.

In May 1970, Simon and Garfunkel's most successful album, titled *Bridge over Troubled Water*, was pegged firmly at the number one position in Hartford. The title track was one of the most depressing releases I'd ever heard. Yet it was appropriate for the times. Its inferred sorrow kept perfect company with the carnage at Kent State and the invasion of Cambodia, which President Nixon announced late in April.

The summer of 1970 was one of more joyful music than the previous four or five. The Blues Image released "Ride, Captain, Ride." Vanity Fair did "Hitching a Ride." Mungo Jerry featured "In the Summertime." And Santana recorded "Evil Ways."

There was *Airport*, the original disaster movie of the sixties featuring Burt Lancaster, Dean Martin, and Jacqueline Bisset. My father and I went to see *Airport* while my mother attended to my grandfather, hospitalized following a stroke.

I loved *Airport*. It portrayed airline pilots as dashing, well-paid individuals (this was long before Jimmy Carter's wonderful program of airline deregulation, sports fans) who always got the great women. *Airport* was like watching coverage of a NASA mission. It got the old blood flowing.

Apollo 14

For anyone who hasn't seen the foliage in New England in September and October, I highly recommend the experience. It is breathtaking. The autumn of 1970 was beautiful. Cool, fresh wind swept away the heat of August as if a giant air conditioner had been quietly set to "low cool."

Progress on the service module redesigned to prevent another explosion like the one that nearly destroyed *Apollo 13* continued, but slowly. It appeared the launch of *Apollo 14* would slip into 1971, which is exactly what happened.

The crew for the upcoming flight was particularly interesting because our first astronaut, Alan Shepard, was slated to fly as the spacecraft commander (Shepard's last-minute substitution as commander of this mission eventually caused Gordon Cooper, who was originally assigned as the mission commander for *Apollo 14*, to leave NASA). Shepard had inner ear problems that had kept him from flying during Gemini and earlier Apollo missions. But the problems were corrected, and Shepard returned to full flight status. It was great to see him on the flight roster again. Dirty laundry concerning crew flight assignments, as in the example of *Apollo 14*, was not readily available to the public.

By Christmas of 1970, we knew the entire crew of *Apollo 14*. Beside Shepard in the command module would be Stuart Roosa and Edgar Mitchell. Roosa was the command module pilot, and Mitchell was slated to walk on the lunar surface with mission commander Shepard in his duties as lunar module pilot.

The final round of SATs was over. Senior year in high school was all but wrapped up, my grades looked pretty good, and I was ready to get to college.

A number one hit at Christmastime of 1970 was "I'm Your Captain" by Grand Funk. At the end of the tune, the lyrics repeated, "I'm getting closer to my home," with the sound of waves crashing in the background. Years later, when the Far East Network—which served U.S. military personnel in Japan and Southeast Asia—played "I'm Your Captain," the tune became a pleasant reminder of the beautiful Connecticut that I missed so badly.

Apollo 14 was launched on January 31, 1971. The mission was highly successful, with Shepard and Roosa utilizing a device that in some ways resembled a rickshaw to transport equipment on the lunar surface.

The command module for *Apollo 14* was named *Kitty Hawk*, and the lunar module was named *Antares*. Shepard flew this mission nearly ten years after his flight in *Freedom 7*, on May 5, 1961. Having overcome his inner ear disorders and having met the grueling training required of a lunar landing commander, Shepard had my total admiration.

It is interesting to note that when *Antares* lifted off the lunar surface to rendezvous with the awaiting *Kitty Hawk* in lunar orbit, the event was accomplished on the first orbit, a difficult maneuver that required keen navigational technique and a second burn of the lunar module's ascent engine.

When *Apollo 14* splashed down on February 9, 1971, only three Apollo missions remained to fly. The next flight, that of *Apollo 15*, was scheduled to fly during the summer months. It was almost like old times, with a late-winter flight and another during the summer. When measured against the pace of Gemini or Apollo in the prelunar landing phase, however, the absence of another springtime mission was obvious.

Summer of 1971 held important expectations: the end of high school, the knowledge of college acceptance, and the flight of *Apollo 15*.

In April, my grandfather, the one who had the stroke the previous summer, died. It was sad to watch him deteriorate from the vigorous man I had known to his final days, spent paralyzed and in pain, trapped within the confines of a putrid, depressing convalescent home. The treatment afforded my grandfather and the other men and women who were suffering slow deaths around him by the staff was abominable. To make matters worse, the cost of his "care" was astronomical. The popular term *rip-off* applied.

Just think, in his lifetime, my grandfather saw Zeppelin launch his dirigibles and he saw the Wright brothers fly. Lindbergh crossed the Atlantic. Hitler's rockets fell on London. And Neil Armstrong hopped off the *Eagle*'s ladder at Tranquility Base. That is incredible!

On a lighter note, I was accepted to all three schools to which I had applied: Southern Connecticut State University, Central Connecticut State University, and the University of Connecticut. Of the three, I selected Southern Connecticut. It was convenient and it was close to New Haven Airport. That was important.

I graduated from Cheshire High School on Tuesday, June 22, 1971. My parents were disgusted because I had grown long sideburns for our senior play, *Once Upon a Mattress*. I must admit I looked pretty shabby.

There was a huge drinking and drug party following graduation. I didn't go. I went out with Lydia instead. She had sat near me back in Mrs. Greenwald's freshman English class. On graduation night, Lydia looked fantastic in her miniskirt and her high-heels.

Listening to the car radio that evening, Lydia and I heard news typical of the times. President Nixon was furious over the recent printing of the "Pentagon Papers," a series of documents outlining U.S. involvement in Vietnam through 1968. Nixon was so disgusted about the revelations in the nation's leading newspapers that his aides began covert "operations" against those who helped make the documents public. Such operations went on to ruin Nixon's presidency.

Secretly, Henry Kissinger in his meetings with Le Duc Tho had already agreed to allow North Vietnamese troops to remain in South Vietnam after the fighting there ceased. After idiots like Jane Fonda went to Hanoi to apologize to the North Vietnamese for our "war crimes" in a degrading attempt to end the mess, people found out that our POWs—many of whom were in captivity for their sixth year by 1971—were being brutally tortured. Pressure on the Nixon administration to determine the plight of our gallant POWs (Prisoners Of War) increased. If you're interested in what life was like for our POWs during the Vietnam War, I heartily recommend *In Love and War*, by Jim and Sybil Stockdale. It will move you.

Meanwhile, the war dragged on through its seventh year.

Apollo 15

A more upbeat topic in the news was the upcoming launch of *Apollo 15*. The *Apollo 15* crew of David Scott (veteran of *Gemini 8* and *Apollo 9*), Al Worden, and Jim Irwin was prepared to use a fancy ground vehicle, jokingly dubbed the lunar rover, for the first time. It promised to be a great mission.

Three rock superstars died of drug-related causes during 1971. Jim Morrison, lead singer of the Doors, was first. His death was followed by those of Jimi Hendrix, of "Purple Haze Fame," and of Janis Joplin (who had sung with Big Brother and The Holding Company). It's ironic that both Joplin and Morrison had hits on the charts at the time of their deaths. Joplin had released "Bobby McGee" in early 1971 and the Doors were high on the charts with their *L.A.*

214

Woman album that featured "Love Her Madly."

The spacecraft blasted skyward on July 26, 1971. The launch, as usual, was awesome. The word from NASA was that this mission was more advanced than any Apollo mission to date.

For starts, *Apollo 15* carried a heavier payload than any previous lunar landing mission. Falcon, the lunar module, had been modified to afford consumables for a longer stay on the surface and also to accommodate the lunar rover.

Additionally, Scott and Irwin wore modified pressure suits, designed to enhance freedom of movement on the lunar surface. The backpacks they wore were designed to permit longer ventures outside of Falcon. And there was more room inside Falcon for samples collected by the crew while on the moon.

Scott and Irwin took three EVAs while they were on the moon's Swamp of Decay. After the EVA, Scott parked the lunar rover in a position from which a remote camera mounted on the vehicle could send television signals of Falcon's departure from the moon.

The lunar lift-off was fantastic! It's one thing to imagine how the LM looked as it blasted away from the descent stage (the bottom half of the LM, which stayed on the moon). But actually watching the event, in color, no less, was phenomenal. It was the first televised coverage of an Apollo lunar lift-off. That alone made the mission worthwhile.

Apollo 15 command module pilot Al Worden made history, too, when, on August 5, 1971, with the spacecraft earthbound, he went EVA to recover film cassettes outside Endeavor. Worden was the first human to walk in "deep" space, some 197,000 miles from earth.

The splashdown of *Apollo 15* occurred on August 7,

on time and on target. Eight American astronauts had walked on the moon. Four more would savor the experience before the Apollo program came to a conclusion. *Apollo 15* was the last manned U.S. mission in 1971.

September 1971. College. Freshman year at Southern Connecticut State University in New Haven. It was difficult and boring at the same time.

First of all, *we had classes on Saturdays*! I had to get up at 6:00 A.M., make the forty-minute commute to school, sit through the most boring English class I'd ever attended—filled with the kind of hippies, junkies, and social dropouts I despised—and proceed back to Cheshire, where I put in the rest of the day at Hutton & Cook, peddling men's clothing.

Because there was no time to change clothes before going to work, I had to go to class dressed in coat and tie, which made me stand out like a sore thumb among the bell-bottomed, army-knapsack-toting students, who hated the very sight of another student dressed in the "establishment uniform," which basically meant anything recently laundered.

Those first months at Southern were pretty lousy. Even the music was lousy. I remember the first day of classes that fall listening to Rod Stewart's "Maggie Mae" screaming from the girls' dorms, where anxious new freshman females thought it chic to place the speakers of their stereos in the windows, just so everyone could hear Rod Stewart.

Then there was "American Pie." God, I hated that song. Every station played it over and over. The other kids thought it was fantastic. They even *sang* it as they walked from class to class. The whole damn thing depressed me. The kids thought they were having a great time! All they talked about was, "Who got stoned at Tina's party?" or,

"Who went to Moratorium Day stoned?" or, "Who screwed Beth, who was stoned, at Tina's party?" Were they kidding? Was *this* college? It was more like "Romper Room" for screwballs!

My expectations for college centered around meaningful classes, some good times, a few beers with the guys, and sex more than once a weekend. None of those expectations was met. I buried myself in books about flying, Apollo, and a new interest: the Marines.

I had been intrigued with the military since childhood. Maybe most guys think the military is neat at one time or another; I really don't know. But after looking at the fruitcakes in high school for four years and then getting into college only to find older fruitcakes vegetating there, those disappointments served as motivational factors as I searched for a personal source of pride and accomplishment.

Almost all of the astronauts had served in the military. A large number of our political leaders had served. Most airline pilots had served. My father served. Most people I admired had clocked some time in the service of his or her country. Despite Vietnam—and this may sound like bullshit—I felt I had an obligation to do the same if I ever expected to get anywhere. I felt I owed something to the United States.

It was either going to be the Navy or the Marines. *The Marines*! I admired them most! In Vietnam, all of our services pulled their weight, but the reports I read about Marine infantry units and Marine air support were startling. What a bunch of guys! Besides, their uniform was a knockout.

I decided to seek a commission in the United States Marine Corps. It was a scary decision. I kept it to myself until I learned more about how one gets a commission in the Marines. Even without a lot of research, I knew it wouldn't be easy.

Officer training programs weren't very popular on campus in the early seventies. Poisoned by the Vietnam experience, student populations across the nation generally despised anything that even faintly resembled a uniform. But there were still individuals in college who appreciated the benefits afforded by serving as officers. It took a degree of individuality and balls.

I qualified for the Marine Corps Platoon Leaders Class (PLC) program. The twelve-week program was outstanding because there was no on-campus drill required. All training took place at the Marine Corps Officer Candidates School at Quantico, Virginia, during the summer. I attended training between my sophomore and junior year for six weeks and returned the following summer for another six weeks.

Marine Corps officer training was extremely difficult and extremely rewarding. Throughout the course, thoughts of the astronauts kept me motivated when the going was rough. At one point, tendonitis nearly prevented completion of OCS. Running, an activity performed in plentiful doses at Quantico, became excrutiating. It was John Glenn, a Marine, who served as my "personal consultant" as I ran mile after mile in the summer heat. Thinking about him motivated me. For Glenn, OCS was only the first step. Glenn did not give up. Nor did I.

Upon graduation from Southern Connecticut State, I was commissioned a second lieutenant in the United States Marine Corps Reserve. It was the proudest day of my life. On active duty from 1975 through 1978, I served as an infantry officer in command of a rifle platoon with the Third Marine Division overseas and in Naval Aviation with the Second Marine Air Wing in North Carolina. I highly recommend the experience.

Apollo 16

In the spring of 1972, as American aircraft bombed Hiaphong Harbor and as I took the written examinations for the Marines, we launched *Apollo 16.*

Aboard for the April 16 launch was spacecraft commander John Young, veteran of *Gemini 3*, *Gemini 10*, and *Apollo 10.* Flying with him were Thomas Mattingly as command module (Casper) pilot and Charles Duke as lunar module (Orion) pilot.

When *Apollo 16* was launched, the vehicle represented the heaviest payload ever boosted toward the moon. Three days after lift-off Casper and Orion arrived in lunar orbit. When Orion separated from Casper for the lunar descent, Duke noted the backup steering system, which gimbaled the lunar module's main engine and allowed the astronauts to "steer" the vehicle, was malfunctioning.

NASA rules were very strict regarding "no-go" conditions for lunar landings. One of them required the backup steering system to function. Without bending the rules, Orion remained in lunar orbit for some seven hours before proceeding. NASA located the problem, and it was determined a safe landing and ascent could be performed with a faulty yaw gimbal actuator.

The flight of *Apollo 16* succeeded. Two hundred and sixty-five and one half hours after lift-off, Casper returned safely to earth. Young and Duke spent over twenty EVA hours on the rocky Descartes region of the moon. Effective use of a lunar rover made three separate EVA periods extremely effective. *Apollo 16* recovered many pounds of priceless lunar samples.

Only one Apollo mission remained. President Kennedy's dream was just about over—with no bold next step to honor the accomplishments of those who made Apollo possible.

The bloodletting had yet to end in the United States. In May, as he campaigned for the Democratic presidential nomination, Alabama governor George Wallace was shot in a shopping center parking lot in Maryland.

More fortunate than President Kennedy, Robert Kennedy, and Martin Luther King, Wallace recovered. Yet the price he paid was dear—he would never walk again. And Wallace's assailant, another real zero, remains in jail where I hope he will spend the rest of his life.

In June 1972, the Democratic National Headquarters in Washington, D.C., was robbed by a group of thugs hired by President Nixon's staff. This event became the Watergate scandal. As the conventions took place that summer, the Nixon White House struggled to keep a lid on the connection between the robbers and the president.

In a cutting fusilade of investigative reporting, correspondents from the *Washington Post* and the *New York Times* refused to let the story die. Their research eventually brought the Nixon Administration to its knees. The year 1972 was not only the year of the final Apollo missions and another year of Vietnam; it was the year Watergate came into our homes like a piece of dirty laundry nobody wanted.

Apollo 17

December 1972. President Nixon had won reelection, and his popularity remained high. After all, it was Nixon who had journeyed to Communist China and the Soviet Union that year. And it was Nixon who appeared to be on the brink of ending American involvement in Vietnam.

Secretary of State Henry Kissinger stated, "Peace is at hand," in October. When the Hanoi regime refused to follow through, Nixon ordered operations Linebacker and Linebacker II, the unrestricted bombing of Hanoi and

Haiphong. Earlier bombing of North Vietnam, called Operation Rolling Thunder, had restricted American pilots from bombing key military targets. The Linebacker operations lifted those restrictions. North Vietnam's war machine crumbled beneath ordinance dropped from American B-52, F-4, A-7, and A-6 aircraft.

To our POWs behind bars in Hanoi the sound of American attack aircraft overhead signaled that their horrible ordeal was almost over.

On December 7, 1972, *Apollo 17* thundered majestically into the heavens. *Apollo 17* was the only U.S. manned mission launched at night. *Apollo 17*'s dramatic departure for the moon was the most awesome, inspiring event I have ever seen. The nighttime launch made it even more impressive than the launch of *Apollo 11*.

Commanding *Apollo 17* was Gene Cernan, who had flown on *Gemini 9* and *Apollo 10*. Cernan, who now works as a science editor for ABC News, earned a reputation as one of the outstanding astronauts of his era. Having met Cernan in 1983, I heartily agree.

Apollo 17's command module (*America*) pilot was Navy Captain Ronald Evans. The lunar module (ironically, the *Apollo 17* LM was named *Challenger*) pilot was Dr. Harrison Schmitt, the first geologist to fly as a crew member. After *Apollo 17*, Schmitt went on to the U.S. Senate, where he was a strong advocate for the space program. Today Schmitt encourages a manned mission to Mars.

Three days after lift-up, *Apollo 17* entered lunar orbit. An advanced scientific package stored in the service module took laser altimeter readings of the lunar surface and highly sophisticated mapping cameras photographed the moon. Additionally, special thermal mapping equipment took millions of temperature samples of the surface. The package was operated by Ron Evans, the command module pilot and Evans retrieved the package during a deep-space EVA as *Apollo 17* made its journey home.

Apollo 17's mission was to explore the rugged Taurus-Littrow Valley of the moon. The flight was the longest Apollo mission and included seventy-five hours on the surface, the longest stay by any Apollo crew.

Aboard their lunar rover, Cernan and Schmitt logged over twenty-one miles. They gathered 243 pounds of lunar samples, another program record.

At 5:55 P.M. on December 14, 1972, *Apollo 17*'s lunar module departed from the surface of the moon, with Cernan and Schmitt safely aboard. The event was bittersweet. There was cause for elation over the mission's obvious success. Yet the elation was tempered by the knowledge that *Apollo 17* was the final mission of the program and that the footprints Cernan and Schmitt left behind were most likely the last American footprints to be made on the moon in this century.

The glorious Apollo program ended on December 19, 1972 when *Apollo 17* splashed down safely. Twelve American astronauts had walked on the moon during Apollo. They were Armstrong and Aldrin (*Apollo 11*), Conrad and Bean (*Apollo 12*), Shepard and Mitchell (*Apollo 14*), Scott and Irwin (*Apollo 15*), Young and Duke (*Apollo 16*), and Cernan and Schmitt (*Apollo 17*). Nearly as impressive, twenty-five Americans had orbited the moon during the program. They were, in addition to the twelve who actually walked on the moon, the crew of *Apollo 8* (Borman, Lovell, and Anders), John Young (command module pilot of *Apollo 10*), Michael Collins (command module pilot of *Apollo 11*), Richard F. Gordon (command module pilot of *Apollo 12*), the crew of *Apollo 13* (Lovell, Swigert, and Haise), Stuart Roosa (command module pilot of *Apollo 14*), Alfred Worden (command module pilot of *Apollo 15*), Thomas Mattingly (command module pilot of *Apollo 16*), and Ronald Evans (command module pilot of *Apollo 17*). And the crews of three other Apollo missions strove to ensure the safety of the lunarbound astronauts. They were Grissom, White, and Chaffee (who died aboard *Apollo 1*), Schirra, Eisele, and Cunningham (*Apollo 7*), and McDivitt, Scott, and Schweickart (*Apollo 9*).

As *Apollo 17* became part of history, the United States should have been prepared to send more astronauts to the moon, with the intention of building a lunar base, within the decade following *Apollo 11*'s first landing in the Sea of Tranquility.

The technology used for Apollo was more than sufficient to begin the journey. Certainly, the United States had the boosting capability and the spacecraft to initiate an "Apollo Phase II": a logical follow-up program to the initial Apollo explorations. The goal of Apollo Phase II would have been short-range occupation of the lunar surface by manned crews and the construction of lunar shelters for future manned expeditions. Ultimately, the program following Apollo Phase II would have seen permanent lunar occupation by American and international crews by the turn of the century.

Instead, NASA turned to Earth orbit, with what little Apollo hardware remained after the Nixon administration financially raped the U.S. space program and, ultimately, the Space Transportation System—more commonly known as the space shuttle.

The Soviets, using the slow-but-sure method of advancement in space they adopted after lunar landing plans were canceled around the time of *Apollo 8*, flew three manned missions in the early seventies. Each mission built Soviet experience toward a manned space station. Their efforts were rewarded when, on June 6, 1971, the crew of *Soyuz*

11 occupied the *Salyut 1* space station (it was unfortunate that the crew of *Soyuz 11* perished during reentry). A new era began.

Apollo marked the end of American domination in space. Stevie Wonder sang "Very Superstitious." It was Christmas of 1972.

Skylab

Just before my first summer of Marine Corps officer training, the last beautiful *Saturn V* thundered into orbit on May 14, 1973. Named *Skylab 1*, the launch placed the heaviest payload ever boosted into orbit. The S-IVB stage, normally home for the lunar module, had been converted into an operational space station. And it was impressive.

The Skylab program which centered around the orbiting S-IVB turned space station, used equipment designated for the Apollo Applications program. This included the remaining *Saturn V*, three *Saturn 1-B* boosters, and three Apollo spacecraft.

The primary purpose of Skylab was to test man's endurance in space in an environment unlike any yet experienced: Skylab, compared to any American or Soviet manned spacecraft, was huge. It contained over ten thousand cubic feet inside, and it weighed one hundred tons. Although cumbersome, Skylab even had a shower on board.

Skylab II

The first Skylab crew consisted of veteran Gemini and Apollo ace Pete Conrad, Paul Weitz, and Dr. Joseph Kerwin. Following their launch atop a *Saturn 1-B* booster on May 25, 1973, they orbited the earth for more than twenty-eight days.

While in orbit, Conrad, Weitz, and Kerwin restored Skylab—which had suffered damaged solar panels during its boost phase—to working condition. Their EVA repair efforts were outstanding; they literally saved Skylab from being abandoned.

Skylab III

The second Skylab mission was launched on July 28, 1973. The crew for this mission was Alan Bean, who had flown with Pete Conrad and Dick Gordon on *Apollo 12* in 1969, Owen Garrett, and Jack Lousma. Both Garriott and Lousma would later fly as space shuttle pilots.

Skylab II lasted for an incredible fifty-nine days. Following intensive scientific experiments aloft, the modified Apollo command module that carried Bean, Garriott, and Lousma to Skylab splashed down on September 25, 1973.

Skylab IV

When Gerald Carr, Edward Gibson, and William Pogue departed from the cape for Skylab on November 16, 1973, they began man's longest journey in space to date. Their mission lasted until February 8, 1974—eighty-four days. The last Skylab flight proved man could exist for extended periods in space.

Skylab was destroyed in July 1979 as it reentered the earth's atmosphere. It was hoped the space shuttle would fly before Skylab's orbit deteriorated. The shuttle was to have moved Skylab into a higher orbit, preserving the spacecraft for future use.

But the space shuttle was running so far behind schedule, because of poor planning and funding, that Skylab died a sad death.

When Carr, Gibson, and Pogue returned to earth in February 1974, they were the last Americans to fly in space for over seven years.

Skylab IV landed during the height of the first Arab oil embargo–related energy crisis. Since we lived in the Northeast, where winters are typically bitter cold, we conserved heating fuel and waited in long lines to buy gas for our cars. The victories of Mercury, Gemini, and Apollo faded in the shadow of economic turmoil.

The Skylab missions took place as a shaky "peace" came to Vietnam. In January 1973, a cease-fire was arranged. Our POWs came home in March (sadly, there are many American servicemen who served in Vietnam who remain unaccounted for), as the Watergate crisis began to cripple the Nixon presidency. The ultimate tragedy of Vietnam had yet to take place.

Almost as soon as our forces withdrew from Southeast Asia, worried diplomats turned their heads toward the explosive Middle East, where Israel and Egypt fought each other. Concerns for Arab-produced oil threatened the global economy. If the space program was already near "the back of the bus" on the administration's list of priorities, it moved back another row in late 1973.

ASTP

When Gerald Ford assumed the presidency in August 1974, national pride was low. The prices paid for Vietnam and Watergate were horrifying. Instead of the gasoline Green Stamps of the sixties there was talk of rationing stamps. Japanese cars were becoming increasingly popular because of their incredible mileage efficiency and because, to our horror, they were built better than American cars.

The last Skylab mission was over. There were no funds for another Skylab mission. Instead, in a political salute to the atmosphere of détente Nixon established with the Soviets, NASA agreed to a link-up in orbit with a Soviet Soyuz spacecraft. Training for the mission began in 1973.

Dubbed the Apollo-Soyuz Test Program (ASTP), the last *Saturn 1-B* booster with an Apollo spacecraft, modified to dock with a Soyuz spacecraft, was readied. The crews were interesting. Flying as the Apollo spacecraft commander was veteran Tom Stafford, who had flown *Gemini 6* in 1965 and commanded *Gemini 9* in 1966 and *Apollo 10* in 1969. Rookie Vance Brand, a future space shuttle pilot, flew on this mission in the traditional command module pilot's role. And finally Deke Slayton, whose irregular heartbeat kept him from flying his Mercury orbital mission in 1962, flew into space for the first time aboard the ASTP.

The Soviet (*Soyuz 19*) spacecraft commander was veteran Alexei Leonov, who was the first man to step into space during his dramatic EVA aboard *Voskhod II* in 1965. Flying with Leonov was Valeriy Kubasov, veteran of the *Soyuz 6* mission that had flown in 1969.

ASTP was a remarkable demonstration of how American and Soviet crews can cooperate. The only way the Apollo and Soyuz spacecraft could dock in orbit was via a common docking aparatus. Such a device was manufactured in the United States, as the result of fruitful exchanges between Soviet space experts and NASA. The device was extremely significant; future crews may well demand transfer capability from U.S. spacecraft to Soviet equipment, or vice versa, in the event of an emergency in orbit. It is sad that our astronauts have only flown with their Soviet counterparts this one time. Think of how much further both nations could be if we worked together all the time!

On July 15, 1975, a mighty Soviet *A-1* booster lofted *Soyuz 19* from the Baikonur Cosmodrome in Kasakhstsan. About seven hours later, the last beautiful Saturn booster to carry Americans into space boosted the ASTP Apollo spacecraft into orbit.

The American and Soviet crew flew together until July 24. A successful docking was performed, and the crews exchanged mementos of the event in flight. When the ASTP Apollo splashed down, it became the last Apollo spacecraft to fly. That represents an utter waste of fine technology that could have been upgraded and retained for use even today.

Karen and Richard Carpenter's recording of "Only Yesterday" was a top forty hit while Americans and Russians flew together in space.

No American flew in space again until 1981.

Prior to the ASTP launch, the result of our efforts in Vietnam became evident. After we bombed Hanoi into submission in late 1972, the North Vietnamese, as industrious as ever, quickly repaired their military organization.

By the spring of 1975, communist forces had pushed far into South Vietnam. One city after another fell to the North Vietnamese forces under General Giap. The South Vietnamese army, whose commitment to the war was never as strong as many assumed, vaporized before the North's superior forces. Vietnamization and American involvement in Vietnam were, in the final analysis, massive failures.

Saigon fell. U.S. Marines from units in which I served helped evacuate the city. The pictures from Saigon were particularly ugly. The communists succeeded after all. Despite eleven years of U.S. involvement and the massive aid to the South Vietnamese government, all was lost.

So many lives were lost in that war. So many lives. . . .

Falling Star

The years between the ASTP mission and the first manned flight of the new space shuttle seemed like a lifetime. During that period, the world—and my perception of it—changed dramatically.

In July 1975 when ASTP flew, I was a brand-new Marine second lieutenant. When *Columbia* hurtled into space in April 1981, I was a civilian again, with my active duty years successfully completed.

Like a secret friend hovering on the perimeter of my life, the space program took me from childhood through high school, college, and military service and into the dollar-chasing years of adulthood.

Events and circumstances led to the world of sales instead of into a NASA spacecraft. It was disappointing to wake up one morning and realize my chances of becoming an astronaut were relatively remote (too much prop time, not enough high-performance jet time). It was even more disappointing to recognize the path to NASA was fraught with financial struggle (poor pay compared to other careers) and came with no guarantee of ever flying in space. By 1980, many astronauts from the Apollo days had left the program. Funding problems abounded. The glories of Apollo were conspiciously absent as the shuttle era dawned.

But money and glory aside, flying for NASA remains, in this author's opinion, the most exciting, rewarding adventure in existence. I would jump at the chance to fly the shuttle or any future NASA spacecraft. Those who have

earned the title NASA Astronaut have my deepest respect—and genuine envy. Who knows? I may yet have the
opportunity to fly in space. It's never too late to try.

During these shuttle years, I tend to relate missions
with family events instead of with pop music, as I did so
often during Mercury, Gemini, Apollo, Skylab, and ASTP.
I am the proud father of two beautiful daughters (no bias
whatsoever), and it is great fun to couple space events, like
the flight of *STS-1*, with domestic triumphs, like the first
successful trip to the movies with Kristen, my oldest daughter, or the satellite repair mission (*Discovery*, 51-I) with the
birth of Lauren, my youngest daughter.

Kristen was born in 1978, as the shuttle fell further
and further behind schedule. Hopes for a Skylab "rescue"
mission were dashed in 1979 as NASA struggled to keep
the heat-resistant tiles from falling off *Columbia*. To make
matters even worse, the SSMEs (Space Shuttle Main Engines) were too balky for a manned launch attempt.

During the 1979–80 period, our national pride suffered through another bout of energy ills, rampant inflation, skyrocketing interest rates, and tension with our
friend the Ayatollah. Recession loomed dark on the hori-
zon. We needed a NASA victory.

STS-1

The story that ended in disaster on January 28, 1986,
began on April 12, 1981, when John Young and Robert
Crippen flew the first space shuttle mission into orbit. It
was the first time American astronauts rode a vehicle into
space that had never been flight tested. (Specifically, only
gliding tests were performed with *Enterprise*, a non–space-
rated orbiter, in 1977.)

Despite the loss of a few precious tiles, the flight of *STS-1* was successful. Young and Crippen landed *Columbia* at Edwards Air Force Base on April 14, 1981. The age of the shuttle began.

STS-2 through STS-4

From November 1981 to July 1982, *Columbia* flew three more crews (consisting of two pilots only) into orbit, to test the shuttle's systems and capabilities. Joe Engle and Richard Truly flew *STS-2* from November 12, 1981 to November 14, 1981. On March 22, 1982, Jack Lousma and Gordon Fullerton rode *STS-3* into orbit. They landed safely on March 30, 1982, after remaining in space an extra day because of poor weather at the landing site. Finally, on June 27, 1982, Thomas Mattingly and Henry Hartsfield flew *STS-4* aloft, and they went on to complete their mission on July 4, 1982.

The shuttle was prounounced "operational" following the flight of *STS-4*. As sales manager for Beech Aircraft Corporation in Atlanta at the time, I was pleased with shuttle's amazing progress. Despite doubts over our lack of lunar or Mars landing programs, I believed what NASA said. I thought the shuttle was indeed "operational."

STS-5 through Mission 61-A

While the shuttle was not nearly as impressive as Apollo, NASA nevertheless achieved an admirable record between November 1982—when the "operational" shuttle missions began—and January 1986, when Mission 51-L ended in disaster. In slightly more than three years, four orbiters—*Columbia, Challenger, Discovery,* and *Atlantis*—flew twenty-one successful missions into orbit. One hundred and twenty-three astronaut-pilots, mission specialists, and payload specialists flew on those missions. Of that number, nine were women. Many represented foreign countries. Two were members of Congress.

Shuttle crews demonstrated their ability to recover and repair satellites in orbit. Hundreds of scientific experiments were conducted. Photographic mapping of earth's surface was conducted with pinpoint accuracy. Although never achieving the "low" cost of access to space originally advertised, commercial payloads were successfully placed into orbit. Important geological research abounded. Prior to Mission 51-L, space shuttle crews accumulated over 17,648 hours in space.

And the Soviets? Between the ASTP mission in 1975 and the Mission 51-L tragedy, Soviet cosmonauts flew thirty-two missions into orbit. Building on their trusty Soyuz design that first flew in 1967, they perfected their rendezvous and docking procedures, lofted several space stations, and occupied those orbiting craft for tens of thousands of hours, surpassing the lead held by American crews since *Gemini VII* in 1965.

The latest Soviet space station achievement, MIR, demonstrates the tenacity and dedication of the Soviet space effort. The brave cosmonauts and their leaders are to be commended for their accomplishments.

In 1987, the Soviets successfully launched Energia, the most powerful booster ever built since *Saturn V.* Energia is capable of lifting roughly the same payload profile as was *Saturn V.* The United States currently possesses no heavy-lift booster like Energia. It is impossible to comprehend, as NASA struggles for additional lift capabilities beyond the shuttle, why we flushed our Saturn technology down the drain. What an awful waste!

Between May 1961 and January 1986, the United States launched fifty-six manned missions, of which fifty-five actually flew in space. The Soviet Union launched sixty missions between April 1961 and September 1985, of which fifty-eight actually flew in space. Total U.S. manned hours in space at the time of the last successful shuttle mission prior to mission 51-L (Mission 61-C) was 40,151 hours and forty-six minutes. Total Soviet manned hours in space at the time of the last Soviet mission to fly prior to the *Challenger* (51-L) disaster was 44,855 hours and fourteen minutes.

Two Soviet missions suffered fatalities in flight, the *Soyuz 1* mission in 1967 and the *Soyuz 11* mission in 1971. A total of four cosmonauts were lost in those tragedies. One American mission ended in disaster, the *Challenger* Mission 51-L flight in 1986, in which seven Americans gave their lives in actual flight. Additionally, one American mission, that of *Apollo 1* (204) burned on the pad during a routine simulation, killing three American astronauts, in 1967.

The most impressive accomplishments of the U.S. program to date were the only manned landings on another celestial body (by Apollo astronauts on the moon) in history and the successful use of a reusable spacecraft capable of flight in the atmosphere (the shuttle). Meanwhile, the Soviet program accomplished endurance records approaching the time in space required of future interplanetary crews and use of not one but several space stations, complete with robot resupply craft and "guest" crews.

While the U.S. program remains in trouble as the result of the Mission 51-L disaster, the Soviet program continues an aggressive schedule.

Earthlight

In testimony at the Iran-contra hearings in July 1987, Marine Corps Lieutenant Colonel Oliver L. North stated, in reference to the Vietnam War, that "[The war] . . . was lost in Washington, not in Vietnam." That is essentially correct.

In the case of our space program, a similar analogy is appropriate. The current sorry state of affairs in which the U.S. manned space program finds itself is not a result of failure at the launch pad; it is the result of failure in Washington. Since 1969, support at the executive and congressional levels for NASA and our manned efforts in space has dwindled. I note with horror that our space program was not even considered a critical issue during the 1988 presidential campaign, and the American people are losers because of it.

Writing in *Aviation Week and Space Technology* (February 2, 1987, p. 104), a West German stated that "America's manned space flight program no longer deserves the name." He continued; "The American spirit of enterprise once stimulated the world. This spirit is history. Now it's the age of the irresolutes—the time of beancounters and bookkeepers."

In the months following the *Challenger* disaster, hundreds wrote in *Aviation Week* of their desires to see our space program return to its proper place on the list of national priorities—at or very near the top. I am encouraged to see people from all walks of life, men and women, children and senior citizens, all expressing dismay at the lack of leadership that led to the tragedy of Mission 51-L.

Concerns over the space program—or lack of one—are not limited to aviation-oriented publications. They appear in newspapers. They appear in magazines oriented toward business, science, health, politics, and education. On television, rarely does a week go by when there is not some reference to our ailing space program and the growing Soviet effort in orbit. As this book went to press, our manned space program, despite the resumption of shuttle operations, remains without proper leadership or direction from Washington.

Is this the "space race" revisited? Not exactly. Times have changed drastically since 1957, when *Sputnik* beeped across the night sky. In the United States, the space race ended in a crescendo of for-the-moment feats, feats of great magnitude but feats without a clear, long-term strategy.

In the race that exists today, if indeed there is a "race" (for what?), it is the turtles (the Soviets) who have taken the lead from the hares (the Americans). The Soviets' slow, plodding experimentation in earth orbit with aging yet proven spacecraft affords them easy access to space. By essentially abandoning our once-formidable arsenal of expendible boosters—Redstone, Atlas, Titan, Delta, Thor, and Saturn—we placed every egg we had in one basket: the shuttle. That bean-counter-oriented philosophy proved costly to the extent of disaster.

In an age where placing blame has become a lucrative occupation for many, it may be easiest to simply point a finger at NASA for all that has gone wrong with our space program. But NASA is not totally to blame. Those legislators who denied NASA its funds while we spent billions on an outrageous war in Southeast Asia are the culprits. Lack of leadership killed the space program.

The Soviet Soyuz spacecraft and the *A-1* booster that

typically lofts it are based upon technology that is over twenty years old. Is that all wrong? Certainly not! It is shrewd.

Take the Gemini spacecraft, for example. Gemini was a natural by-product of Mercury. And Apollo was designed based upon knowledge gained during both Mercury and Gemini. While the Mercury spacecraft may have been used to its maximum during its 1961–63 program endurance, Gemini certainly was not.

Gemini could still be in service today, in a modified, improved version. The spacecraft could easily provide access to an orbiting space station, as was once envisioned by those who designed, on paper, the Manned Orbiting Laboratory for the Air Force. Able to achieve orbit via the relatively inexpensive *Titan II*, a dependable booster that entered service in the early sixties, Gemini was scrapped before its time was up. The *Soyuz TM* spacecraft the Soviets use to transport MIR crews into and out of orbit is based upon a design that first flew in 1967. That's pretty efficient.

And what of Apollo? The case for Apollo is more salient still. Apollo hardware, once redesigned, was perhaps the best equipment to ever carry humans. In eleven manned missions covering millions of miles—many of them into deep space—no man ever failed to return safely to earth in an Apollo spacecraft. In the case of *Apollo 13*, the spacecraft suffered a catastrophic explosion enroute to the moon and the basic system was hearty enough to bring its crew home.

The Boeing 727 entered scheduled airline service in 1964. Hundreds of them are still flying today—twenty-five years later—with updated avionics, new engines, and new interiors. They are among the safest aircraft to ever fly. We owed at least the same treatment to Apollo. With new computer capabilities and updated systems, Apollo could have paved the way to an early lunar base. Via a second

Skylab, American crews could be orbiting the earth right now, in search of new energy or a way to cure AIDS via medical science in zero-G. Why not? The Soviets have been doing it for years!

And what of the boosters? More specifically, what of the mighty Saturn? When Washington failed our national interest in space, it failed most severely when our Saturn technology was cast aside for the space shuttle.

In Saturn we possessed the strongest, most reliable booster rocket man had ever created. Even the magnificent new Soviet booster, Energia, only compares with but fails to outclass the awesome lift capability of *Saturn V*. Saturn could be at work today, providing commercial communications lift ability while "cocking the fist" for the United States military. And Saturn could have been improved upon many times, via solid rocket motors, or even better, via development into the Nova-class ultra-heavy booster once envisioned for the direct-ascent scenario to the moon.

Why be in space in the first place? Because it is there? Because the Soviets will use it against us if we fail to maintain a strong presence there? Because someday there may be no place left to go?

The answer to each question is *yes*!

Man wasn't placed on this earth to while away his time. Men and women were given the mental capacity to reach out beyond their caves, huts, and houses. If there is an ultimate duty, it is to provide a better place for our children in which to live. And that comes only at the cost of exploration, of our land, of our seas, and in space.

The exploration of space and the planets is the answer to man's future. The solutions to dwindling energy and cures for disease lie in our ability to extend outward, toward the stars.

As results of manned space exploration, we already take for granted calculators, computers, open-heart and micro-surgery, efficient air conditioning and heating, stereo sound systems the size of paperback books, plastics and alloys unknown only twenty-five years ago, clothes that keep us warmer in winter and cooler in summer, cars that burn less gasoline and cover longer distances, commercial aircraft capable of landing themselves in conditions of zero-visibility, and a communications network so vast we can talk to nearly any location on earth with startling clarity. Did we get all this despite the space program? Hardly.

And what of the Soviets? It is commendable that, in this nuclear age, the United States and the Soviet Union have never fired an atomic shot at each other. Despite all the idiotic bickering, that fact is evidence that somewhere some people are thinking clearly.

But the fact that although we have come close on at least one occassion (the Cuban Missile Crisis of 1962), no one has fired a nuclear warhead at the other is based upon a delicate balance of deterrence. And in our age the space programs of competing systems are ultimate signs of techological achievement that support the "balance of power."

In this author's opinion, we, as a nation, cannot afford *not* to have a vigorous space program. It is the space program that will keep our minds prepared for what our adversaries may have planned for us! Space provides a peaceful, productive way for the superpowers to compete. It is far better to see who may get to Mars first than to annihillate each other. Even better, we may find it's more fun to go to Mars *together*! We all breathe the same air, use the same water, and burn the same oil. We might just need each other.

The Ride Report

In her report to the president, *Leadership and America's Future in Space*, astronaut Dr. Sally K. Ride comments: "For

two decades, the United States was the undisputed leader
in nearly all civilian space endeavors. However, over the
last decade the United States has relinquished, or is relin-
quishing, its leadership in certain critical areas . . . " Among
those "critical areas," according to Ride, are the exploration
of Mars and the continued occupation of low-earth orbit.
Ride warns: "The United States has clearly lost leadership
in these two areas, and is in danger of being surpassed in
many others during the next several years."

Dr. Ride's report is an outstanding piece of research.
It offers realistic options the United States could execute
to regain its position of leadership in space. Her objectives
include a more intense earth orbital program, a new program to explore the solar system, a lunar base, and manned
exploration of Mars. These options take us from the space
station to deep-space exploration by American astronauts.
All of them are important; certainly a combination of them
should be mandatory policy of the federal government.

Just think of the positive consequences of a manned
American mission to Mars! Dr. Ride sums up this mind-
boggling possibility well. She comments:

> This leadership intiative declares America's intention to
> continue exploring Mars *[we landed our Viking robot
> spacecraft there in 1976]*, and to do so not only with space-
> craft and rovers, but also with humans. It would clearly
> rekindle the national pride and prestige enjoyed by the
> U.S. during the Apollo era *[and just think, we wouldn't
> have a war in Vietnam to ruin it]*.* Humans to Mars would
> be a great national adventure; as such, it would require a
> concentrated massive national commitment—a commit-
> ment to a goal and its supporting science, technology, and
> infrastructure for many decades . . . A successful Mars in-
> itiative would recapture the high ground of world space

*Author's comments.

leadership and would provide an exciting focus for creativity, motivation and pride of the American people. The challenge is compelling, and it is enormous.

What could the "average American" hope to gain from such an endeavor? Plenty. Our schools would respond to this goal as they did when President Kennedy announced our lunar landing objectives in 1961. A lofty goal such as manned Martian exploration will require tens of thousands of highly motivated Americans, from many different fields of expertise. Physicians, mathematicians, dieticians, writers, politicians, pilots, aquanauts, manufacturing experts, geologists, paleontologists, systems analysts, computer experts, programmers, design engineers, teachers at every level, training experts, human resources specialists, and multitudes of support personnel will be needed. Hundreds of thousands of jobs will be created. Entire new fields will develop. The positive by-products from this program alone would be staggering. Every American would, either directly or indirectly, benefit considerably from such an effort.

In the final analysis, we owe our children and all the future inhabitants of this planet the knowledge to be derived from a renewed, aggressive manned space program. We owe them the pride and satisfaction to be gained from performing incredible feats, and we owe them the motivation to get them there.

I want that pride—that choked-up feeling of awe that washed over me like a bracing wave from the cold Atlantic every time I saw Americans roar into space atop a mighty rocket—back. I want that example of everything great that men and women can achieve together to be there for my children and for theirs. Their horizons should be, literally, endless. I wish for them a life in a land where dreams and astronauts have replaced hate and war.

Sources

Of Dreams and Astronauts is a personal narrative. It is not a scholarly research paper on the manned space program. The effort is based upon personal experience and a compendium of sources, many of them interviews with relatives, friends, and individuals associated with aviation and space.

I drew heavily upon my memories of the period, constantly checked against fact to ensure accuracy. Dozens upon dozens of books and articles were consulted. Some are strictly concerned with spaceflight, while others are histories of the Vietnam War, the Kennedy-Johnson years (for example, I paid several visits to the magnificent John F. Kennedy Library in Boston, an outstanding resource), and countless other topics that are associated—directly or indirectly—with the story of our space program.

Several general sources were invaluable. They are Loudon Wainwright and the editors of LIFE magazine, *Life in Space* (Little, Brown, 1983); numerous issues of *Aviation Week and Space Technology*; *National Geographic*; *Air and Space* Magazine; John Noble Wilford, *We Reach the Moon* (New York: New York Times, 1969); Michael Collins, *Carrying the Fire* (Farrar, Straus, Giroux, 1974); Michael Maclear, *The Ten Thousand Day War* (Avon, 1981); Michael Cassutt, *Who's Who in Space* (G. K. Hall, 1987); and Neil McAleer, *The Omni Space Almanac* (World Almanac, 1987).

I also relied upon many issues of *NASA Facts* and *NASA Information Summaries* and Dr. Sally K. Ride, *Leadership and*

America's Future in Space: A Report to the Administrator (Aviation Week and Space Technology, 1987).

Research involving popular music at the time of each mission included the expertise of Frank Holler, program director of WDRC Radio, Hartford, Connecticut. Frank supplied *Hartford's Best Selling Hits* for each year from 1961 through 1975, the period of Mercury, Gemini, Apollo, Skylab, and ASTP. Debbie Moore Nugent of Infomart/ Dallas provided important research where the lyrics of popular hits were relevant to the description of a particular mission or period. Joel Whitburn's *Billboard Book of Top 40 Hits* (Billboard Publications, 1987) also supplied critical data for research concerning the popular music of the era.

In addition to the works referenced above, the following chapter-by-chapter discussion includes other references that were extremely useful.

Chapter 1

The demise of the orbiter *Challenger* is perhaps best described by the editors of *Aviation Week and Space Technology* in *Shuttle 51-L Loss*, (McGraw-Hill, 1986). For nominal shuttle prelaunch activities I referred to Joseph P. Allen, *Entering Space* (Stuart, Tabori and Chang, 1985). Also, I found Joseph J. Trento, *Prescription for Disaster* (Crown, 1987); Richard S. Lewis, *The Voyages of Columbia, the First True Spaceship* (Columbia University Press, 1984); and Marshall H. Kaplan, *Space Shuttle: America's Wings to the Future* (Aero Publishers, 1983) useful.

Chapter 2

Aside from the extensive research into old family records, picture albums, and countless memorabilia, I referred to Mitchell R. Sharpe, *The Rocket Team* (Thomas Y. Crowell, 1979) and to James and Alcestis Oberg, "Nostalgia for Sputnik," *Space World*, October 1987. As background information on the presidential campaign of 1960 I found Theodore H. White, *The Making of the President, 1960* (Atheneum House, 1961) invaluable.

Chapter 3

I wanted to capture the magic of the Kennedy presidency as it mingled with our first daring manned ventures into space in this chapter. The hope and romance of the Kennedy years is portrayed well by William Manchester, *One Brief Shining Moment* (Little, Brown, 1983). Additional references concerning President Kennedy were Arthur M. Schlesinger, Jr., *A Thousand Days* (Houghton Mifflin, 1965); Robert F. Kennedy, *Thirteen Days* (Norton, 1968); and William Manchester, *The Death of a President* (Harper and Row, 1967). Details of Project Mercury were plentiful within Lloyd Swenson, *This New Ocean: a History of Project Mercury* (NASA, 1966). *We Seven* (Simon and Schuster, 1962), which was penned by M. Scott Carpenter, L. Gordon Cooper, Jr., John H. Glenn, Jr., Virgil I. Grissom, Walter M. Schirra, Jr., Alan B. Shepard, Jr., and Donald K. Slayton, the "Original Seven" Mercury astronauts themselves, was tremendously informative. I also found Tom Wolfe, *The Right Stuff* (Farrar, Straus, Giroux, 1979), a key to the inside story on Project Mercury.

Chapters 4, 5, and 6

U.S. combat involvement in Vietnam escalated as Project Gemini began in 1965. We remained in Vietnam throughout the Gemini and Apollo programs. Since the war so heavily influenced those years, I relied on several additional sources. They are Philip Caputo, *A Rumor of War* (Holt, Rinehart and Winston, 1977); Dave R. Palmer, *Summons of the Trumpet* (Presidio Press, 1978); Al Santoli, *Everything We Had* (Random House, 1981); and William Broyles, Jr., *Brothers in Arms* (Alfred A. Knopf, 1986). Of particular interest, Caputo and Broyles were commissioned in the Marine Corps via the same program through which I earned my commission in 1975. I also referred to John Trotti, *Phantom over Vietnam* (Presidio Press, 1984); Robert Mason, *Chickenhawk* (Viking Press, 1983); Michael Lee Lanning, *The Only War We Had* (Ballantine, 1987); Stephen Coonts, *Flight of the Intruder* (United States Naval Institute, 1986); David Butler, *The Fall of Saigon* (Simon and Schuster, 1985); and Jim and Sybil Stockdale, *In Love and War* (Harper and Row, 1984) for background information. On the Johnson presidency I found Merle Miller, *Lyndon* (G. P. Putnam's Sons, 1980); Eric F. Goldman, *The Tragedy of Lyndon Johnson* (Alfred A. Knopf, 1969); and Lyndon B. Johnson, *The Vantage Point* (Holt, Rinehart and Winston, 1971) necessary reading. On the impact Robert F. Kennedy had upon my generation I referred to Jack Newfield, *Robert F. Kennedy: A Memoir* (E.P. Dutton, 1969) and to Arthur M. Schlesinger, Jr., *Robert F. Kennedy and His Times* (Houghton Mifflin, 1978). Extra research on Project Gemini included *Gemini* (Macmillan, 1968), by Virgil I. "Gus" Grissom, who commanded *Gemini 3*, the first manned mission of the Gemini series. *On the Shoulders of Titans*, by Barton C. Hacker (NASA, U.S. Government Printing Office, 1977), was also helpful. As insight concerning the *Apollo 1* tragedy Erik Bergaust, *Murder on Pad 34* (Putnam, 1968) was valuable. For additional background on the ASTP mission I read Edward Ezell, *The Partnership* (NASA, 1978). I also referred to notes taken from conversations with Eugene Cernan, who flew aboard *Gemini 9*, *Apollo 10*, and *Apollo 17*, and with John Young, who is our nation's most experienced astronaut, having flown aboard *Gemini 3*, *Gemini 10*, *Apollo 10*, *Apollo 16*, STS-1, and STS-9.

Chapter 8

I found Michael D. Lemonick and Dick Thompson, "Surging Ahead," *Time*, October 5, 1987, particularly informative regarding the current state of the Soviet space program. I was also inspired by several writers whose opinions appeared in *Aviation Week and Space Technology*. Among them are Eugen K. Reichl, in the February 2, 1987, edition, Bill Yenne, in the September 14, 1987, edition, George F. Rugge, in the August 17, 1987, edition, Pepper P. Powers in the July 20, 1987, edition, and Frank Sietzen, Jr., in the May 4, 1987 edition. I also consulted *Should the U.S. Federal Government Significantly Increase the Exploration and/or Development of Space Beyond the Earth's Mesosphere?* (Congressional Research Service, 1985) for background data.

Appendix A

Soviet Manned Missions into Space Prior to U.S. Mission 51-L

MISSION	DAYS	HOURS	MINUTES	NOTES
Vostok 1		1	48	
Vostok 2		25	18	
Vostok 3	3	22	22	
Vostok 4	2	22	57	
Vostok 5	4	23	06	
Vostok 6	2	22	50	
Voskhod 1	1	0	17	
Voshkod 2	1	2	02	
Soyuz 1	1	2	48	Crew perished
Soyuz 3	3	22	51	
Soyuz 4	2	23	21	
Soyuz 5	3	0	54	
Soyuz 6	4	22	43	
Soyuz 7	4	22	40	
Soyuz 8	4	22	51	
Soyuz 9	17	16	59	
Soyuz 10	1	23	46	
Soyuz 11	23	18	22	Crew perished
Soyuz 12	1	23	16	
Soyuz 13	7	20	55	
Soyuz 14	15	17	30	
Soyuz 15	2	0	12	
Soyuz 16	5	22	24	
Soyuz 17	29	13	20	
Soyuz 18	62	23	20	
Soyuz 19	5	22	31	ASTP mission

MISSION	DAYS	HOURS	MINUTES	NOTES
Soyuz 21	49	06	23	
Soyuz 22	7	21	52	
Soyuz 23	2	0	07	
Soyuz 24	17	17	26	
Soyuz 25	2	0	46	
Soyuz 26	96	10	0	
Soyuz 27	5	22	59	
Soyuz 28	7	22	17	
Soyuz 29	139	14	48	
Soyuz 30	7	22	03	
Soyuz 31	7	20	49	
Soyuz 32	175	0	36	
Soyuz 33	1	23	01	
Soyuz 35	184	20	45	
Soyuz T-2	3	22	20	Upgraded Soyuz
Soyuz 37	7	20	42	
Soyuz 38	7	20	42	
Soyuz T-3	12	19	08	
Soyuz T-4	74	17	38	
Soyuz 39	7	20	43	
Soyuz 40	7	20	38	
Soyuz T-5	211	08	05	
Soyuz T-6	7	22	42	
Soyuz T-7	7	21	52	
Soyuz T-8	2	0	18	
Soyuz T-9	149	09	46	
Soyuz T-10-1	0	0	0	Pad abort
Soyuz T-11	7	21	41	
Soyuz T-13	112	03	13	
Soyuz T-12	11	19	14	
Soyuz T-13	112	03	13	
Soyuz T-14	64	21	52	
	1829	928	1874	

U.S. MANNED SPACE FLIGHT LOG

Mission	Crew	Date	Mission elapsed time, hr:min:sec	Cumulative U.S. manned hrs in space hr:min:sec
Mercury-Redstone 3	Shepard	May 5, 1961	00:15:22	00:15:22
Mercury-Redstone 4	Grissom	July 21, 1961	00:15:37	00:30:59
Mercury-Atlas 6	Glenn	Feb. 20, 1962	04:55:23	05:26:22
Mercury-Atlas 7	Carpenter	May 24, 1962	04:56:05	10:22:27
Mercury-Atlas 8	Schirra	Oct. 3, 1962	09:13:11	19:35:38
Mercury-Atlas 9	Cooper	May 15 and 16, 1963	34:19:49	53:55:27
Total - Project Mercury				53:55:27
Gemini-Titan III	Grissom, Young	Mar. 23, 1965	04:53:00	63:41:27
Gemini-Titan IV	McDivitt, White	June 3 to 7, 1965	97:56:11	259:33:49
Gemini-Titan V	Cooper, Conrad	Aug. 21 to 29, 1965	190:55:14	641:24:17
Gemini-Titan VII	Borman, Lovell	Dec. 4 to 18, 1965	330:35:31	1302:35:19
Gemini-Titan VI-A	Schirra, Stafford	Dec. 15 and 16, 1965	25:51:24	1354:18:07
Gemini-Titan VIII	Armstrong, Scott	Mar. 16, 1966	10:41:26	1375:40:59
Gemini-Titan IX-A	Stafford, Cernan	June 3 to 6, 1966	72:21:00	1520:22:59
Gemini-Titan X	Young, Collins	July 18 to 21, 1966	70:46:39	1661:56:17
Gemini-Titan XI	Conrad, Gordon	Sept. 12 to 15, 1966	71:17:08	1804:30:33
Gemini-Titan XII	Lovell, Aldrin	Nov. 11 to 15, 1966	94:34:31	1993:39:35
Total - Gemini Program				1939:44:08
Apollo-Saturn 7	Schirra, Eisele, Cunningham	Oct. 11 to 22, 1968	260:09:03	2774:06:44
Apollo-Saturn 8	Borman, Lovell, Anders	Dec. 21 to 27, 1968	147:00:42	3215:08:50
Apollo-Saturn 9	McDivitt, Scott, Schweickart	Mar. 3 to 13, 1969	241:00:54	3938:11:32
Apollo-Saturn 10	Stafford, Young, Cernan	May 18 to 26, 1969	192:03:23	4514:21:41
Apollo-Saturn 11	Armstrong, Collins, Aldrin	July 16 to 24, 1969	195:18:35	5100:17:26
Apollo-Saturn 12	Conrad, Gordon, Bean	Nov. 14 to 24, 1969	244:36:25	5834:06:41
Apollo-Saturn 13	Lovell, Swigert, Haise	April 11 to 17, 1970	142:54:41	6262:50:44
Apollo-Saturn 14	Shepard, Roosa, Mitchell	Jan. 31 to Feb. 9, 1971	216:01:57	6910:56:35
Apollo-Saturn 15	Scott, Worden, Irwin	July 26 to Aug. 7, 1971	295:11:53	7796:32:14
Apollo-Saturn 16	Young, Mattingly, Duke	April 16 to 27, 1972	265:51:05	8594:05:29
Apollo-Saturn 17	Cernan, Evans, Schmitt	Dec. 7 to 19, 1972	301:51:59	9499:41:26
Total - Apollo Program				7506:01:31
Skylab SL-2	Conrad, Kerwin, Weitz	May 25 to June 22, 1973	672:49:49	11518:10:53
Skylab SL-3	Bean, Garriott, Lousma	July 28 to Sept. 25, 1973	1427:09:04	15799:38:05
Skylab SL-4	Carr, Gibson, Pogue	Nov. 16, 1973 to Feb. 8, 1974	2017:15:32	21851:24:41
Total - Skylab Program				12351:43:15
Apollo-Soyuz Test Program (ASTP)	Stafford, Brand, Slayton	July 15 to 24, 1975	217:28:23	22503:49:50
Total ASTP				652:25:09
Space Transportation System				
STS-1 (OFT)	Young, Crippen	April 12 to 14, 1981	54:20:53	22612:31:36
STS-2 (OFT)	Engle, Truly	Nov. 12 to 14, 1981	54:13:12	22720:58:00
STS-3 (OFT)	Lousma, Fullerton	March 22 to 30, 1982	192:04:49	23105:03:38
STS-4 (OFT)	Mattingly, Hartsfield	June 27 to July 4, 1982	169:11:11	23443:22:40
STS-5	Brand, Overmyer, Allen, Lenoir	Nov. 11 to 16, 1982	122:14:25	23932:19:40
STS-6	Weitz, Bobko, Peterson, Musgrave	April 4 to 9, 1983	120:23:42	24413:54:28
STS-7	Crippen, Hauck, Ride, Fabian, Thagard	June 18 to 24, 1983	146:23:59	25145:54:23
STS-8	Truly, Brandenstein, D. Gardner, Bluford, W. Thornton	Aug. 30 to Sept. 5, 1983	145:08:40	25871:37:43
STS-9	Young, Shaw, Garriott, Parker, Lichtenberg, Merbold	Nov. 28 to Dec. 8, 1983	223:47:24	27214:22:07
41-B	Brand, Gibson, McCandless, McNair, Stewart	Feb. 3 to 11, 1984	191:15:55	28170:41:42

Mission	Crew	Date	Mission elapsed time, hr:min:sec	Cumulative U.S. manned hrs in space hr:min:sec
41-C	Crippen, Scobee, van Hoften, G. Nelson, Hart	April 6 to 13, 1984	191:40:05	29129:02:07
41-D	Hartsfield, Coats, Resnik, Hawley, Mullane, C. Walker	Aug. 30 to Sept. 5, 1984	144:57:00	29998:44:07
41-G	Crippen, McBride, Ride, Sullivan, Leestma, Garneau, Scully-Power	Oct. 5 to Oct. 13, 1984	197:23:37	31380:29:26
51-A	Hauck, D. Walker, D. Gardner, A. Fisher, Allen	Nov. 8 to Nov. 16, 1984	191:44:56	32339:14:06
51-C	Mattingly, Shriver, Onizuka, Buchli, Payton	Jan. 24 to 27, 1985	73:33:27	32707:01:21
51-D	Bobko, Williams, Seddon, Hoffman, Griggs, C. Walker, Garn	April 12 to 19, 1985	114:23:54	33507:48:39
51-B	Overmyer, Gregory, Lind, Thagard, W. Thornton, van den Berg, Wang	April 29 to May 6, 1985	168:08:47	33772:21:22
51-G	Brandenstein, Creighton, Lucid, Fabian, Nagel, Baudry, Al-Saud	June 17 to 24, 1985	169:39:00	34620:36:22
51-F	Fullerton, Bridges, Musgrave, England, Henize, Acton, Bartoe	July 29 to Aug. 6, 1985	190:45:26	35955:54:24
51-I	Engle, Covey, van Hoften, Lounge, W. Fisher	Aug. 27 to Sept. 3, 1985	170:27:42	36808:12:54
51-J	Bobko, Grabe, Hilmers, Stewart, Pailes	Oct. 3 to 7, 1985	97:14:38	37294:26:04
61-A	Hartsfield, Nagel, Buchli, Bluford, Dunbar, Furrer, Messerschmid, Ockels	Oct. 30 to Nov. 6, 1985	168:44:51	38138:50:19
61-B	Shaw, O'Connor, Cleave, Spring, Ross, Neri-Vela, C. Walker	Nov. 26 to Dec. 3, 1985	165:04:49	39129:19:13
61-C	Gibson, Bolden, Chang-Diaz, Hawley, G. Nelson, Cenker, B. Nelson	Jan. 12 to 18, 1986	146:03:51	40151:46:10
51-L	Scobee, Smith, Resnik, Onizuka, McNair, Jarvis, McAuliffe	Jan. 28, 1986	00:01:13	40151:54:41

U.S. Man-Hours in Space

Program	Mercury	Gemini	Apollo	Skylab	ASTP	STS
Man-hours in space	54	1 940	7 506	12 351	652	1 428
Number of manned flights	6	10	11	3	1	25
Crewmembers	1	2	3	3	3	Varies 2 - 8
Cumulative man-hours in space	40,151 hours 54 minutes 41 seconds					

Courtesy of NASA

Sources: NASA Information Summary PMS-020 (JSC) of August, 1986; *The Omni Space Almanac.*

Appendix C

Hartford's Best Selling Top Ten

1961

Title		**Artist**
1.	Michael	Highwaymen
2.	Hello Mary Lou/Travelling Man	Ricky Nelson
3.	I Fall to Pieces	Patsy Cline
4.	Runaround Sue	Dion
5.	Runaway	Del Shannon
6.	Quarter to Three	U.S. Bonds
7.	Baby Sitting Boogie	Buzz Clifford
8.	Big Bad John	Jimmy Dean
9.	Blue Moon	Marcels
10.	Calcutta	Lawrence Welk

1962

Title		**Artist**
1.	Stranger on the Shore	Acker Bilk/Andy Williams
2.	Alley Cat	Bent Fabric
3.	Roses Are Red	Bobby Vinton
4.	Limbo Rock/Popeye	Chubby Checker
5.	Ramblin' Rose	Nat King Cole
6.	Wolverton Mountain	Claude King
7.	The Twist	Chubby Checker
8.	All Alone Am I	Brenda Lee
9.	Let's Dance	Chris Montez
10.	The Wanderer/The Majestic	Dion

1963

Title	Artist
1. I Love You Because	Al Martino
2. Maria Elena	Los Indios Tabajares
3. Sugar Shack/Surfin' USA/Shut Down	Jimmy Gilmer/Beach Boys
4. Blue Velvet	Bobby Vinton
5. The End of the World/Wipeout/ Surfer Joe	Skeeter Davis/Surfaris
6. Be My Baby	Ronettes
7. The Bounce	The Olympics
8. Deep Purple	Nino Tempo & April Stevens
9. Rhythm of the Rain	Cascades
10. Blowing in the Wind	Peter, Paul and Mary

1964

Title	Artist
1. Pretty Woman	Roy Orbison
2. Hello, Dolly	Louis Armstrong
3. She Loves You	The Beatles
4. I Want to Hold Your Hand/ I Saw Her Standing There	The Beatles
5. Everybody Loves Somebody	Dean Martin
6. Java	Al Hirt
7. Love Me Do/P.S. I Love You	The Beatles
8. Do Wah Diddy Diddy	Manfred Mann

1965

Title	Artist
1. The Wooly Bully	Sam the Sham & Pharaohs
2. Hang on Sloopy	McCoys/Ramsey Lewis Trio

	Title	Artist
3.	Help	The Beatles
4.	Satisfaction	Rolling Stones
5.	Downtown	Petula Clark
6.	Can't You Hear My Heartbeat	Herman's Hermits
7.	I Got You Babe	Sonny & Cher
8.	Let's Hang On	Four Seasons
9.	You Were on My Mind	We Five
10.	Red Roses for a Blue Lady	Wayne Newton/Bert Kaempfert

1966

Title		**Artist**
1.	When a Man Loves a Woman	Percy Sledge
2.	Good Lovin'	Young Rascals
3.	California Dreamin'	Mamas & Papas
4.	Last Train to Clarksville	Monkees
5.	Sunny	Bobby Hebb
6.	These Boots Are Made for Walking	Nancy Sinatra
7.	Strangers in the Night	Frank Sinatra
8.	You Can't Hurry Love	Supremes
9.	Paint It Black	Rolling Stones
10.	Cherish	The Association
	Reach Out, I'll Be There	Four Tops

1967

Title		**Artist**
1.	To Sir, With Love	Lulu
2.	The Letter	Box Tops
3.	Ode to Billie Joe	Bobbie Gentry
4.	Windy	Association
5.	I'm a Believer	Monkees
6.	Light My Fire	Doors
7.	Somethin' Stupid	Nancy & Frank Sinatra

8.	Happy Together	Turtles
9.	Groovin''	Young Rascals
10.	Can't Take My Eyes Off You	Frankie Valli

1968

Title		**Artist**
1.	Hey Jude	Beatles
2.	Love Is Blue	Paul Mauriat
3.	Honey	Bobby Goldsboro
4.	(Sittin' On) The Dock of the Bay	Otis Redding
5.	People Got to Be Free	Rascals
6.	Sunshine of Your Love	Cream
7.	This Guy's in Love with You	Herb Alpert
8.	The Good, the Bad, and the Ugly	Hugo Montenegro
9.	Mrs. Robinson	Simon & Garfunkel
10.	Tighten Up	Archie Bell & the Drells

1969

Title		**Artist**
1.	Sugar, Sugar	Archies
2.	Aquarius/Let the Sunshine In	Fifth Dimension
3.	I Can't Get Next to You	Temptations
4.	Honky Tonk Woman	Rolling Stones
5.	Everyday People	Sly & the Family Stone
6.	Dizzy	Tommy Roe
7.	Hot Fun in the Summertime	Sly & the Family Stone
8.	I'll Never Fall in Love Again	Tom Jones
9.	Build Me Up, Buttercup	Foundations
10.	Crimson and Clover	Tommy James & the Shondells

1970

Title	**Artist**
1. Bridge over Troubled Water	Simon & Garfunkel
2. (They Long to Be) Close to You	Carpenters
3. American Woman/No Sugar Tonight	Guess Who
4. Raindrops Keep Fallin' on My Head	B.J. Thomas
5. War	Edwin Starr
6. Ain't No Mountain High Enough	Diana Ross
7. I'll Be There	Jackson 5
8. Get Ready	Rare Earth
9. Let It Be	Beatles
10. Band of Gold	Freda Payne

1971

Title	**Artist**
1. Joy to the World	Three Dog Night
2. Maggie May/Reason to Believe	Rod Stewart
3. It's Too Late/I Feel the Earth Move	Carole King
4. One Bad Apple	Osmonds
5. How Can You Mend a Broken Heart	Bee Gees
6. Indian Reservation	Raiders
7. Go Away Little Girl	Donny Osmond
8. Take Me Home, Country Roads	John Denver with Fat City
9. Just My Imagination (Running Away with Me)	Temptations
10. Knock Three Times	Dawn

1972

Title	Artist
1. First Time Ever I Saw Your Face	Roberta Flack
2. Alone Again (Naturally)	Gilbert O'Sullivan
3. American Pie	Don McLean
4. Without You	Nilsson
5. Candy Man	Sammy Davis, Jr.
6. I Gotcha	Joe Tex
7. Lean on Me	Bill Withers
8. Baby, Don't Get Hooked on Me	Mac Davis
9. Brand New Key	Melanie
10. Daddy, Don't You Walk So Fast	Wayne Newton

1973

Title	Artist
1. Tie a Yellow Ribbon 'Round the the Ole Oak Tree	Tony Orlando and Dawn
2. Bad, Bad Leroy Brown	Jim Croce
3. Killing Me Softly with His Song	Roberta Flack
4. Let's Get It On	Marvin Gaye
5. My Love	Paul McCartney & Wings
6. Why Me	Kris Kristofferson
7. Crocodile Rock	Elton John
8. Will It Go Round in Circles	Billy Preston
9. You're So Vain	Carly Simon
10. Touch Me in the Morning	Diana Ross

1974

Title	**Artist**
1. The Way We Were	Barbara Streisand
2. Seasons in the Sun	Terry Jacks
3. Love's Theme	Love Unlimited Orchestra
4. Come and Get Your Love	Redbone
5. Dancing Machine	Jackson Five
6. The Loco Motion	Grand Funk Railroad
7. TSOP	MFSB
8. The Streak	Ray Stevens
9. Bennie and the Jets	Elton John
10. One Hell of a Woman	Mac Davis

1975

Title	**Artist**
1. Love Will Keep Us Together	The Captain & Tennille
2. Lady Marmalade	LaBelle
3. One of These Nights	Eagles
4. Feelings	Eagles
5. Miracles	Jefferson Starship
6. Kung Fu Fighting	Carl Douglas
7. Philadelphia Freedom	Elton John
8. Mandy	Barry Manilow
9. Pick up the Pieces	Average White Band
10. Who Loves You	Four Seasons